Psychoanalysis, General Custer, and the Verdicts of History

And Other Essays on Psychology in the Social Scene

SEYMOUR B. SARASON

Psychoanalysis, General Custer, and the Verdicts of History

And Other Essays on Psychology in the Social Scene

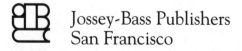

Jossey-Bass Publishers
San Francisco

Copyright © 1994 by Jossey-Bass Inc., Publishers, 350 Sansome Street, San Francisco, California 94104. Copyright under International, Pan American, and Universal Copyright Conventions. All rights reserved. No part of this book may be reproduced in any form—except for brief quotation (not to exceed 1,000 words) in a review or professional work—without permission in writing from the publishers.

Credits are on page 265.

> Substantial discounts on bulk quantities of Jossey-Bass books are available to corporations, professional associations, and other organizations. For details and discount information, contact the special sales department at Jossey-Bass Inc., Publishers.
> (415) 433–1740; Fax (415) 433–0499.

For international orders, please contact your local Paramount Publishing International office.

Manufactured in the United States of America. Nearly all Jossey-Bass books and jackets are printed on recycled paper containing at least 10 percent postconsumer waste, and many are printed with either soy- or vegetable-based ink, which emits fewer volatile organic compounds during the printing process than petroleum-based ink.

Library of Congress Cataloging-in-Publication Data

Sarason, Seymour Bernard, date.
    Psychoanalysis, General Custer, and the verdicts of history and other essays on psychology in the social scene/Seymour B. Sarason. — 1st ed.
        p.   cm.—(A joint publication in the Jossey-Bass social and behavioral science series and the Jossey-Bass education series)
    Includes bibliographical references.
    ISBN 0-7879-0004-4 (alk. paper)
    1. Psychology—United States—History. 2. Psychoanalysis—History. I. Title.
II. Series: Jossey-Bass social and behavioral science series. III. Series: Jossey-Bass education series.
BF108.U5S27 1994
150' .973—dc20
                                        94-14345
                                           CIP

FIRST EDITION
HB Printing   10 9 8 7 6 5 4 3 2 1   *Code 9474*

Contents

For my Esther
December 14, 1918 – June 7, 1993

Preface

Each essay in this volume could well be expanded into a book. At my stage of life, however, such expansion was very unrealistic. And, yet, each contains ideas or points of view I wanted to state because (obviously) I thought they were worth stating. This is not to say that others have not dealt with the issues, but rather that I wanted to present my perspectives without having to conform to the requirements of journals in regard to format, length, and taking the views of others into account. That may sound self-indulgent, narcissistic, and arrogant to some people, which is why I resisted writing these essays.

But intimations of mortality suggested that I overcome that resistance. In struggling to make a decision, I came to the conclusion that I had, so to speak, paid my dues to the field and had earned the right to write these essays in the way I have. This is not to say that the dues I paid and the essays in this book have caused or will cause more than a ripple in the field, if that. I write for a variety of reasons, not the least of which is the desire to tell my many friends what I have been thinking about. Living as we do in times when those you know, respect, and love are scattered in distant states and lands, publishing one's thoughts is the best way I know to keep in touch with them. Needless to say, if what I write gains me new friends, my cup runneth over.

I did not intend these essays to be thematically related. Perhaps they are not, but as I now read them it seems clear (to me) that, as in my earlier writings, several themes emerge: the nature and consequences of social change, the American worldview, the limitations of an individual psychology, and the perils of an ahistorical stance. If at the point of a gun I had to state most briefly the underlying theme in this volume, it would be that the human mind is our greatest ally and foe.

If writing for friends has always been important to me, it pales before the fact that I always wrote primarily for one person: Esther, my wife, who was killed in a car crash two weeks (June 7, 1993) after the celebration of our fiftieth wedding anniversary. I briefly mention the dimensions of my loss in the essay "The Blind Spot in the Health Care Nonsystem." I had great difficulty being brief. Not because it was so painful (it was worse than that) but because I lacked the literary skill to convey what she was like: utterly without guile; sensitive to the needs and feelings of others; secure in her Jewish-Brooklyn background; devoted to her patients whether they could pay or not; a mature adult who had a childlike zest for living; a person for whom family (nuclear and extended) was all-important; and who, despite the fact that I am a slob, organized, decorated, and graced a house that I and others considered a work of art. I am one of those fortunate men who with each passing year of marriage found his admiration, love, and respect for his wife escalating. Most of my books were dedicated to Esther, usually with a sentence or two that may have seemed ritualistic to some people. What I have said here about her will, I hope, prevent such a reaction in readers of this volume. I wish I had ways of describing my love and loss more adequately.

All but one of these essays were written for this volume. The exception, "American Psychology and the Needs for Transcendence and Community," was added because it was written a year before Esther's death and contains thoughts unfortunately prodromal of what her loss has stirred up in me.

As before, this book would not have received the light of published day without the gracious help of Lisa Pagliaro, not only as secretary but as friend. I wish also to thank three people at Jossey-Bass who during some very difficult days made sure that I knew they were on my side: to Lesley Iura, Currie McLaughlin, and Christie Hakim, I express my appreciation for their support and encouragement.

New Haven, Connecticut   Seymour B. Sarason
June 1994

The Author

Seymour B. Sarason is professor of psychology emeritus in the Department of Psychology and at the Institution for Social and Policy Studies at Yale University. He founded, in 1962, and directed, until 1970, the Yale Psycho-Educational Clinic, one of the first research and training sites in community psychology. He received his Ph.D. degree from Clark University in 1942 and holds honorary doctorates from Syracuse University, Queens College, Rhode Island College, and Lewis and Clark College. He has received an award for distinguished contributions to the public interest and several awards from the divisions of clinical and community psychology of the American Psychological Association, as well as two awards from the American Association on Mental Deficiency.

Sarason is the author of numerous books and articles. His more recent books include *You Are Thinking of Teaching? Opportunities, Problems, Realities* (1993), *The Case for Change: Rethinking the Preparation of Educators* (1993), *Letters to a Serious Education President* (1993), *The Predictable Failure of Educational Reform: Can We Change Course Before It's Too Late?* (1990), *The Challenge of Art to Psychology* (1990), and *The Making of an American Psychologist: An Autobiography* (1988). He has made contributions in such fields as mental retardation, culture and personality, projective techniques, teacher training, the school culture, and anxiety in children.

1

Psychoanalysis, General Custer, and the Verdicts of History

Beginning in the sixties, and in part because of what was happening in that decade, psychoanalysis as therapy, theory, and research came under critical scrutiny as never before. Criticism and rejection were by no means absent features in the history of psychoanalysis, but in the pre–World War II era, psychoanalysis was never in the mainstream of academic psychiatry and psychology. That is to say, psychoanalysis had been institutionalized in independent institutes quite content to remain uncontaminated by what they perceived to be disciplines uncomprehending of and hostile to the contributions of psychoanalysis.

World War II changed all that. I consider it both amazing and regrettable that we still do not have the story of how and why psychoanalysis began to be legitimated in the university *during World War II and in the immediate years after the war*. I observed and in a very minor way participated in that process, but the story is not central to the purposes of this essay. Suffice it to say, it is a story in which certain individuals, psychoanalytically trained, play important, policy-making roles in the military, roles requiring them to plan for a dramatic increase in the number of mental health professionals coming out of university departments to care for an unprecedented number of psychiatric casualties directly or indirectly related to war experiences. Another part of the story is that during the war some psychoanalytically trained or oriented individuals had

1

developed or experimented with approaches to the handling of casualties that were informed by psychoanalytic theory, the results of which were encouraging, practical, and persuasive. Related to this was another part of the story: academic psychology and psychiatry were unprepared to deal with the *clinical* aspects of battle casualties except in ways that exacerbated the manpower problems of the military. And all of these parts appeared in a zeitgeist, by no means peculiar to professionals, that the world had changed and should change, that what was was no warrant for its continuation; the sacred cows defined by custom and tradition were not only not sacred but impediments to the forging of a better world.

When the full story is told, if it ever is by the ahistorical mental health professions, it will be a contribution to the understanding of social and institutional change. If I emphasize the significance of "the story," it is because the current backlash against psychoanalysis fails to distinguish between the validity of psychoanalytic theory and practice, on the one hand, and the ways in which psychoanalysis brought attention to some core problems that no alternative approach can ignore, on the other hand.

Nothing is more representative of the backlash than Frederick Crews's (1993) extended essay reviewing four recent books, and it contains references to many more. After an introductory paragraph in which he writes that psychoanalysis as a therapy "has proved to be an indifferently successful and vastly inefficient method of removing neurotic symptoms," Crews goes on to summarize his major points:

> Freud's doctrine has been faring no better, in scientifically serious quarters, as a cluster of propositions about the mind. Without significant experimental or epidemiological support for any of its notions, psychoanalysis has simply been left behind by mainstream psychological research. No one has been able to mount a successful defense against the charge, most fully developed in Adolph Grunbaum's meticulous *Foundations of Psychoanalysis*, that "clinical validation" of

Freudian hypotheses is an epistemic sieve; as a means of gaining knowledge, psychoanalysis is fatally contaminated by the inclusion, among its working assumptions and in its dialogue with patients, of the very ideas that supposedly get corroborated by clinical experience. And Grunbaum further showed that even if Freud's means of gathering evidence had been sound, that evidence couldn't have reliably yielded the usual constructions that he placed on it. We cannot be surprised, then, by Malcolm Macmillan's recent exhaustive demonstration that Freud's theories of personality and neurosis—derived as they were from misleading precedents, vacuous pseudophysical metaphors, and a long concatenation of mistaken inferences that couldn't be subjected to empirical review—amount to castles in the air. [p. 55]

Let me now list Crews's major criticisms, for each of which he goes into detail:

1. The image of Freud as "a fearless explorer, a solver of deep mysteries, a rigorously objective thinker, and an ethically scrupulous reporter of both clinical data and therapeutic outcomes" is a false one given to us by "loyalist biographers" whose loyalties led them to exclude data that would tarnish Freud's image. Crews is quite aware of how damaging this criticism is, and he draws upon many sources to buttress his conclusion.

2. The writings of loyalist psychoanalysts (e.g., Jones, Gay) reflect the censorship of a "secretive psychoanalytic establishment" responsible for locking away in the Library of Congress many of Freud's papers and letters until as long as the twenty-second century. "But as some sensitive documents, having already served their Sleeping Beauty sentences, make their way into the light and as serendipity turns up others from outside sources, Freud's fallibilities become disturbingly clear. A blatant example from previously unexamined but not suppressed documents concerns Freud's relations with Hordel Frink, a psychoanalyst who was Freud's patient and

who was having an affair with one of his patients." I quite agree with Crews that the events in this relationship are "scarcely believable": Freud's dogged persistence in telling Frink that he was a latent homosexual, he should divorce his wife, marry the patient whom Freud urged to divorce her husband even though Freud had never met either of the presumed unsuitable spouses, and since Frink's patient was a bank heiress, Freud suggested (brazenly if perhaps semifacetiously, Crews says) that Frink's fantasy of making Freud a rich man should eventuate "into a real contribution to the Psychoanalytic Funds. . . . The divorce and remarriage did occur—soon followed by the deaths of both of the abandoned, devastated spouses, an early suit for divorce by Frink's new wife, and the decline of the guilt-ridden Frink himself into a psychotic depression and repeated attempts at suicide" (Crews, 1993, p. 56).

3. Freud's celebrated paper on the "Wolf Man," in which he regarded his therapeutic efforts as very successful, contained contradictions and implausibilities never discerned by the analytic establishment. Also, it turns out, the patient was in and out of analytic treatment for seventy years, an embarrassment that the analytic fraternity (and Freud) sought to keep from being uncovered. Central to Freud's etiological diagnosis in this case was a dream the patient (Pankeev) remembered from age four, a dream from which Freud deduced a primal scene at age one when Pankeev observed his parents copulating, doggy style, several times while he watched from his crib and soiled himself in horrified protest. Crews brings together evidence both from the patient and others to support two conclusions: the assumption about the primal scene in this instance was gratuitous and absurd, and it was characteristic of Freud to misinterpret and distort in the service of ideas he passionately held. Crews does not depend on an *argumentum ad hominem* (although that is not completely absent) but on the face invalidity of Freud's claims and illogic. Crews is not interpreting; he is reporting and collating what recent investigators have turned up.

4. The case of "Dora," which Erik Erikson said was "the classical analysis of the structure and genesis of hysteria." At the very

least, Crews is convinced that Freud's hectoring and badgering of the young woman was at best mammothly insensitive and at worst bordered on the unethical.

5. Esterson's *Seductive Mirage: An Exploration of the Work of Sigmund Freud* is one of the four books reviewed in Crews's essay.

> Except for an incisive discussion of the Wolf Man case establishing that Freud must have invented one of its key figures, the servant girl Grusha, *Seductive Mirage* does not add to our factual knowledge about Freud. Rather, it combines a close scrutiny of his ethics and rhetoric with criticism of his original "seduction theory" and its putative correction, his major case histories, his theories of neurosis and dream formation, his several reformulations of metapsychology, and his clinical technique and its results. Esterson's book, I should emphasize, is not a polemic written by a long-time foe of psychoanalysis. It is a piece of careful and sustained reasoning by a mathematician who happens to be offended by specious means of argumentation. And its eventual verdict—that every notion and practice peculiar to psychoanalysis is open to fundamental objection—rests on evidence that any reader can check by following up Esterson's cited sources. [pp. 60–61]

6. There is a parallel between psychoanalysis and a modern totalitarian regime "in which propaganda campaigns and heresy trials come to preempt free debate." In 1912 Ernest Jones, Freud's official biographer-to-be, convened a committee whose mission was to protect Freud from criticism and to derogate his critics. "This Orwellian project, which continued until 1926 and remained undisclosed until 1944, guaranteed that the sounding board for Freud's newest fancies, like those of any insecure dictator, would be an echo chamber."

7. In a footnote in his review-essay, Crews (1993) gives a most succinct and concrete list of criticisms:

The movement's anti-empirical features are legion. They include its cult of the founder's personality; its casually anecdotal approach to corroboration; its cavalier dismissal of its most besetting epistemic problem, that of suggestion; its habitual confusion of speculation with fact; its penchant for generalizing from a small number of imperfectly examined instances; its proliferation of theoretical entities bearing no testable referents; its lack of vigilance against self-contradiction; its selective reporting of raw data to fit the latest theoretical enthusiasm; its ambiguities and exit clauses, allowing negative results to be counted as positive ones; its indifference to rival explanations and to mainstream science; its absence of any specified means for preferring one interpretation to another; its insistence that only the initiated are entitled to criticize; its stigmatizing of disagreement as "resistance," along with the corollary that, as Freud put it, all such resistance constitutes "actual evidence in favour of the correctness" of the theory and its narcissistic faith that, again in Freud's words, "applications of analysis are always confirmations of it as well." [p. 62]

I have given enough excerpts from Crews to convey the substance and flavor of his criticism. These excerpts are a sample of much more contained in his review-essay. Putting the critics and the partisans of psychoanalysis aside, it would be surprising if readers of the review-essay would not conclude that Freud was an overzealous, obsessed, fame-seeking, power-aggrandizing, unlikable, data-manipulating and -distorting, complex individual who foisted on the world a theory and a therapy it could have well done without. Most critics seem to accept such a conclusion. The partisans of analysis (none of whom to my knowledge has written an essay comparable to that of Crews) present no evidence refuting the many critics Crews cites. They probably would, as Crews suggests, argue that psychoanalysis as theory and therapy has come a long way from Freud's formulations. And in the unlikely case that these partisans were knowledgeable about research outside the establishment but informed by this or that aspect of analytic theory, they could argue that this body of research contradicts the philistine notion that analytic ideas are, as Crews says, "castles in the air." Not surprisingly, the analytic establishment has and probably never will confront the criticisms Crews and others have amassed. Like General Custer they see themselves surrounded by opponents intent only on wiping psychoanalysis off the theoretical and therapeutic map.

There is not all that much new in the current backlash except for the large numbers of scholars who have contributed to it and, of no small importance, their goal to base their conclusions not on opinion but on historical evidence, conclusions they have made public and, therefore, subject to scrutiny. From its earliest days many of the criticisms being made today were articulated but without depth or systematic scrutiny. One thing the early critics did not know or ignored or glossed over: in institutionalizing psychoanalysis in the form of training institutes, the candidates selected were (willingly) subjected to an indoctrination that was as narrow and parochial as that experienced by those seeking to become clerics in a religious sect. There is a difference between training and education.

My first professional job was in a training school for retarded individuals, and the label *training* was used advisedly. The residents were told how they should think, what they should do and precisely how to do it, and the penalties for not conforming. What was going on in their heads was irrelevant and unimportant. It was not an educational institution in the sense that a college and university are educational institutions. Our public schools are called *educational sites*, and if they are currently under fire for their inadequacies, it is because in practice they do not educate—"get out" or capitalize on the interests, questions, and motivations of children— but rather pour into presumably empty heads a predetermined curriculum unrelated to the lives of students. The public school student is compelled to attend school. The student in the analytic institute

willingly seeks to be there, to be told how to think and act in conformity with the "truths" of psychoanalytic theory and therapy. By
the time he or she finishes training, the indoctrination is complete,
in principle as complete as in the case of individuals who are graduated from a vocational school for plumbers, carpenters, and elec-
tricians. (If my academic friends in law and medicine are to be
believed, those professional schools are steadily becoming trade
schools in which memorizing the "tools of the trade" are swamping
educational goals.) At its best, education is a process that *liberates*
you to go beyond the confines of your personal experience, to see
yourself and your ideas from new perspectives, and to see yourself
in the context of a social and intellectual history that is the opposite of parochial.

I focus on the analytic institutes in order to raise a question the
answers (and they are plural) to which are not as self-evident as the
earlier discussion would suggest. Before doing so, however, I have
to say that the negative verdict of history about the psychoanalytic
enterprise is one with which I largely agree but with significant
exceptions I will take up later. Here I ask, Why were psychoanalytic institutes deemed necessary? The answer given in the current
backlash is that Freud and his circle, in the spirit and tradition of
fundamentalist sects, could not tolerate the possibility that what
they considered as truths would be contaminated by intellectual
viruses from outside sources. Not only from outside sources but also
heresy from within. The picture we are given is that of "true believ-
ers" never in doubt that they possessed truths that would change
the world, some day, but until that day their obligation was to keep
doctrine pure, to seek and train adherents, and not to be daunted
or discouraged by the slow pace of the movement's progress. As
individuals they varied widely and wildly in background, personality, personal stability, creativity, and more. But they had several
things in common: they had no doubt that Freud had discovered
momentous truths (with which, of course, Freud agreed), and they
were incapable of that kind of self-criticism, that kind of sociological understanding and imagination, that sense of the history of past

revealed "truths," and that kind of humbleness that allows one to say that the human mind is our greatest ally and foe, and what does that mean for the path being taken?

In rendering this negative verdict, it is too easy to overlook a point wrapped up in the maxim "Even paranoids have enemies." That point is that in its early years psychoanalysis did not exist in a hospitable environment. The academic community, both in Europe and America, was not at all disposed to study, research, and evaluate analytic theory and claims. Yes, an academic here and an academic there would say that psychoanalysis was opening new vistas, but that did not mean that academia was about to roll out the welcome mat. In his review-essay Crews (1993) questions Freud's reality testing. In regard to the creation of the analytic institutes Freud's reality testing was pretty good. It would be wrong to suggest that Freud wanted to be isolated, that there were no conditions in which he would expose his ideas to academic scrutiny. When he was invited by G. Stanley Hall to participate in 1909 in Clark University's twentieth anniversary, his fantasies of fame and influence through this window of opportunity were quite explicit. The point I am emphasizing here is that it is much too one-sided to attribute the analytic debacle only to the personalities of Freud and his circle. There was, so to speak, an external "compliance" factor that played into the personality vulnerabilities of those analysts. Critics have done a remarkable job in uncovering and describing those vulnerabilities, but that is no warrant for assigning blame unidirectionally, as if the societal surroundings played a neutral role. It never does. And, let us not forget, there were more than a few people who characterized Freud and his writings as what one would expect from a Jew, in Vienna, no less, where leading political figures were blatantly *and* publicly anti-Semitic. I trust I do not have to convince the reader that I am not excusing Freud and his circle but rather putting the creation of the analytic institutes in its social-historical context.

In one very important respect Freud boldly took a stance counter to the parochialism of analytic institutes, especially those formed in America. Freud was opposed to a criterion for selection of analytic candidates that for all practical purposes restricted opportunity for training to physicians. Whatever blame is assigned to Freud and his circle for their secretiveness, General Custer stance, obsession with purity of theory, and expulsion of schismatics, one must not overlook the fact that Freud truly desired that psychoanalysis should be known to and absorbed by all disciplines concerned with understanding human behavior in its diverse aspects and accomplishments. He did not take this position lightly; he knew that it was a position critical of the institutes he had spawned. For psychoanalysis to become a medical specialty was the kiss of death. If one criticizes Freud for his grandiosity and intellectual imperialism, that is no basis for overlooking the courage it took for him to take a position running counter to what was becoming the norm in analytic institutes. If his criticisms and arguments went unheeded, it was not for want of his trying.

What also went unheeded was a position he took late in his life as he surveyed the analytic community and was dismayed at what he saw as the inevitable, unwitting, corrupting consequences of being an analyst to whom patients attributed, on the one hand, the most divine-like wisdom and powers and, on the other hand, rage, fury, and disappointment. Or both. He recommended that analysts be reanalyzed every five years, a recommendation that had all of the ballast of a lead balloon. In the current backlash against psychoanalysis, the criticisms are mostly in regard to the relatively early Freud, and they are largely valid. At least as I read the later Freud, he was far from satisfied with what he had institutionalized. It is hard for me to avoid the conclusion that he looked at the analytic institutes from the perspective of the saying "With friends like that, I need never worry about enemies." I am in no way suggesting that Freud went through an intellectual change of life. What I am saying is that the uncovering of the frailties of Freud should not blind us to some important personal virtues. He was a complex, imperfect person.

Insufficient attention has been given to the analytic institutes. If we knew absolutely nothing about the context from which the institutes emerged, critics would still have a field day examining institutes as educational organizations. Let me relate one story. In 1986 I attended a workshop in Boston by Peter Sifneos, a psychiatrist-analyst very well known today for his work on brief psychoanalytical therapy. He told the following story, which starts with a horrendous catastrophe in Boston: the fire in the 1942 Coconut Grove nightclub in which many hundreds of people were killed. Dr. Eduard Lindemann, a noted figure in preventive mental and public health, immediately set up "stations" around the city to deal with individuals and families directly or indirectly affected by the catastrophe. Sifneos, who was either a medical student or psychiatric resident at the time, participated in the effort and was very much influenced by how helpful one can be in brief contact with trauma-affected people—so much so, that when he later began his analytical training (I am understandably not sure of the chronology), he also began to experiment with brief therapy. His analytic supervisor told him that such experimentation would not sit well with the establishment figures of the Boston Institute, a bastion of orthodoxy if ever there was one. But then as now, Sifneos was his own person, and despite warnings about his future in the institute, he began a program of research. He wrote a paper, which was accepted for the convention program of the American Psychiatric Association. His anxiety level escalated when he found out that Franz Alexander would be a discussant of his paper. Alexander was one of the foremost figures in psychoanalysis, and to a beginner like Sifneos, Alexander represented mainstream thinking. Sifneos expected a very rough time.

Why did Sifneos relate this story at the workshop? *During his analytic training, he had never heard of Alexander and Thomas French's work and book on brief psychoanalytic therapy. He had to go to the convention to learn about their work.* In the cathedrals of psychoanalysis, there is no place for heresies. Nonbooks and nonpersons receive their status from closed minds, a lesson I had learned in my Trot-skyite days when Trotsky's name and role were erased from Russian history except for mention of his status as a traitor. In the past decade, French and Alexander have been "rediscovered" by researchers, mostly clinical psychologists, who have sought to eval-uate the efficacy of brief therapies, analytic or otherwise.

We are told that history is written by the victors, but it is also the case that histories written by victors are supplanted by new his-tories that cast the previous ones in a very different light. Freud and his epigones wrote their histories secure in the belief that psycho-analytic theory had been established as a valid, general theory of the human mind, a belief mightily reinforced by the acceptance of the theory in diverse university disciplines in the two decades fol-lowing World War II. The pendulum has swung, and today the wit-ting and unwitting distortions and omissions these writings manifest have seriously, if not fatally, impaired them as credible scholarly sources. Is it likely that the current backlash—characterized as it is by passion, disdain, and a seemingly wholesale rejection of Freud's *theories*—will in future histories come to be regarded as incomplete, or misleading, or even unfair? Granting as I do that the criticisms of his theories are largely correct, and granting as I do that the psy-choanalytic movement contained more than its share of fools, nuts, and zealots and gave rise to organizations that were caricatures of the root meaning of the concept of education—does granting all that mean that Freud is undeserving of a major place among those who illuminated the mysteries of human behavior? My answer is in the negative, and in the rest of this essay I shall explain why, his warts and all, I regard Freud as preeminent in this century because he thoroughly changed "the nature of the conversation." I shall briefly describe five phenomena that to the more youthful reader, professional or not, will be familiar or even old hat, even though that reader probably is unaware or underappreciative of the role Freud played in putting these phenomena on the table for discus-sion. If Freud's theories about these phenomena have not withstood damning criticism, his identification of these phenomena have withstood the tests of time.

1. As no one before him, Freud directed attention to infantile and childhood sexuality. That the more mature organism experienced and wrestled with the different modes of sexual feeling and expression was well known in human history (and, I assume, in prehistory). Freud's contribution inhered in his claim that from birth sexual feeling and response are in the developmental drama. That claim was not rejected by people on theoretical grounds but on the basis that the claim was on its face absurd, evil, and ridiculous. Machiavelli was and continues to be vilified because of the ways he described actions in the political arena and in the advice he gave to his prince to deal with the way things are and not with what the prince would like them to be or hopes they are. Similarly, there are people today who still cannot forgive Freud for his writings about infantile and childhood sexuality, and if today they are fewer in number than when Freud was writing, it is because what he said came to have the ring of truth and stimulated observational studies that indicated that Freud's claim was not concocted in an armchair. Eschewing his explanations could not get rid of the phenomena.

2. Again as no one before him, Freud made the world aware of how complicated, nuanced, and multimotivated interpersonal and family relationships are. Even those who do not accept his formaltheoretical explanations of the origins, vicissitudes, and development of those relationships cannot deny that he made it impossible to ignore how what we call "relationships" reflect or contain contents and processes Proustian in scope, depth, and complexity. Transference and countertransference, primary and secondary process, oral and anal, ego, superego, and id—these and other kinds of labels, concepts, or abstractions directed attention to phenomena in relationships. If Freud's theoretical explanations are dissatisfying, the fact remains that the concrete, observable phenomena

he sought to interrelate and explain could not be glossed over; they became "facts of life" that students of human behavior had to confront and explain. It is fair to say that he made us sensitive to self and others in ways that changed the nature of our conversation with ourselves and others.

3. The nature and function of dreams have always been a source of fascination. Freud's contribution inhered in his attempt to interrelate the manifest properties of dreams to nonobservable psychological processes in the human mind, processes within the mind but always in transactions with internal and external factors. For Freud, dreams were not random affairs, and they did not have simple explanations, which is why it is misleading to say that he regarded dreams as *only* caused by the pressures of wish fulfillment, as if between the wish and the dream there was, so to speak, empty space. If one does not accept Freud's emphasis on wish fulfillment, one is still left with the task of explaining how the "data" of the dream reflect and transform past internal and external imagery. He took those data seriously, no less so than the early Greeks who took "matter" seriously and sought to explain its nonobservable composition. Freud put dreams on the scientific-psychological agenda as no predecessor did. If his explanation has been or will be superseded, one has to credit him for describing and posing the problem in ways that stimulated discussion and research. The theory may be consigned to the dustbin of history; the problem cannot.

4. There were writers before Freud who emphasized the irrational in human beings, but it was Freud who attempted seriously and systematically to describe why and how that irrationality was inevitable, untamable, and frequently explosively destructive. To the American ear, so attuned to hear messages of optimism, onward and upward progress, and humans' perfectibility, Freud's "pessimism" was, initially at least, perceived as unwarranted and gratuitous, an example of the European proclivity to take a cynical view of human potential, to dismiss the possibility that internal destructive forces were stimulated and fed by old, historical patterns of social organization that guaranteed a misreading and derogation of the nature

of the human organism. Matters were not helped any by Freud's metaphorical theorizing or his semimystical musings in *Beyond the Pleasure Principle*, the book in which he clearly states that irrationality and destructive aggression are part and parcel of human heritage. In dismissing his theorizing, early critics also dismissed the problem with which Freud was grappling: how to explain people's inhumanity to people. But the problem has not gone away. Witness the fact that the twentieth century has been the most destructive in human history.[1] Today, even in America, people are reluctantly and anxiously finding themselves drawn to the problem as Freud was, although they are unaware of kinship with him, an unawareness that pays homage to Freud the pessimist, Freud the problem identifier.

The preceding four points are to suggest that the current verdict of history about Freud and his theories is subject to the criticism that it fails to distinguish between the problems he identified and the explanations he offered. In saying that, I am implicitly assuming that future verdicts will be far more favorable to Freud the problem identifier who changed the nature of the conversation.

I now turn to a criticism of Freud and his followers hardly alluded to in the current backlash. Indeed, it is a criticism more justly made of his critics than of Freud because his critics are writing at the end of the century rather than, as in the case of Freud, in the late nineteenth and the early decades of this century. Put in another way, what have we learned about the social-political, economic, religious arenas that should inform *any* psychology? Leaving psychology aside, have the social sciences given us knowledge that should inform how we should conceptualize human behavior?

---

[1]If I had to recommend one book on this point, it would be *"The Good Old Days": The Holocaust as Seen by Its Perpetrators and Bystanders* (Klee, Dressen, and Reiss, 1991). The historian Hugh Trevor-Roper begins his foreword with these words: "This is a horrible book to read, and yet one that should be read—not in order to revive old enmities (after all, it has been compiled by Germans and published in Germany), but in order that we do not forget the most somber lesson of the Second World War: the fragility of civilization, and the ease and speed with which, in certain circumstances, barbarism can break through that thin crust and even, if backed by power and sanctified by doctrine, be accepted as the norm" (p. x).

However you characterize and judge psychoanalysis, in the past and today, one cannot ignore that it is quintessentially a psychology of the individual and his or her family. Obsessively so. It is as if the larger social world does not exist. Freud was quite clear that psychology was not sociology and so forth. And it was not anthropology except insofar as anthropological studies were a means of validating Freud's individual psychology. And he was not interested in understanding religion except (again) as illustrative material for proving what he had learned about the individual mind. (More of this in a little while.) It is not unfair to say that Freud gave us a picture of the self-absorbed, family-encapsulated, socially unrooted individual. Let me illustrate this by a personal account.

I entered psychoanalytic therapy in my mid twenties. I needed and wanted to understand myself, to "find myself," and I had no doubt whatsoever that psychoanalysis would provide the answers. Just as I had earlier regarded Leon Trotsky as the fountain of knowledge, I had also come to regard Freud. As I have put it elsewhere (Sarason, "Some Reflections on the APA Centenial," 1993):

> I have learned a great deal about myself in the course of being psychoanalyzed. But as the years went on I became increasingly aware that what I had been and was both as person and psychologist was by no means explainable by what I had learned in the analysis. It could be argued that psychoanalytic theory is not intended to be an encompassing framework of human development and behavior, valid regardless of where the development occurred and the behavior patterns which it shaped. And it could be argued that Freud was quite aware that psychoanalytic theory was not sociology, political science, or any other conventional discipline but rather a set of principles and processes which undergirded those disciplines. Absent that undergirding, these disciplines will remain superficial and fruitless.
>
> There are some who would argue both points today but that would be an example of reading the present into the past.

In those earlier days psychoanalytic theory was presented as encompassing and, therefore, in a "successful" analysis the patient knew why and how he or she had become the person he or she was. The possibility that the origins, substance, and development of psychoanalysis were themselves unexplainable by the theory—that religion, ethnicity, national history, national politics, for example, were parts of an explanation—could not be considered by partisans of the theory.

For example, why did Freud dislike America and, I think, Americans? That question intrigued and bothered me. It reminded me of a letter Freud wrote to Saul Rosenzweig, who was my dissertation advisor at Clark University. Rosenzweig had written Freud about his experimental studies of repression. It was a relatively brief letter in which Freud expressed something akin to disdain for Rosenzweig's misdirected efforts. It was not a cordial letter. If the history of psychology I learned at Clark never explained national differences, that letter hanging in Rosenzweig's office was further evidence that national origin was a very important variable. How important it was became compellingly clear when in my first position after leaving Clark I developed a friendship with Henry Schaefer-Simmern, a political refugee who was an artist, art historian, art theorist, and art educator. I wrote about him in my autobiography and in my recent book *The Challenge of Art to Psychology*. The chasm between his European and my American mind was indeed wide. Whatever psychoanalytic theory could demonstrate about our kinship as two humans was more than rivalled by the differences in our world view. It was Schaefer who subtly and indirectly forced me to confront the fact that I was not a psychologist but an *American* one. [pp. 101–102]

I can understand why Freud paid no attention in his writings to what I shall, for the sake of brevity, call the societal matrix. In the past there have been critics of that omission, but with rare exceptions, those critics did not indicate in any detail or a systematic way how a general psychology would look—and a general psychology was Freud's overarching goal—if it took seriously what has been learned since Freud about the social matrix. Little or nothing is said about this in the current backlash, focused as the critics have been on the invalidity of the theory and how that invalidity in part reflects peculiarities and shortcomings in the personalities of those who contributed to the theory. What most critics have uncovered and concluded is praiseworthy, but, I would argue, they may have contributed to the current situation in which attempts to forge a general theory—let alone one that takes the social matrix seriously—are notably absent. As a result, we have a fraction of a theory here, a fraction there, and there is no way or basis on which to add them up. This situation goes unrecognized by the critics who in demolishing a psychoanalytic theory point us to a directionless future. Freud's theorizing has been characterized by some as grandiose. You could say it was a courageous but flawed effort that deserves to be superseded. But that supersession is not on the horizon because of centrifugal forces, reflective of the social matrix, operative in the psychological and social science communities.

What do the critics have to say about Freud's oft-quoted (with approval) assertion that the two major tasks or problems in living are loving and working? I ask that question because I know of no critic who has taken note of how that assertion is so revelatory of how the social matrix is absent in Freud. For one thing, Freud said little or nothing about the nature, place, and changes in work in the social matrix of his time. One would expect that having placed as much importance on working as on loving, he would say something about working, if not as much as about loving. Can it be that by work he was referring to himself, his colleagues, and his and their patients, a most atypical sample of workers? I have to conclude that Freud was utterly insensitive to how the experience of work—how it is associated with personal identity, stance toward one's future, personal and material security, loving and aggression, and more—varies fantastically in different parts of the strata of the social matrix. But if the social matrix was not an interest of Freud's, it apparently is of little interest to his critics who, unlike Freud, should not be expected to be ignorant of the role of work in the psychological makeup of people. Freud was absolutely correct in putting work on a par with love, but neither he nor his critics conceptualized their interrelationships. It is too easy and grossly superficial to say that a person's early development influences or determines how he or she will experience work, as if young children never work, as if the definition of work refers only to what adults do. It will take someone as "grandiose" as Freud—and no such person is on the horizon, let alone in our midst—to attempt to conceptualize how the social matrix inevitably interrelates loving and working.

Somewhere in the corpus of his work, Lewis Mumford said that if you needed to assign blame for many of the personal and social ills of the modern world, it should be the person or persons who invented the way of transporting steam over distances, which thus severed the tie between home and work and radically transformed not only the nature of work but family relationships as well. The *industrial* revolution ensured a revolution in the *family* and everything else in the *social matrix*. And in that "everything else" was a phenomenon as central to the human organism as loving and working, a phenomenon that by its increasing absence since the industrial revolution has had destabilizing and destructive effects in the lives of people. I refer to the psychological sense of community: the sense that one belongs and is rooted in a network of relationships characterized by obligations, mutuality, and dependability. If the price paid for that sense has its drawbacks, they pale before the price paid for loneliness and an unwanted privacy. I am saying nothing that was not said in and before Freud's time and that has not been said since by many writers (among whom I regard no one as highly as Robert Nisbet). The lack of a sense of community is in every sense of the word a symptom not only *in* individuals but *of* the social matrix, but it is a symptom about which psychological theorists, beginning with Freud, say nothing. Psychological theories are about encapsulated individuals in very encapsulated settings. It would be more correct to say that the theories are about parts of people, a fragmentation isomorphic with the social matrix.

It should be obvious that at the same time that I largely agree with the current verdict on psychoanalytic theory and therapy, I hold the view that future verdicts will be less severe on Freud for the reasons I have already given. I am justly severe on his critics for their misplaced emphases; their criticisms were largely valid but, in the spirit of "Adelaide's Lament" in *Guys and Dolls* when Adelaide eschews medical diagnoses of her upper respiratory tract infections in favor of "where the real problem is," her unmarried status, the critics never got to the "real" problem. To the reader unfortunately unacquainted with that song, let us just say the future verdict will be that the critics missed the forest for the trees. They will have to console themselves with being half right, which is not an unimportant feat.

2

Posterity, the Cruelest of Critics

There are two ways a university discipline (e.g., psychology, biology, English literature, physics) is "understood." From the perspective of someone outside the discipline, especially if outside the university, those who bear the label of that discipline tend to be viewed as homogeneous (at least relatively so) in interests and goals. If forced to reflect on their view and the outsider becomes aware that the label masks heterogeneity, that realization is transitory. We are all quite capable of indulging the Aristotelian tendency to attribute to all people in a labeled group a degree of similarity that reality disconfirms. And if we overlook or are insensitive to that reality, history will correct the misperception. To those in the discipline in the university, and to those "practicing" it outside the university, the discipline contains individuals and groups bewilderingly heterogeneous in interest, goals, and modes of practice—so diverse as to make serious substantive discussion among them either difficult or impossible.

In the case of psychology, nothing illustrates this more clearly than the perusal of the contents of the convention program of the American Psychological Association. I am probably right in stating that there is only one thing the thousands who attend the convention have in common: the belief that the association is too large, too carved up into specialties, possessed of too many different "languages" to permit one to see a common core. If that belief is understandable, it is wrong to the extent that it rests on the assumption that what someone termed an academically sanctioned Tower of Babel is due only to untrammeled growth and size. The fact is that from its earliest days—when its annual meetings could be held in a large seminar room—there were already sharp cleavages in regard to what was judged to be *the* important problems psychology had to address if it was to be a scientifically and socially productive discipline. Like our political founding fathers, those who founded the American Psychological Association were not homogeneous in terms of their personalities, values, outlooks, and conception of psychology as a discipline. However, unlike our founding political fathers, they were not under the gun of having to forge a constitution by which all would be governed. On the contrary, those early psychologists steered clear of any suggestion that the American Psychological Association say or do anything that would suggest that not all problems were of equal significance for psychology's future. Private opinions were quite another matter. James, Hall, Titchener, Dewey, Witmer, Cattell: among them were clear differences about the path psychology should take and how the future would pass judgment if this or that path was not taken.

If no consensus was sought about ordering problems in terms of their importance in the long term, there was consensus, indeed unanimity, about several nonsubstantive matters. And by nonsubstantive I mean matters that were neither peculiar to nor unique to the understanding of human behavior. The first was that to the extent that psychology was undergirded by the canons and ethos of science, it stood a chance of illuminating the nature and organization of human behavior. Regardless of the substantive problem (e.g., color vision, reaction time, perception, learning), the methods, analysis, and conclusions of investigations would be judged by the traditions and morality of science and its logic. Related to this was another belief: Although scientific methodology was not monolithic, "in the final analysis" experimental methodology was most decisive for establishing laws of human behavior. Put in another way, although in principle no methodology was off-limits, experimental methodology was the king of methodologies.

The third part of this nonsubstantive core of psychology was both a belief and an obligation. The belief was that a scientific psychology could contribute knowledge about human behavior that society could utilize for the betterment of its citizens. It was considered a glimpse of the obvious that ascertaining basic laws of human behavior would be appropriately accepted and utilized by society. Beyond this belief was an obligation: psychology *should* have an obligation to contribute to the public welfare. When or how these contributions would be employed was unpredictable. Nevertheless, psychology had a dual obligation: to science and society.

So, from its institutional-organizational origins in the late nineteenth century, the common core of American psychology was nonsubstantive in content. Why was there no consensus about important versus trivial, productive versus unproductive substantive problems? To the ears of Americans, psychologists that question will sound silly and stupid. They may even sound dangerous because questioning suggests that perhaps there should be an agreed-upon priority list that tells us that this problem is more worthy than that one, and those who choose the less worthy problems are less worthy psychologists.

But I did not raise the question because I think such a consensus is either necessary, feasible, or productive. (Not at this point in the argument, at least!) I raised the question for several reasons. The first was to indicate that today, as in the early years, such a consensus does not and cannot exist. The second was to suggest that this state of affairs was and is not determined by American genes but by American history, culture, and democratic ethos. It is a state of affairs markedly different from the characteristics of psychology in the former Soviet Union as well as in certain theocratic countries. It is a state of affairs well described and justified by one of my colleagues: "The game of science is a crapshoot. You can never know who will come up with new ideas, theories, and techniques that will render conventional wisdom wrong and obsolete. God help American psychology if it only travels in a mainstream, putting down anyone who meanders away from the mainstream. Staying only in the mainstream can have unintended, tyrannical consequences. If psychology ever loses its democratic *and* anarchic features, the crapshoot is over." I intend no derogation whatsoever when I characterize my colleague's utterance as quintessentially American rhetoric. "Doing your own thing"—whether it was youth in the sixties or the robber barons of the nineteenth century—is an obligation we have to ourselves and one that society is obliged to protect. It is not an aspect of our worldview conducive to consensus about substantive cores. At the same time psychologists bemoan the absence of a common core, they are under the sway of a worldview antithetical to a consensus about a common core.

If the common core of psychology has been and still is nonsubstantive, that is true only in terms of its national, professional organizations. In terms of departments of psychology, it is and has been another story. There are departments whose graduate curricula leave no doubt about what they consider productive and unproductive theories, which are the important problems and which are trivial, which problems have solutions that will contribute to understanding and eliminating human misery, and which problems are best consigned to the dustbin of history. On the surface as well as in rhetoric, these departments pay respect to coverage of areas and theories, but in diverse ways their faculty and students are in no doubt about what the core of psychology should be. That is most clearly revealed by the criteria they employ for selecting faculty and students (i.e., criteria reflecting a consensus about the substantive core of psychology). Anyone who has advised his or her undergraduates about applying to graduate school knows well how departments differ in regard to their views about "core psychology." Indeed, departments will give more weight to an applicant from advisor A than from advisor B because they know that A shares the same view of core psychology as the department does.

We know precious little about the culture of departments, and what we know derives from personal anecdote and, occasionally, departmental histories written many decades after the department has changed radically. Having listened for decades to these anecdotes from diverse people in diverse departments, and having read the too few autobiographies and biographies of psychologists, I am forced to the conclusion that at the same time psychologists are in principle opposed to straitjacketing the field by advocating or adapting a substantive common core, they are as individuals quite clear that not all substantive problems are equally worthy in contributing to understanding human behavior and to improving the public welfare. For many psychologists, however, their individual convictions exist side by side with the perception that there is nothing resembling a consensus about the worthiness of problems being posed and studied. And it is that perception that gives rise to the feeling that there *should* be some basis that could serve as a unifying point, a kind of general factor, enabling one to identify other than with a discrete specialty. As a student of mine said after attending her first American Psychological Association convention, "Isn't there *any* basis that connects or could connect these specialists?" It was not helpful to the student to be told that that was the question that almost everyone at the convention asked at least once. Nor did it appear to be helpful when someone in our lunch group said to her, "It is only through specialization that we can get the hard scientific building blocks from which a viable house of psychology can be built." To which another member of the group plaintively replied, "Since when can you build a house when there is no one to tell the electrician, plumber, mason, carpenter, roofer, painter, and others where each fits in? Your metaphor substitutes one form of homelessness for another." It was quite a conversation, which ended with agreement that the student's question was unanswerable—at lunch, at least.

In the rest of this chapter, I shall attempt to *begin* to answer the student's question, which I regard as a legitimate one precisely because so many psychologists ask it. Indeed, I would argue that any discipline that cannot publicly deal with a question so troublesome to its members is in deep trouble and that posterity, the cruelest of critics, will render an unfavorable verdict. That, I hasten to add, does not mean that psychology will not have made productive contributions to understanding human behavior and contributing to the public welfare. What it does mean is that its actual contributions will be far less than its potential ones. Voltaire said that history is written by the victors. Posterity has a way of turning the victors into the vanquished. Unfortunately, that is a message to which an ahistorical American psychology is hugely insensitive. I am not talking about history as it is popularly regarded, that is, the onward and upward kind that studiously avoids the warts and blemishes, the kind that presents partial pictures that posterity derides, amends, and recasts. Posterity has not been kind to the omissions, caricatures, and untruths of historians in regard to women, minorities, immigrants, Indians, and slavery. Posterity has not been kind to individuals and collectivities too smug to be capable of honest self-scrutiny.

The possibility that posterity may render a relatively unfavorable verdict about psychology today encounters two related arguments. The more narrow of the two is that "it is in the nature of things" for older psychologists (e.g., me) to view change as a departure from an earlier state of grace (i.e., the good old days). That is the generational argument, identical in principle and rhetoric to explanations of why parents and their children cannot talk with or understand each other. They hear each other only by shouting across a mammoth divide that is as frustrating as it is unbridgeable. In regard to the issue of a common substantive core, that argument is irrelevant because, as I have indicated, there never has been a common core. That kind of state of grace never existed. The good old days were not all that good.

The more general form of the argument is that it has always been the case in human history that there have been prophets of doom and gloom who could not recognize or tolerate changes in custom, practice, and thought; like Henny-Penny they saw the skies as falling. What they saw as disaster others saw as progress. It is an argument quite convincing to those who choose their examples in a nonrandom, selective way. In its most blatant form it is an argument resting on the axiom that what is is better than what was, and what will be will be better than what is. They would deny that their argument would warm the cockles of Dr. Pangloss's heart because Voltaire's doctor said that every *day* in *every* way we are getting better and better; the proponents of the argument clearly do not intend the Panglossian message. On the scale anchored on one end by hopelessness and on the other by undiluted optimism, the good doctor is off the distribution, and the proponents of the argument have no intention of joining him. If they are not off the distribution, they are certainly on the high end.

On numerous occasions I have encountered the general argument in response to my doubts about the onward-upward course of American psychology. When possible, I have asked my critic this question: "Would you deny that there have been times in human history when prophets of doom and gloom were absolutely right that their society was going to hell and indeed went to hell not for a day, or month, or year but for a long period of time?" No one answered the question in the affirmative. I would then ask, "Why, then, can you not consider the possibility that, generally speaking, American psychology has not been on an onward-upward course, that on balance posterity will not be kind to us?" Please note that my question had to do with a possibility—whether it had ever occurred to the critic that *maybe* psychology was a misdirected enterprise.

Their answer was in two parts. The first was that there was much in American psychology, past and present, that was unworthy, or unproductive, or pathetically trivial—a drag on psychology's scientific and societal contributions. The second part was that despite these drags, American psychology had been and still is on an onward-upward course. *Self-evidently so!* In short, they could neither articulate nor examine the possibility that what is self-evident may be illusory. We are not surprised when nonpsychologists unreflectively accept what to them is self-evident. Indeed, if psychology has demonstrated anything it is that what is evident to the self should never be confused with the "truth." But that caveat was known long before the discipline of psychology was born. We should be surprised when we hear psychologists talk about the onward-upward course of psychology as a self-evident feature.

I am reminded of recent surveys of people's judgments of the quality of our public schools. As one would expect today, a very large number of people consider our schools to be inadequate. When they were asked to judge the schools their children attend, these parents offered opinions that were far less dysphoric. That is the type of discrepancy I have encountered among psychologists: they feel far more positive about their specialty than they do about the overall enterprise of psychology. Their area in psychology is on an onward-upward course. The rest of psychology is an inkblot they find uninterpretable.

How *should* we begin to try to understand why so many psychologists feel unconnected to the overall enterprise of psychology? I italicize should for the simple reason that when the feeling of disconnectedness is so general, it requires pursuing understanding. I would go further and say that inability or failure to seek that understanding is not only symptomatic of the consequences of an absence of a common core but is the starting point for identifying a common core that, in my opinion, is the relation of American psychology to American history and culture.

There are two characteristics that American psychologists have in common: they are psychologists and they are Americans. Psychologists (at least most of them) are quite aware that they desire their field to have an impact on their society. They are far less aware of how American history and society have shaped their field generally than they are of how the substance of and contexts in which what they think and do are justified *primarily*, if not exclusively, on the basis of and respect for knowledge gained by the rationality, logic, and morality of science. If I left out the word *primarily* in that sentence, there is nothing in the assertion with which I would quarrel. But it is precisely that word that belies the belief that the substantive concerns of psychologists have been and can be explained independent of American culture. If that belief is invalid, in whole or in part, it means that it has never been the case, and cannot today be the case, that the theories, methods, and formulated problems in psychology are independent of the nature of American society. Substance aside, it also means that institutional contexts in which psychologists do what they do—in their national organizations, university departments, clinics, private and public settings, laboratories, private offices—are not comprehensible apart from the nature and dynamics of American society.

I shall now try to buttress my argument both by personal experience and selections from the writings of some deservedly well known psychologists. Let me first state the argument as succinctly as possible.

1. The common core in psychology is in the transactions between that field and American society. No psychologist, regardless of specialty, operates without a conception of the nature and dynamics of the human organism that bears the imprimatur of American society.

2. Unless and until psychologists self-consciously seek to understand those transactions, their feeling of disconnectedness will become stronger, and they will feel increasingly like strangers in the field.

3. Posterity, the cruelest of critics, will unfavorably judge psychology for its blindness to the fact that it inevitably reflected a particular society.

When I was in graduate school, I read somewhere in the corpus of William James's writing something that went like this: Only German psychologists could devise the mind-numbing experiments they did. I cottoned to that for two reasons. The first was that, since I was Jewish, James's putdown was grist for my personal anti-Nazi mill. The second reason was that it fit in with an attitude I was absorbing, although none of my teachers ever stated it baldly. The attitude was that *of course* American psychology was incomparably superior to any European psychology. It would be more correct to

say axiom rather than attitude because it was so self-evident—so
right, natural, and proper—as not to require articulation. With one
major exception (to come later) we learned American psychology,
and that meant theories of human development and behavior by
psychologists like Thorndike, Guthrie, Tolman, Hull, Gesell,
Woodworth, and similar eminences. (Piaget got passing mention.)
We did read Henry Murray and Gordon Allport. In the case of Allport, whose book *Personality* was one of the bibles of the time and
rightly so, his respect for some European trends (e.g., phenomenology) was unmistakable, but those trends went unpursued and undiscussed. They were treated as "philosophy," a quite characteristic
American way of dealing with ideas seemingly incompatible with
the nonsubstantive core of American psychology. No one was in
doubt that Allport was presenting us with a way of thinking about
and studying how to make *unified* sense of the characteristics of and
forces in a person (i.e., his or her development and life). A person
was not a laundry list of characteristics, dynamics, or unrelated
parts. The whole was indeed more than the sum of its parts. If we
were not in doubt about what Allport's goal was, no one ever
pointed out that his position was, implicitly at least, a very sophisticated critique of an American psychology comprised of parts or
specialties for which there was no common core—or if there was
one, no one seemed interested in conceptualizing it. Except, of
course, for Allport's Harvard colleague, Henry Murray, who was one
of psychology's most creative people, a characteristic not unrelated
to the fact that he saw American psychology as misdirected precisely because it was so American.

Murray's *Explorations in Personality* (1938) is dedicated to five
people, three of whom were European: Freud, Whitehead, and Jung.
(The number would be four if you included L. J. Henderson,
another nonpsychologist Harvard colleague, who "insisted" that
Murray read Pareto's *The Mind and Society*). If this dedicatory fact
is insufficient to convince one that Murray was uncomfortable with
American psychology, a reading of the first fifty pages of his book
will erase any doubt that the major intellectual-conceptual influences on his thinking were European. It is noteworthy that in a

book of 761 pages there are few footnotes of a substantive nature (i.e., nonbibliographic). Of the few, the longest one states:

> This may be regarded, perhaps, as one of many manifestations of a general disposition which is widespread in America, namely, to regard the peripheral personality—conduct rather than inner feeling and intention—as of prime importance. Thus, we have the fabrication of a "pleasing personality," mail courses in comportment, courtesy as good business, the best pressed clothes, the best barber shops, Listerine and deodorants, the contact man, friendliness without friendship, the prestige of movie stars and Big Business, quantity as an index of worth, a compulsion for fact-getting, the statistical analysis of everything, questionnaires and behaviourism. [p. 9]

Murray was not being contentious or snide. He was, in his own inimitable way, saying that features of America suffused the substantive bloodstream of American psychology and that the field would pay dearly for its lack of awareness of that fact. Murray was not a mindless critic. What is obvious in that book is the seriousness with which he sought to employ the methodological-experimental traditions of American psychology. The important point is that he zealously avoided remaining imprisoned in a view of the world and persons that was quintessentially American. That effort ran headlong into a problem that was characteristically American: America was wondrously, bewilderingly, frustratingly pluralistic, a fact mirrored in the group Murray assembled at the Harvard Psychological Clinic. Put in another way, the centripetal conceptual forces in that group were more than matched by the centrifugal ones. Intent as he was on achieving consensus about a comprehensive theory of personality, Murray (1938) knew that consensus was literally impossible:

> It is true that we never completely succeeded in merging our separate ideologies. How could such a thing come to pass in a

group composed of poets, physicists, sociologists, anthropologists, criminologists, physicians; of democrats, fascists, com-
munists, anarchists; of Jews, Protestants, Agnostics, Atheists;
of pluralists, monists, solipsists; of behaviourists, configura-
tionists, dynamicists, psycho-analysts; of Freudians, Jungians,
Rankians, Adlerians, Lewinians, and Allportians? To the fact
that we never found a language suitable to all, that some of
the experimenters entertained reservations to the last, the
reader can ascribe some of the annoyance or pleasure he may
experience when here and there throughout the book he
encounters varieties of terminology or theory. [p. xi]

For Murray consensus was not inherently virtuous. What was virtuous was the goal of seeking communalities, of avoiding the traps
of narrow special viewpoints, of undoing the parochialism of American psychology.

No person I would consider literate in psychology—an essen-
tial feature of which is knowledge of the history of American psychology—would deny that Allport and Murray had lasting impacts.
What I find interesting about almost all literate psychologists is how
they explain the impacts. Basically, their explanations are in terms
of Allport's and Murray's ideas, conceptions, theories, and the
research they did and the research of others they brought to bear
on their distinctive positions. It would be fair to say that the explanations are in the tradition of intellectual history. I have absolutely
no quarrel with that tradition. Would that such a tradition be other
than a small tributary in the river of American psychology! My
quarrel with the tradition is in what is omitted in the case of Allport and Murray, especially Murray, whom I knew, not as well as I
would have liked, but well enough to assert that his achievements
are not understandable apart from two related characteristics. The
first was that Murray had a generalizing mind powered by a boundless curiosity that served as a magnet drawing his attention to ideas,
events, and people relevant to his goal of a comprehensive statement of human behavior. He was no indifferent eclectic. Indeed,

he was a man possessed of a vision that made damned near every-thing in his experience and observations have meaning for that vision.

American psychology has had its generalists but very few with Murray's range, which brings me to the second factor: Murray was agonizingly aware that American psychology was a misdirected enterprise to the extent that it ignored the obvious fact that it had, so to speak, been born and reared in a literally unique society, a uniqueness that had its positive and negative consequences.

I said earlier that American psychology has not been without its generalists.[1] Indeed, one of the most frequent complaints of psychologists over fifty years of age is that the number of generalists is far fewer today than when they entered the field. They look back nostalgically at a past dominated by a dozen or so people whose work and writings had to be digested by anyone who wanted to be considered literate in the field. They bemoan the replacement of the generalist by the specialist; at the same time they accept the inevitability and virtues of specialization. But, yet, they yearn for a past when the substance and boundaries of the field were largely defined by a few people. I shall return to this yearning later after discussing a recent chapter by Garner (1994) with the arresting title "Psychology Has a Rosy Past, Present, and Future."

Briefly but incisively Garner (1994) destroys "the myth of the past."

---

[1] One such generalist was Roger Barker, who over several decades took on the awesome task of describing the human and physical ecology of an American town. In numerous ways he demonstrated how ecological features of environments are related to regulari-ties in human behavior independent of individual differences in personality among par-ticipants. It is to his everlasting credit that he undertook to test his conceptions and findings by studying a British town. Murray riveted on the internal and external mani-festations of personality—that is, the structure of personality, not the structure of envi-ronments. I have long entertained the fantasy that someone will come along masochistic, creative, and knowledgeable enough to attempt to integrate the two approaches. That kind of generalist is missing in American psychology not only because that level of integrative thinking has always been rare but also because the education of psychologists is inimical to that kind of approach. You can say that Murray and Barker were specialists as long as you go on to say that they had fertile, generalizing minds. Parochial specialists they were not.

Thus the idea that the past was filled with generalists and that specialists have only recently come to dominate psychology is basically false. What is true is that psychologists involved in these various systems of psychology simply asserted that their system was true for all of psychology. I hope I have shown that only James, the Dynamic Psychologists, and the Functionalists were open to any subject matter, and that even with these systems (James excluded) the individual researchers were as specialized as they are now.

I have been making the argument that the idea that essentially all psychologists of the past (i.e., before Heidbreder) were generalists is a myth. With few exceptions, psychologists have always been specialized in their research, and of necessity. On more than one occasion I have wandered through the psychology section of the library, and randomly picked up journals from the early part of this century. I highly recommend this activity for anyone who has not done it, because it is very illuminating. Articles published then seem much the same as they do today: They deal with highly specialized topics, and are very data oriented. The statistical treatment was less sophisticated, but there was more than ample attention to the statistical techniques available at that time. In some real sense, then, the actual doing of psychological research has not changed much for nearly a century.

Yet despite my disclaimer about the specialist being a relatively new development in psychology, there is a reality that makes the specialist more necessary today than in earlier decades. That reality is the sheer volume of research being carried on, a volume that has made it increasingly difficult for any single researcher to keep up with the literature except in a narrower field of research. So being a generalist, in the sense of knowing a very broad field of research, has become nearly impossible; the generalist in breadth of knowledge is, of necessity, a dying breed. But it is truly of necessity, not desire, since many psychologists would prefer to be more general.

To emphasize this point about the sheer quantity of research preventing anyone today from being a generalist in breadth of knowledge, simply consider the sequence of three books, each entitled "Experimental Psychology." The first is the justly famous book by R. S. Woodworth, published in 1938. Written by a single author then, that book was revised sixteen years later, but this time with a co-author, H. Schlosberg (Woodworth & Schlosberg, 1954). One man could no longer handle the breadth of coverage that Woodworth alone had in 1938. And in the next revision, an edited volume (Kling & Riggs, 1971), each chapter was written by a different author. So just thirty-three years after Woodworth's epic volume, the book had become a handbook written by many different authors. The second two books are titled as editions of Woodworth's original work. I have not listed them as such in the references because in fact they are not revised editions. Each was an entirely new and different book. The amount of knowledge had indeed forced a change from the single generalist in breadth to an edited book.

It would appear from that quotation that Garner is throwing in the sponge in regard to a common core in psychology. So let us listen again to what he says:

Is specialization necessarily bad? I think not, and speaking at the same conference (Garner, 1986), I prefaced and closed my talk with the argument that the basic problem for psychologists was to determine the relative contributions to behavior of the organism and the environment. While my talk was on problems of perception, this basic issue is valid not only for all aspects of perception, but indeed for all of psychology. *Sarason (1988), having read the book which contained the proceedings of the conference, noted (pp. 409–411) that of all the experimental papers given, mine was the only one that stated or implied that there is a common theme for all of psychology, and this common theme, according to Sarason, provides at least the basis for a core of psychology.* Agreeing with him, I argue that specialization does not guarantee that psychology will disappear, and that in its stead there will appear a large number of subspecialties, each operating in total ignorance of all the others. In my view, psychology will be held together by one or more conceptual themes that apply to all of psychology, such as the organism-environment theme that I used.

The italics are mine, not to parade my position but to emphasize something Garner is understandably reluctant to say: he may be unique among today's most eminent experimentalists in asserting that there is or should be a common core in psychology. Garner was writing an article, not a book, and he does not expand on his assertion. But anyone familiar with his work will agree on two aspects of his thinking. The first is his prepotent skepticism of dichotomies, especially in regard to methodological parochialism, best demonstrated in what I consider a classic article (Garner, 1972). The second is that our perceptual environment is structured; it is not a random assemblage of stimuli. That may seem to be a glimpse of the obvious but in regard to the environment, *any* environment, few take the obvious seriously. So, when Garner says that the core problem in psychology is the organism-environment transaction, he means that regardless of specialization, psychologists should be obliged to address the structure and bidirectionality of the transaction. For Garner, specialization in no way justifies isolation or tunnel vision or dependence on a single methodology—hence his insistence on the employment of "converging operations."

Despite the fact that Garner and I have been longtime colleagues and dear friends at Yale, I have been unsuccessful in persuading him to write a book based on his seminar "Contemporary Viewpoints." I have known at least half of the graduate students who have taken the seminar. With few exceptions (I assume there were exceptions, but none comes to mind!) they found it an unsettling, exciting experience precisely because of the way Garner got them to take seriously the organism-environment transaction in regard to all major areas in psychology. In that seminar, at least, they saw psychology as a home, not just a house for strangers.

It is not fortuitous that in the chapter from which I have quoted, Garner devotes several pages to Heidbreder's deservedly classic *Seven Psychologies* of 1933. Garner implies that writing a comparable book today would be a daunting if not impossible task. I agree, but not on the basis of the galactic increase in specialties and accumulated knowledge. That basis strikes me as too healthy and optimistic a conclusion, making a virtue out of apparent necessity. If the task is one no psychologist will undertake, it is in part because of how psychologists are socialized into the field. Put in stark terms, I would argue that if students are not exposed to generalizing minds, why should one expect that way of thinking to be absorbed by those entering the field? If they learn that each major area has its own common core, why should one expect them to look beyond their area? Now for some musings on "socialization" from a senior citizen in the field.

When I went to graduate school I wanted to be a psychologist, period. Not a clinical or social or developmental, or any other kind of psychologist. I wanted to and expected to learn what psychology was about. I was by no means atypical in this respect among graduate students. The application for admission did not require me to indicate my choice of area of specialization. What was made clear was that we were going to learn psychology—if not the whole schmear, most of it. It is a very different story today. In applying for admission, the student declares, is expected to declare, his or her area of specialization. The applicant who cannot make a declaration, or in regard to interests appears to the selection committee to be wishy-washy, has two and three quarter strikes against him or her, regardless of college grades or test scores or even letters of recommendation. Self-selection and institutional selection begin with the writing and reading of applications. Specialists select specialists. This is also the case in choosing faculty. When advertising for a departmental opening, there is no doubt what kind of a psychologist is being sought. Worse yet, frequently a specialist within a specialty is sought. It is fairly common that graduate students in area X will take (and then only because they are required) a single course, perhaps two, in areas Y or Z. And it is not unusual for students to complain about spending time in areas outside their specialty. Needless to say, faculty are not expected, let alone required, to be conversant with other major areas. What students and faculty have in common is proficiency in statistics and research methodology, the nonsubstantive core of American psychology.

Garner is right, of course, in saying that this state of affairs reflects the knowledge explosion that began during and after World War II. But that is only part of the story. In his classic essay, Garner (1972) gives concrete instances of how that explosion started by virtue of problems the military was encountering. And in his long research career, it was the military and other governmental agencies that supported his work with enthusiasm. And that is my point: *with the best of intentions public policy stimulated and supported the specialization explosion.* It was a public policy in regard to research, not education in a broad sense. It was not a public policy about a field but about discrete problems. The education of a psychologist was a responsibility of university departments; they had to determine what a psychologist is or should be. They had to do the defining and to develop an educational program consistent with the definition. It should occasion no surprise that a field in which there was no consensus about a core problem went along, eagerly and entrepreneurially, with a policy that seemed so right, natural, and proper—a policy powered in the two decades after the war by the perception of a bottomless pit of money.[2]

---

[2]Anyone doubting this point should read *The Degradation of the Academic Dogma* by Nisbet (1971). Nisbet is regarded as a sociologist and social historian, but those labels hide the fact that many of his superb books are directly relevant to and illuminating of the organism-environment problem. If labels serve a necessary function, they too frequently reinforce the worst features of specialization and parochialism. Garner was right in saying that specialization is no excuse for intellectual isolation.

It went relatively unremarked that psychology was being influenced by nonuniversity funding sources not only in terms of the
substance of the field but also in its educational-institutional
arrangements. Psychologists liked to believe that the generous support their research was receiving was due to, and only to, the importance of the problems they proposed to study in the ways they
would study it. Psychologists did not like to confront the fact that
more than a few psychologists researched problems *because* there
was money to support those problems and not because they had a
burning interest in them. If promotion and visibility depend on the
number of publications, the psychologist was under pressure to
become entrepreneurial, a characteristic we associate with those in
business, not in the university. For example, we are used to hearing
that one index of the knowledge explosion is the fantastic growth
of specialized journals. There is truth in that, but there is also truth
in the assertion that in a fair number of instances a journal has been
started less because its special focus is of indubitable importance and
more because of the need for outlets for the publish-or-perish
dynamic.

Whatever the undeniable virtues of specialization, we should
not overlook its untoward consequences deriving from its origins
and embeddedness in a distinctive society in a distinctive era. No,
American psychology today is not explainable only in terms of a
knowledge explosion with its consequent growth in specialization.
It is explainable (only in part, but a crucial part) by three related
factors. The first is that there has never been a consensus about a
common core with which all psychologists can identify. The second and related factor is that the strength of *individualism* in the
American ethos has always been reflected in the substance of psychological theories and in the organizational-institutional contexts
in which psychologists are trained-educated or work. The third factor has been unreflective acceptance of the unarticulated null
hypothesis: "The substance of American psychology is unrelated to
its origins and development in America." On the countless occa-

sions I have sampled opinion about that hypothesis, I have gotten two reactions. Not always, but in most instances, the hypothesis is rejected. The second reaction given by respondents is that they have given little or no thought to how being American suffuses the substance of psychology. However you judge Freud, you have to give him credit for demonstrating that what people do not allow themselves to think or talk about may be as or more revealing than what they can or do think and talk about. Another way of putting it goes this way: If we learn anything over a lifetime, it is that what we took for granted, we should not have. Like our posterity, each of us can be a cruel self-critic.

One final point I will illustrate in a way many readers will understand. Recall the first time you went abroad. Let me answer that for myself. Our late and lamented travel agent was an Italophile. So he arranged a five-week stay in Italy. I went to the library and took out a book on Italy. It is hard for me to convey the impact of the first sentence in the book: "Remember, every Italian is two thousand years old." In some inchoate way I knew that that declarative statement contained an encyclopedia of truth. I could not get that sentence out of my head. If an Italian wrote a comparable tour book about America, would he or she begin with "Remember, every American is a young person, no more than three to four hundred years old"? Does a "young" American look upon the world and the behavior of its people the way an "old" Italian does?

I met with a number of Italian psychologists. On the one hand, they were impressed, indeed overwhelmed, by the size and diversity of American psychology, and they were respectful of efforts to establish universal laws of human behavior. On the other hand, they saw those efforts as misguided, or woefully narrow, or inadequate in some ultimate sense because they were so asocial and ahistorical in nature. As one of them said, "I doubt that what American learning and personality theorists are saying explains the American mind. I am certain they are not helpful in explaining the Italian psyche. I have been in America several times. In all candor I have to say that

I found de Tocqueville far more helpful to me in understanding what I saw, heard, and was told about Americans than from any American psychologist I have read or met." When we returned home I read de Tocqueville's *Democracy in America* for the first time. *That* was an experience. Here was a young Frenchman, more than a hundred years ago, and who only spent nine months here, describing the "American mind" in ways that had the ring of obvious truth. I understand why that book is regarded by political scientists as a classic. What I could not understand was why I was never asked or required to read a book that should be regarded as a classic in psychology. And the wisdom contained in what the Italian psychologist said was confirmed in spades when years later I read a book about American Italians by an American sociologist (Gambino, 1974).

Posterity has done nothing to dim the significance of de Tocqueville's contribution. On the contrary, with each passing decade his penetrating observations and explanations gain increasing attention and respect. One would have hoped and expected that American psychology would have confronted the question, What enabled him to take seriously (and apparently unreflectively) that the American psyche, any psyche, is never independent of social contexts (local, regional, and national) and social history? For him, it was inconceivable that one could arrive at laws of human behavior that gave second place to the fact that the external world is structured and has a history suffusing the present. He took seriously that the organism-environment transaction was the core problem, in precisely the way that Garner indicated. It was not a side issue. It was the core problem.

If posterity has been kind to de Tocqueville, I venture to predict that the basis for that kindness is precisely the basis on which our posterity will judge American psychology unkindly. As I have said, that does not mean that American psychology will be judged as having been without virtues but rather that it was wanting in regard to the core problem. Unless, of course, you regard that problem as but one problem in a sea of equally important problems. If you so regard it, it has the considerable virtue of not engendering any plaintive misgivings about attending a convention of the American Psychological Association.

In this chapter I have talked about American psychology. If what I have said has any validity, it should be applicable to other fields. If my informants in other fields are to be believed, then what I have said is applicable. It so happens that many of my friends are in medical fields, either on the level of practice or so-called basic research. From what they have told me, the situation in medicine may be even more serious than in psychology. As one physician said to me, "A common core? Are you serious? There are several *thousand* medical journals, and if you peruse a random sample of them, there is one conclusion you come to: there not only is no common core, but no one is trying to conceptualize one. Medical specialists are like strangers passing each other in a foggy night. If you do not like that metaphor, there is another one that views medicine as an extended family in which no one knows or seeks to identify his or her nuclear core, however much each member of the family yearns for that nuclear core without which they feel unconnected, isolated, and periodically in the midst of an identity crisis." Another physician said, "Of course there is a common core in medicine, but it is not substantive but rather the desire to be protected from or to be rid of any societal tendency to restrict [physicians'] rugged, American individualism." I shall resist the temptation to repeat what I said earlier.

3

Thoughts About Robinson's *Love's Story Told:* A Life of Henry A. Murray

From the standpoint of science, biographies of scientists are interesting, but they do not advance the course of the science. At their most revealing, they shed light on how a particular scientist came to make his or her contributions that changed the field in some acknowledged way. Biographies are not written about "garden variety" scientists but about major figures who were household or semihousehold names. Even so, the number of these biographies is small. The reason, I suspect, is that very few major scientists led lives so florid, or lurid, or fascinating, or atypical as to expect that the biography will find a market of readers.

So, for example, modern physics is not comprehensible apart from the work of Josiah Gibbs in the latter half of the nineteenth century. He was a giant on whose shoulders succeeding generations stood and saw new horizons. But Josiah Gibbs was a "conventional" Yale professor who led a quiet, conventional life that is not the stuff of biography. Absent compelling, titillating, curiosity-arousing events and experiences, how does one justify writing a book about him? That he deserves a biography goes without saying, but that is not the bottom line of publishers unless there is a subsidy to cover the costs of publication. Whatever else it is, biography is not considered science. It is commentary on science, but it is not science. Josiah Gibbs is important for what he thought, did, and wrote as a scientist. His personal development, his family relationships, his quotidian style of living, his "psychology" are in some ultimate sense nothing compared to his scientific contributions. No scientist would say that those contributions are completely independent of what Gibbs was as a thinker, a person. But the "cash value" of Gibbs the person inheres in his scientific deeds. All else is commentary—interesting, but commentary nevertheless.

It is a very different ball game for psychology. For the psychologist (this one, at least!), the final score of the game is known, the contributions of the biographees are acknowledged. How did they, living when and where they did in circumscribed contexts, having describable interpersonal and social structure and dynamics, come to make their contributions? It is axiomatic for the psychologist that, for example, Piaget's contributions, anyone's contributions, are neither random events nor independent of the person. In the realm of human affairs, there are no virginal births. For the psychologist, the questions are, what was the ball game, what were the rules and who set them, who was on the biographee's "side" and who were the "opponents," what and who contributed to the outcome, and how do we explain why it was this person and not others in the ball game who turned out to be the most valuable player?

For the psychologist, those questions are not for the purpose of commentary. I said earlier that scientists do not assert that outstanding contributions are completely independent of "personal variables" that play no role whatsoever in the theories and methodologies of the particular science. Far from asserting it, it is the raison d'être, the stock-in-trade, of the psychologist. How do you explain any distinctive behavioral feature or accomplishment of any human being? What do you have to know to make sense of a person's life? What mysteries does that sense illuminate, and how applicable and productive is it for explaining the lives of others? Biographies begin and end with hypotheses and theories, usually implicit and hardly spelled out, not dreamed up to account for one, and only one, person. They are hypotheses and theories—*pictures* would be more appropriate—assumed to hold for the explanation of any life. That is why for some outstanding figures there is more than one biography; each biographer has a different emphasis or point of view, a different "truth" about the number, substance, and weight of factors one has to employ to explain a life, not only *this* life.

Unless my experience over the decades has misled me, psychologists tend to be avid readers of biographies. They also tend to be severe critics of biographies because they regard the underlying hypotheses and theories to be too incomplete or too partisan to a particular theory (e.g., psychoanalytic) or so mechanically or arbitrarily employed as to be more confusing than illuminating, as to explain everything and, therefore, nothing (or very little). Psychologists are interested in lived lives, a glimpse of the obvious. But if that is obvious, it is no less so that very, very few psychologists have written biographies as a way of illustrating and testing hypotheses and theories. That is unfortunate but not surprising. For one thing, in the education of psychologists conceptualizing and writing biographies is not a recognized methodology for developing and testing theories of human development. Clinical psychologists are taught to take case histories. If you sample among those histories and then read John Dollard's 1935 classic *Criteria for the Life History*, you will be comparing a shack in a third world ghetto to a Frank Lloyd Wright house. For Dollard—sociologist, anthropologist, psychoanalyst, and psychologist—the life history was a preeminent way of studying, clarifying, testing theories of human behavior. His book is an indictment of psychology then and now. Posterity has been on Dollard's side.

But there is a more seriously insidious reason for psychology's neglect of biography. Writing a biography is a very time-consuming, horribly complex and demanding task, especially if it is an explicit attempt to illustrate and test competing theories. Given the publish-or-perish dynamics in the university, for a young psychologist to attempt a biography is academic suicide. That also explains why longitudinal studies are so rare in psychology. Anyone who

believes that the substance of psychology and the worldview of psychologists are unrelated to America and the American university
still believes in Santa Claus.[1]

Writing a biography requires confronting the organism-environment transaction. However diverse writers may be in their conception of the human psyche, each is aware that that psyche is a
wondrously complicated affair that develops and changes over time,
becomes increasingly differentiated, and comes to have what may
be termed "style," that is, a pattern of regularities unique to a person at the same time that it has features common to others in a particular collectivity. Although in their heart of hearts biographers
know better, they proceed on the assumption or with the hope that
the psyche is a jigsaw puzzle that can be completed (i.e., understood
and "solved"). The better the biographer, the more respect he or
she has for how complex and differentiated the human psyche is.
And if that respect is great when biographers begin, it is boundless
when they are through because they know that being "through" is
not the "end" they imagined when they started. Too much mystery
remains.

A similar respect is rarely accorded the environment. Indeed,
the word *environment* is usually used in a vague, global way to refer
to an "out there" (e.g., parents, siblings, living conditions, neighborhood, regions, schools). What biographers usually rivet on is the
family because it is considered self-evident that the family is the
most important part of the "environment," that part without which
one cannot explain why a person became what he or she became.[2]
Biographers know, of course, that the context of the family is one

[1]I have advocated that the training and education of psychologists should include the
writing of an autobiography. How does the student explain him- or herself to others,
and what is the relation of this explanation to what the student is learning about psychological theory? I have no reason to believe that my suggestion will be either discussed or taken seriously.

[2]The word *environment* is part of the problem. A far better word or concept is *ecology*
because it confronts us with systems within systems so that a change in one place or
system correlates with changes in another or larger system; that is, no conceptualized

within larger physical and social psychological contexts. These other contexts are "ground" to the "figure" of the family.

Two questions arise. How is the figure related to and a reflection of the ground in ways that are psychologically absorbed by the central character of the biography? Are these ways and their substance or contents encompassed within our conceptions of what a human being is? For example, every human being comes to have a distinctive conception and way of experiencing and explaining time, space, the nature of sex differences, climate, dying. Put in another way, there are universal problems that every human being confronts and answers in some way. Those problems and answers are never experienced as trivial, and they cannot be understood only in terms of the family context.

How these problems are experienced and answered also have to be seen in terms of a larger physical and human context. If natives on a South Pacific island experience and answer these problems differently than Americans do, it is not only because their family contexts are different. If to natives on the island of Truk wind, clouds, and water color almost everything they think and do, it says more about the physical ecology than it does about family context or personality. Each Trukese is unique, but no Trukese is understandable apart from an ecology all Trukese have in common. It is not an ecology that is just "out there"; it is an ecology absorbed in ways and with an efficiency that leaves no doubt in the minds of the Trukese that they possess a psychological identity quite different from that of the Germans, Japanese, and Americans who serially ruled their islands. The worldview of a Trukese is not that of an

---

system is understandable only in its own terms. We know this in matters of weather, air quality, economics, bodily systems, and the like. It is something Freud tried to cope with in his "topography" of the mind in which a change in one place became both cause and effect of changes elsewhere. He riveted on the ecology of the intrapsychic world and, relatively speaking, was unconcerned with the ecology of the "out there." His "in there" was comprised of systems within systems. In that respect, he took ecology most seriously. It was as if the ecology of the "out there" did not require a similar respect. I can excuse that in Freud but not in his epigones.

American, and the same is true for that of the American Indians who have not assimilated the American worldview.

All this is obvious. But if it is obvious, it has not been taken seriously by very many biographers of Americans they seek to understand. Undoubtedly, this is in large part because biographers seek to understand the personality and accomplishments of an individual, and they take for granted that their American readers, like the biographers, "know" the larger context and its impacts. Is there any doubt that to a Trukese who became capable of reading these biographies what we think we know, what we take for granted, would be the parts of the puzzle without which Americans and their worldview would be utterly incomprehensible to that Trukese? What would a Trukese want to know to be able to say "I now understand the American worldview?"

These are the questions anthropologists ask when they study the Bongo-Bongos of this world. They are not the questions Americans ask about Americans. When we say we are Americans, we imply or assume that the label refers to a congeries of concrete referents that are very distinctive. If you, as I have, press someone to define or list those referents, you can count on two reactions. The first is a kind of startled response followed by silence and then "I've never really thought about that." The second reaction is "The answer or answers should be obvious but, surprisingly, they are not." The exceptions have been from those adults who became naturalized citizens. If their answers were incomplete, they knew what few Americans know: there is a distinctive American worldview independent of personality and family context. As one of them said, "Just as you can count on finding a McDonald's or Burger King or Wendy's in San Francisco, or Peoria, or Sioux Falls, you can expect Americans to see themselves, in comparison to those elsewhere, as living in a Garden of Eden. And to prove the point some will point to the fact that a large number of people on this planet would love to live here." This was said by a political refugee from Nazi Germany who went on to say, "What Americans have trouble understanding is that people like me *want* to live in America, but that does not mean we want to be Americans, that we want to or could be other than what we have been." This person became a very dear friend and a major influence on my thinking, not least because he, like my anthropologist friend Thomas Gladwin, kept forcing me to examine my American worldview. More correctly, to understand that I was not explainable only by my family context. Let me illustrate with an anecdote about Henry Schaefer-Simmern.

I visited him and his new wife in their Manhattan apartment. When I walked in, the electricity in the air was palpable. Obviously, Schaefer and Gudrun (an American) had quarreled. Before I knew it, Schaefer said to me in his Prussian-like way, "Seymour, you will be an objective judge." He then related that the previous night Gudrun's close friend from Cleveland had come to meet Schaefer for the first time. When she saw Schaefer, she exclaimed, "Henry, I am so glad to meet you." I looked at Schaefer, waiting for him to go on with the story. He saw my puzzlement and then blurted, "She called me *Henry*. This woman who had never known me called me by my *first* name. Even *you* do not call me by my first name." Having taken German, I knew that the personal pronouns *du* and *Sie* reflect or are applicable to different degrees of interpersonal intimacy. I knew the "rule," but I had never encountered its interpersonal significance. Over the years I learned from other German refugees that it took years for them to get accustomed to what someone called "too breezy American familiarity."

I suppose that from the standpoint of understanding a personality, this will be considered a trivial example. But if your concept of personality encompasses how worldviews are assimilated, it is far from trivial, and we are far from understanding how that assimilation takes place.[3] Biographies rarely illuminate the process. My argu-

---

[3] I wrote my autobiography (Sarason, 1988) as a way of taking seriously what I say in this chapter. Needless to say, when I was through with the writing, I was by no means satisfied with my accomplishment, despite very favorable reactions from others. The one part of the book I felt most good about concerned how in the Brooklyn-Manhat-

ment is not that biographies do not intend such illumination but rather that they do not see it as important or relevant to explaining a person. Neither as goad or guide is American psychology of help. If it were, we would be farther down the road of a general, not an American, psychology. To the extent we illuminate the substance and acquisition of the American worldview, we will better comprehend people anywhere. Theories of human development and behavior are ambitious affairs intended as explanation of people anywhere. If they deserve brownie points for ambitiousness, they deserve demerits for their parochialism.

In the decade after World War II, it appeared that an integration was taking place between psychology and anthropology, between those concerned with personality and those concerned with culture. Personality and culture had long been slippery, inkblottish concepts that made their relationships in conception and study both fascinating and murky. It seemed in that decade that American psychology was beginning to confront the fact that anthropologists had demonstrated the salience and role of worldviews (i.e., their substance, processes of acquisition, force, and omnipresence). What was the American worldview, and how should psychology study and take it into account? What could psychologists gain and apply to understanding how Americans become Americans? If those questions got raised, they failed to have staying power. Why?

That is not an easy question to answer, but I offer two aspects of an answer. The specific aspect was the fact that the "integration" of psychology and anthropology was powered on both sides by an interest in psychoanalytic theory: more correctly, by the aim of

---

tan-Newark physical and cultural ecology in which I was born and reared, I absorbed a sense of place that forever stayed with me. My personality is not understandable apart from that sense of place. The concept of the sense of place does not figure in our theories. I can never forget the first time (in the late 1940s) I drove across Nebraska and appointed myself president of the National Association for the Immediate Sale of Nebraska. *That* was an experience for Brooklyn-Manhattan-Newark me. In less stirring or frightening ways, I reacted similarly to my first trip to Europe.

proving or evaluating the validity of psychoanalytic hypotheses. Since the concept of worldview was absent in that theory, the emphasis was on what the theory contained, not on what was absent, even though what was absent was precisely what anthropology had demonstrated to be no less crucial than the oedipal complex, breast feeding, child-rearing practices, sexual development, and much more.

The more general answer is that examining the sources, nature, and acquisition of our "Americanness" has never been one of our notable characteristics. That may not be peculiarly American, but that kind of examination cannot be avoided by a profession devoted to understanding human development and behavior. European observers have described Americans as not being introspective. What they mean, I think, is that we are not introspective about our Americanness. Living as they did or do on a continent comprised of many *contiguous* countries differing from each other in all kinds of ways, it is not surprising that these observers are practically every day reminded of their Germanness, Frenchness, Italianness, Spanishness, Russianness, and so forth. Separated as we are by two oceans from most of the world, we have not, so to speak, had need to examine our Americanness. Indeed, up until this century, Americans felt divinely blessed by their isolation. That situation has changed somewhat, but only somewhat. In an age of global television, Americans are being reminded daily that who and what we are are differences that literally make a world of difference. If worldviews change very slowly—more by a geological scale of time than by our conventional calendar time—the study of that change is not around the corner.

Henry Murray was one of my heroes in psychology. So, when Robinson's (1993) *Love's Story Told: A Life of Henry A. Murray* was published, I bought and read it. The title of the book was, to say the least, intriguing. But more intriguing were two reviews I read before the book was available to me. The first was the lead review by Alfred Kazin (1993), a noted author and literary critic, in the *New York Review of Books*. Here are the opening paragraphs:

Love's Story Told is a remarkable biography, with a startling
tale to tell about the man who is its subject, the woman he
loved, and the literary presences and psychological myths that
dominated their lives.

One August morning in 1924, when the Cunard liner
Scythia was on its way from Boston to Liverpool, its captain
came down with acute appendicitis. As luck would have it,
Sir John Bland-Sutton, president of the Royal College of Sur-
geons, was on board and was able to operate successfully on
the captain. The chloroform was administered by a thirty-
one-year-old American physician, Henry Alexander Murray, a
well-to-do and extremely engaging New Yorker accustomed to
regular holidays in Europe.

After the operation the two medical men relaxed over
drinks in the lounge and it turned out that Sir John was
addicted to the work of the largely forgotten American novel-
ist Herman Melville. He had come over for just four days to
explore New Bedford, the port from which Melville had
embarked on his whaling voyage in 1841. *Moby Dick* "was a
kind of Bible" with him. He kept it at his bedside, and of
course had the book with him. He urged it on Murray.

Many a book is said to have "changed" someone's life. The
charming, easygoing Murray, whose most obvious social trait
was a regal tendency to flatter people and to get on with them
all too easily, was so transformed, shaken-up, and galvanized
by the force of *Moby Dick* that both his professional and his
personal life were to be redirected by the book. The immediate effect of *Moby Dick* on Murray was to make him identify
with Melville. He acclaimed Melville as a prophetic and
unafraid discoverer of the unconscious, and saw Melville's
inner life as his own. (I am informed by several Harvard
Ph.D.s in Psychology that as future director of the Harvard
Psychological Clinic, Murray strenuously pushed for incorporating theories of the unconscious in psychological studies at
Harvard.) Melville provided Murray with his first happy shock
of recognition of himself. I met him just a few times, and was

always exhilarated by his intellectual enthusiasms. Visiting him when he was a very old man (he lived to be ninety-five) I was not surprised to see pictures of whales mounted around his front door in Cambridge.

The second and much briefer review was by a psychiatrist, Anna Fels (1993), in the *New York Times Book Review*. Here, less one paragraph, is her review:

On first glance, "Love's Story Told: A Life of Henry A. Murray" is the biography of a man who was a distinguished professor of psychology at Harvard University from the 1920's to the 1960's, one of the creators of a widely used psychological test and the author of a respected but never completed biography of Melville.

The book, however, is really the story of how this talented, wealthy man from a society family pursued his fantasies on such a grand scale that he wound up in a mythologized sadomasochistic relationship replete with whips and knives.

Although Murray maintained a conventional marriage and social life, the center of his life, and of Forrest G. Robinson's biography, is Murray's affair with Christiana Morgan, a married aristocrat who shared his interest in Carl Jung. For 40 years, the two of them devoted themselves to "the dyad"—a relationship based on the Jungian idea of the symbiosis between animus, the male spirit, and anima, the female spirit. Typical of his psychological extravagance, Murray arranged for Jung to analyze not only himself and Morgan but his wife too—giving new meaning to the idea of family therapy. . . .

What emerges from this bizarre saga is a vision of Murray's disturbing intellectual and emotional limitations. For all his energy and enthusiasm, he left a swath of damaged lives: his wife's, his lover's, his lover's husband's and more.

I shall return to these reviews later.

Each of us reads a biography for different reasons. Here are the questions for which I sought answers when I read the Murray biography:

1. Murray was the first American psychologist to develop a comprehensive, systematic theory for studying and explaining personality. More than that, it was in the most explicit way not only a departure from mainstream psychology but a criticism of it. How can this be explained? Is it unimportant that Murray had no formal education and training in American psychology, that he had little to unlearn?

2. He had a boundless curiosity about himself and others. I would call it a "robber baron" mentality: to seize and interconnect ideas and experiences regardless of where or from whom they came, to appropriate and put his stamp on them. This curiosity and searching had no geographical boundaries. Intellectually he was an expatriate. Like the American robber barons who sought to control everything they surveyed, Murray sought to understand and explain everything about the human psyche. He was not in the tradition of a William James or John Dewey but in that of a Karl Marx, a Sigmund Freud, or a Carl Jung who sought to explain everything. If Murray's curiosity was boundless, so was his ambitiousness. Is Murray understandable apart from his ambivalence about and disdain for American intellectual and social parochialism? Is he understandable apart from his coming of age in the American 1920s, the roaring twenties, when the Puritanical streak in American ideology and rhetoric weakened, when Paris was the Mecca for rebellious Americans?

3. Precisely because of the first two points, how do we explain why Murray's comprehensive theory of personality says little or nothing about American society? Is that because his aim was to arrive at a *general* theory independent of national or cultural contexts, time, and place? Was he unaware that *his* theory was insufficient to explain *him* or the substance and boundaries of *his* theory?

4. Why is it that Murray is being remembered in psychology for developing the Thematic Apperception Test, not for his theory

of personality? That undeserved fate is in startling contrast to the recognition accorded Murray for rescuing Herman Melville from obscurity, despite the fact that he never saw fit to publish his mammoth-sized study of the author of *Moby Dick*. Is it possible that his reluctance to publish that study derived, in part at least, from an awareness that his theory was inadequate to explain Melville the American, just as his theory was inadequate to explain Murray the American? If, as it has been argued, Murray saw himself in Melville, that in studying Melville he was exploring himself, would he not have become aware that he had to come to terms with what it meant to be American?

Having read Robinson's biography twice, I still had difficulty deciding on a starting point to get answers, however partial, to my questions. My questions were not Robinson's. More correctly, my questions pointed in directions that the biography goes only a little way and, in my opinion, superficially.

I decided to start with Murray's *Explorations in Personality* (1938), a book, I had to conclude, that neither Robinson nor the two reviewers quoted earlier ever read. One would never describe the 761-page book as an easy read, not because there were multiple authors but because of the ambitiousness of the project. Let us listen to Murray in his opening paragraphs of the preface:

> This is a book of many authors. But in writing it our purpose was to make an integrated whole, not a mere collection of articles on special topics. The planned procedure for achieving unity was this: to have all experimenters study the same series of individuals with the same concepts actively in mind, and then in assembly—a meeting being devoted to each case—to report their findings and collaborate in accomplishing a common purpose: the formulation of the personality of every subject. The degree of unity attained is for others, not us, to judge. Diversity is certainly conspicuous in spots; so difficult is it, particularly in psychology, for a group of men to reach and hold a common outlook. Indeed, what is now so

hard for us to realize is that the job was done at all, that for
three years the many authors of this book were able to work,
think and talk together with enjoyment and some measure of
productiveness.

Four years ago every investigator at the Harvard Psychological Clinic was a pioneer with his own chosen area of
wilderness to map. Each area was an aspect of human personality—a virgin forest of peculiar problems. Here he lost and
sometimes found himself. Though there were plenty of opportunities for communication, his obligations to other experimenters were minimal and he was free to follow the wilful
drifts of his own elusive thought. He enjoyed, in other words,
relative autonomy in a Jeffersonian democracy of
researchers—an atmosphere that is breath to the nostrils of
every seeker after hidden truth.

All we workers were bound by a common compulsion: to
inquire into the nature of man; and by a common faith: that
experiment would prove fruitful. We devoted ourselves, therefore, to the observation of human beings responding to a variety of controlled conditions, conditions which resembled as
nearly as possible those of everyday life. Our emphasis was
upon emotional and behavioural reactions, what previous
experiences determined them, to what degree and in what
manner. This preoccupation set our studies somewhat outside
the university in tradition. For it has been the custom in academic psychology to concentrate upon the perceptive and
cognitive functions of the human mind or, more recently,
upon the behaviour of animals. [pp. vii–viii]

"Indeed, what is now so hard for us to realize is that the job was
done at all"—it was and remains a unique "job" in American psychology, or psychology anywhere. Nowhere in the book is this better illustrated than in four Murray-written chapters totaling 360
pages: "Proposals for a Theory of Personality," "Variables of Personality," "Judgments of Personality," and "The Genetical Investi-

gation of Personality: Childhood Events." You cannot read these chapters in any ordinary way, for example, the way you would and can read Freud. Freud had a "system" that compared to Murray's was a piece of cake. What we are asked to absorb in these chapters are *scores* of defined variables, their interrelationships, their dynamics, their intrapersonal and interpersonal causes and consequences, their ties to specified life events and developmental processes, and more. You do not read these chapters—you study them. Initially, you do not absorb their contents—you are overwhelmed by them: the specificity, the labels, the permutations and combinations, the scores of new labels for "needs and presses."

When I read the book as a graduate student (four years after it came out), I had a reaction that everyone else who read it had (and has): it is so goddamned detailed and complicated as to tax memory beyond the breaking point. And yet, I could not point to one variable, one need or one press, or to *any* one thing, that was excess baggage. I reacted as I had on first reading Darwin's *The Origins of Species*: I could never know other than a minuscule fraction of what Darwin knew; I did not possess that type of mind that could keep and utilize so many variables in the forefront of my thinking. Murray knew what he was asking of the reader because several times in those chapters, he explicitly says that the complexity is not of his doing but a requirement for taking complexity seriously. His plea has fallen on deaf ears.

Those chapters are as intellectually ambitious a feat as exists in psychology (broadly defined), ambitious in terms of scope and organizing principles as well as in the goal of incorporating the concepts of others in psychology *and* in the biological sciences. Murray was not only a physician—he was a Ph.D. in physiology and had a proven track record in medical research. One cannot read those chapters, and the preceding ones by him, without recognizing the obvious: Murray was out to milk, to integrate, all of his experience and knowledge to explore and map the human personality. And in doing so he was quite aware, it was his intention, that with the publication of that book American psychology would have to deal with

Henry Murray. Personal ambition was part of the picture, but that took second place to his obsession: to explore and map the human personality, to change the course of American psychology.

Up until Robinson's biography the title "Explorations in Personality" seemed apt and even modest. Strangely (perhaps not), Robinson does not connect the title of the book to the fact that in his childhood Murray's heroes were explorers of what were then unexplored areas of the planet. Indeed, Murray seriously wanted to follow in their footsteps. Living as we do at the end of the twentieth century, it is hard for us to comprehend the impact of Murray's heroes (Nansen, Grenfell) on the people of the day. At five, Murray "felt a burning need to climb Mt. McKinley." Murray pleaded with his mother to name his newborn brother Nansen. These may seem trivial points. After all, grandiose fantasies of fame and achievement were not then or now absent in young children, *especially young American boys*. But Henry Murray was not any American boy. He was born into and reared in a very rich American family. If there was any message young Murray absorbed in his high society, rich-rich, influential upbringing, it was that money would be no bar to becoming what you wanted to become. That is putting it crassly and even unfairly because along with seemingly unlimited resources, there was another message: the obligation to use one's resources in ways contributing to knowledge and the public welfare.

In any event, young Murray's desire to be an explorer had a Walter Mitty quality, but he had no reason to believe, no one told him, that reality would bar him from acting on that desire. Beginning early in his youth, traveling in foreign countries was "one of those things," not a fantasy to be postponed because of life circumstances. You could do what you wanted to do; you could become what you wanted to become. If that was part of the American rhetoric, if that was a rhetoric propelling millions of immigrants to these shores, it was not rhetoric for the likes of Henry Murray. It was a message absorbed by him in ways and with a force unaccountable by his theory of personality. What his theory can illuminate, in part at least, is the psychology, the uniqueness, of his personality. But his theory leaves out the social-national "ground" that placed its imprimatur on Henry Murray as "figure." As Murray very well knew, figure is incomprehensible apart from its ground: the subtle, silent, historically structured ground containing values and axioms making up a worldview. However you care to label it, it is not Freud's or Jung's unconscious. But it is no less fateful for how psyches come to be what they are. We know that ground has structure, but the tendency to rivet on figure leads us not only to ignore ground and its impacts but to mislead us about how we regard "human nature." Let me illustrate this point.

I was brought up in psychology to believe that for the neonate the world was a blooming, bloody confusion. Somehow or other that confusion tends to dissipate, a process that occupied the attention of theorists and researchers. When, why, and how did the organism begin to show differential responses to external stimuli? How does perceptual order emerge from confusion? It was assumed that the neonate was biologically incapable of differential perceptual response. It was *not* assumed that the immediate ecology into which the newborn was catapulted had a structure inimical to demonstrating a different perceptual response (i.e., the possibility that it was less the biological immaturity of the organism than it was the structure of that ecology). When that assumption was challenged and tested, we had to change our minds about who had been confused. Granted that it takes special "out there" conditions to elicit a differential perceptual response, but that is precisely the point: we had taken "our" ground for granted, a kind of ground we did not have to think about, as a result of which our explanations of the newborn psyche were faulty, misleading, and incomplete.

I am trying to explain the ambitiousness and intellectual heroism powering Murray's effort to develop an encompassing theory of personality and its development. I have suggested that early on in his life, his need for achievement and fame were already strong, part of his motivational makeup, and reinforced by the realities of his social background. That suggestion runs counter to the picture Robinson gives us. What he gives us is a young lad completely at home in the encapsulated, upper reaches of high society, dutiful and respectful of parents and family, God fearing, attending the best of private schools, a very likable, affable social creature, a sports enthusiast, a leader more than a follower in his cohort, intellectually and academically undistinguished, a reader, most happy when he was out of doors.

When Murray entered Groton in 1906, his father,

> pleading his son's youth and inexperience, persuaded school officials to admit him to the second form and not the third. Grafton Minot, a classmate, remembered Harry as "straight and well-formed, carrying himself with style. His manner was open and agreeable, and I can remember no temper or ill-nature. He was not conceited, but had a certain reasonable dignity. The foregoing is almost negative, an attractive boy from the 'right sort of people' growing up in the 'right sort of way,' but there was much more to him than that." Having said this much, however, Minot neglects to mention what it was that set Harry apart. "Brains? Not much visible interest in scholarship, probably in the first quarter of the class in marks, which did not mean much in our case." Harry was a bright, privileged boy among others of his kind. He was a solid student with strengths in History and French, less evident aptitudes for English and Latin, whose grades never wandered too far from the middle of the class. The Rector's brief comments on Harry's report cards—"A very satisfactory boy," "Good, as usual," "Deserves credit for having taken so high a place in this form," "Came very near to disobedience the other day"—indicate steady progress, never brilliant, but with occasional lapses, toward graduation. [Robinson, 1993, pp. 21–22]

As to his years at Harvard:

> Harry once jested that at Harvard he majored in the three Rs—Rum, Rowing, and Romanticism. He hardly exaggerated.

His undergraduate days were a happy round of pleasures, most of them harmless enough. It did not occur to him at the time that he was wasting himself in shallow frivolity. A certain obliviousness to such right-minded perspectives was doubtless integral to the fun. Privilege had no obvious cost to those who did not share it. Conflict in Europe was still a remote rumbling, almost welcomed by the collegiate crowd as a summons to heroic exploits. Meanwhile, life in Cambridge at once defined and fully satisfied Harry's youthful expectations. He was socially prominent, a celebrated athlete, and blissfully in love. [Robinson, 1993, p. 27]

I think it fair to say that Robinson's brief account of early Murray is intended to emphasize the discontinuity between early Murray and what began to happen when he entered medical school. (Despite an undistinguished academic record, he was admitted to Harvard and Columbia medical schools. We are given no hint whatsoever that Murray had any doubt about being admitted in either place. *You could become and do what you wanted to become and do*, a psychological axiom basic to Murray's worldview.)

I suggest that the discontinuity is not as dramatic as it appears in regard to Murray's ambitiousness, needs for achievement and excelling, and the obligation to serve and to justify one's existence. Of the many facts that Robinson gives us but does not explore, here are a few:

1. In his pre-Groton, private school in New York, he was an editor of the school magazine, "a monthly compendium of school gossip, sporting news, execrable (mostly ethnic) jokes, brief essays (on the evils of socialism, for example), and tips on the best books and plays" (Robinson, 1993, p. 18). He was elected captain of the football team; he "most enjoyed playing quarterback" (p. 18).

2. He enjoyed books, "though he was not always willing to follow his father's lead into Scott and Dickens. Left to himself, he gravitated to narratives of adventure and heroism (Nansen was pre-

eminent in this category), nature stories for boys (Ernest Seton Thompson was a favorite), fairy tales (the collections by Andrew Lang were best remembered), and, rather oddly, the Horatio Alger novels" (p. 24). I find it strange that Robinson considers reading Horatio Alger to be odd, even though his knowledge of what Murray read came to him from an aged Henry Murray.

3. At Groton he played football and golf, enjoyed cross-country running, and became a skilled oarsman on the varsity team. In his *regular* letters home to his father:

> [h]e makes frequent mention of his many activities—debating, choir, stage managing class plays, teaching at a local Sunday school, serving as sports editor for the *Groton Weekly*—but never complains of boredom or fatigue. "I am terribly busy now," he wrote in early October 1910. "Football takes every afternoon. Then there is missionary [Episcopal church work] to Shirley, Pres. of the Museum Society, Grotonian, stage manager for two plays, rehearsals, Camp committee & Civics club, beside my regular studies which are very hard." But such constant, *unreflecting* motion was entirely to his taste. "The sixth form year is swell," he closed. [p. 22]

I italicize *unreflecting* because I regard its implications as gratuitous. One could as well say that seeking and soaking up new experience was already evident in the young boy. If you take Murray's theory of personality only half-seriously, you could not employ the word *unreflecting*.

4. Murray took pride in his Groton essay on the rebel John Brown, a celebration of "heroic idealism" that won the history prize. Writing was never a problem for him.

5. Influenced as he was by the legendary Endicott Peabody, the Groton rector, "He was ambitious for a while to become a medical missionary in the style of Wilfred Grenfell of Labrador" (p. 25). He regularly attended chapel and taught Sunday school in the nearby town of Shirley.

6. In his later years Murray described himself as a loner in his school days. That self-judgment is in dramatic contrast to how others saw him as a youth. But, at the least, one can say that the young Murray—who so easily adapted to whatever milieu he found himself in, who to his cohorts was an affable, likeable, cheerful, humorous, self-confident youngster—saw himself as different, as in some distinctive way apart from others. "Moreover, he had a large, warm circle of friends at Groton. Grafton Minot recalled nothing of the recluse in Harry. Nor did Dean Acheson, his third-form roommate, who remembered him as the 'outstanding' member of the class 'in the sense of originality of mind, curiosity about everything, sympathetic personality, catholicity of taste, cultural breadth'" (p. 25).

Coming as that does from Dean Acheson, I regard his assessment of Murray's intellectual characteristics as confirmation of my conclusion, quite in line with Murray's theory, that he was already an explorer in his youth. He may have appeared as intellectually undistinguished and "unreflecting," but the seeds for his later blooming had already begun to sprout, awaiting full bloom for when he would move to new milieus that would stimulate and reinforce his boundless curiosity. I find it puzzling that when Robinson describes Murray coming to Harvard, he mentions his "well-concealed intelligence." Robinson does not prepare the reader for such a conclusion, suggesting as it does a marked discontinuity between the early and later Murray.

It may sound like a clang association when I say that the Murray biography reminded me of the problems people had in explaining why Harry Truman came to be one of our great presidents. I remember well how puzzled people were when Franklin Roosevelt chose Truman as a running mate in his campaign for a fourth term. Truman was a serious, hard-working senator but by no means distinguished in terms of leadership, and he was not regarded as possessing intellectual-cultural depth and scope. Besides, he was a "product" of the Prendergast political machine not noted for its adherence to virtue in action. If Harry Truman was seen as somewhat more than a cipher, no one described him as being distinguished. If he had a "well-concealed intelligence," it was very well concealed. And when President Roosevelt died, the nation's grief was exacerbated by a not concealed anxiety about the competence of Harry Truman. The discontinuity between what Truman seemed to be and what he needed to be was upsetting; *frightening* would not be too strong a word.

With each passing decade, explaining Harry Truman has occupied many historians and political scientists. Their emphasis has been on Truman the person, his personality, his combination of independence, forthrightness, courage, honesty—a symbol, so to speak, of his early twentieth-century upbringing in a small, midwestern town still reflecting (psychologically and otherwise) a semipioneer tradition and outlook. Shades of Abe Lincoln!

Forget for the moment Harry Truman the person. What do we learn about Independence, Missouri, from McCullough's (1992) recent biography? It had a library, cultural clubs, a new high school, two book stores, theaters, an opera house, and private schools. It was a place in which education and "culture" were respected and fostered. It was a place in which people were aware of "the better things in life." Even if one assumes that it was a town having *some* kinship to Sinclair Lewis's *Main Street*, it was kinship and not identity. It was quintessentially American in attitude in several respects: America was different from the rest of the world, you should strive to become what you want to become, and you should expose yourself to "the finer, higher things in life" even if they had foreign origins (e.g., music). That Harry Truman wanted to be a musician, that he willingly and enthusiastically embraced the piano, that he traveled to Kansas City for advanced lessons say a lot about Truman and his very far from rich family, but these points also say a lot about Independence where such pursuits were judged as worthy, not a sign of uppityness. That a student in high school took Latin, English literature, and a good deal of "foreign" and ancient history required no special explanation. That Harry Truman had a passion for history was recognized *and* applauded. (No president since the founding fathers read *and* knew as much history as he did. His heroes were Andrew Jackson, Hannibal, Richard E. Lee, Scipio, and Cincinnatus.)

I am not suggesting that Independence was Periclean Athens, just as it would be grossly incorrect to suggest that Henry Murray's rich-rich, high-society ambiance was an intellectual-cultural wasteland. What I am suggesting is that the personality *and* accomplishments of Truman and Murray are not explainable apart from the national and local ecologies in which they were reared. If you apply Murray's personality theory and framework to the lives of both men, much about them becomes explainable; that is, continuity rather than discontinuity is apparent. What we get is a feel for their uniqueness. What we do not get is a feel for how the uniqueness of each of their outlooks or worldviews was shaped in the most silent and subtle ways by what on the surface appears to be wildly different *American* contexts. I offer the hypothesis that although these contexts were phenotypically different, they genotypically had several features in common, American features: you should strive to become what you want to become; there is a world to conquer; you should seek and soak up experience; you have to justify your existence by accomplishment and service; Horatio Alger is more than a character in fiction; you are responsible for yourself as well as responsible to others; optimism about your future is right, natural, and proper; Mount Everest is there to be climbed; Abe Lincoln is as quintessentially American as patricians Theodore and Franklin Roosevelt; nothing succeeds like success.[4]

Knowing what we know of the ecology of Independence and the rich-rich section of Henry Murray's Manhattan does not alone explain, of course, why either of these men became what they became. But knowing the ecology of these places should prevent us

---

[4]It is, I think, distinctively American that so many colleges and universities (as well as foundations) have the names of those individuals who gave part of their fortunes (however achieved) to the creation or sustenance of those institutions. If their motivations were often mixed, they nevertheless reflect an American attitude to education as salvation as well as to service as a form of repayment. And not a few of these donors were poorly educated or self-educated.

from being surprised that from them emerged a Henry Murray or a Harry Truman. Granted their unique personalities, and granted that they were very different from each other (let us not count the ways), the fact remains that they had in common *some* aspects of a worldview absorbed in and from ecologies distinctively American. Murray's theory of personality was a heroic attempt to explain personality development and dynamics in terms of intimate and very circumscribed interpersonal contexts shaping intrapsychic structure. He *was* in that respect in the tradition of Freud and Jung. And precisely because he was so steeped in that tradition (what someone called the imperialism of the intrapsychic), he could not give weight to how national and local ecologies come to be absorbed and part of a worldview in subtle and silent ways. That is what I meant when I said that Murray's theory cannot explain his Americanness, just as Freud's theorizing cannot explain his Viennese-European Jewishness. Like Freud and Jung, Murray intended an *encompassing* theory of personality, one applicable to people anywhere. But "anywhere" is a horribly complicated physical, cultural, psychological ecology that puts its stamp on personality "anywhere." It may be labeled "ground," but it is no less impactful than the people, the "figures," we seek to explain. We are quite aware that personality is a horribly complicated affair, and we understand and applaud efforts to make sense of it. But in riveting on the figure and discounting the ground, we have been prevented from seeing relationships vital to clarifying aspects of that complexity.

Another clang association. In 1892 George Santayana, the great Harvard philosopher, visited Yale over a weekend and wrote a brief article in *The Harvard Monthly* titled "A Glimpse of Yale." Here is his opening paragraph:

The ideas which have most influence over our feelings are sometimes the vaguest and the phrases most often on our lips have the least definable meaning. Such, for the Harvard man, is the idea conveyed by the short word YALE. We know what emotion belongs to it, and if we were not afraid of wounding polite ears we might readily enough supply its appropriate context. If we attempted, however, to explain this irritation to a stranger, or to justify it to ourselves, we should soon be involved in difficulties. We feel that Yale is at once most similar and most opposite to Harvard, that she is not only a rival in those things, such as athletics, which are common to both colleges, but at the same time an embodiment of what is most hostile to our spirit. Yet this feeling, even if it should prove justifiable, is not generally grounded on any actual knowledge. It is a vague intuition which experience has never tested. If we knew Yale better, should we not feel all our mistrust dissolve and our coldness thaw? Should we not feel the substantial identity of our aims and history? Should we not marvel that mere rivalry in sport, which ought to be above all things good-natured and friendly, should have produced such an unnatural prejudice between two neighboring colleges? [pp. 48–49]

It is a fascinating article because in it Santayana contrasts the Harvard-Boston-Cambridge and the Yale–New Haven ecologies. Although Santayana is quite aware of commonalities, his purpose is to "explain" why it is not surprising that people at Yale and Harvard see themselves and the world so differently. Let us listen to Santayana on the newly arrived Yale freshman:

The first ingredient of the Yale Spirit is of course the raw material of the students. They come, as is well known, from many parts of the country, and this diversity of origin and associations would seem at first sight to be an obstacle to unity. But it is not. Each boy in his distant high school or academy has been looking forward to the day when he should find himself in the great college; this has been the dream of his boyhood. When he arrives he comes upon entirely strange scenes, where he is dependent for all his pleasures and successes on his ability to make new friends and to play an indispensable part in the undergraduate world. The traditions of the place become sacred to him and he vies with his fellow students in proving that he understands them. His family and early friends are far away. The new influences soon control him entirely and imprint upon his mind and manner the unmistakable mark of his college. College ideals are for the time being his only ideals, college success the only successes. The Yale man is not often such by halves or incidentally; he does not so often as the Harvard man retain an underlying allegiance to the social and intellectual standards of his family, by virtue of which he allows himself to criticize and perhaps to despise the college hero. Divisions of wealth and breeding are not made conspicuous at Yale as at Harvard by the neighborhood of a city with well-marked social sets, the most fashionable of which sends all its boys to the college. These boys—so much does extreme youth prevail among us—form the most conspicuous masculine contingent of Boston society, and the necessity falls upon them of determining which of their college friends are socially presentable. This circumstance brings out at Harvard an element of snobbery which at Yale is in abeyance. The college hero is there most unreservedly admired, and although it is not true that the most coveted societies are open to everyone who gains distinction in scholarship or athletics, other considerations have relatively much less weight than among us. The relations of one Yale student to another are comparatively simple and direct. They are like passengers in a ship or fellow countrymen abroad; their sense of common interests and common emotions overwhelms all latent antipathies. They live in a sort of primitive brotherhood, with a ready enthusiasm for every good or bad project, and a contagious good-humor. . . .

In fact, Yale is in many respects what Harvard used to be. It has maintained the traditions of a New England college more faithfully. Anyone visiting the two colleges would think

Yale by far the older institution. The past of America makes itself felt there in many subtle ways: there is a kind of colonial self-reliance, and simplicity of aim, a touch of non-conformist separation from the great ideas and movements of the world. One is reminded, as one no longer is at Harvard, of Burke's phrase about the dissidence of dissent and the Protestantism of the Protestant religion. Nor is it only the past of America that is enshrined at Yale; the present is vividly portrayed there also. Nothing could be more American—not to say *Amurrcan*—than Yale College. The place is sacred to the national ideal. Here is sound, healthy principle, but no over-scrupulousness, love of life, trust in success, a ready jocose-ness, a democratic amiability, and a radiant conviction that there is nothing better than one's self. It is a boyish type of character, earnest and quick in things practical, hasty and frivolous in things intellectual. But the boyish ideal is a healthy one, and in a young man, as in a young nation, it is perfection to have only the faults of youth. There is some-times a beautiful simplicity and completeness in the type which this ideal produces. One of the most impressive things I saw at Yale was the room officially occupied by the secretary of the Young Men's Christian Association. It was a pretty room, the windows high in the wall, as a student's windows should be. There were books and teacups and a pot of white chrysanthemums in bloom. The stove alone might have dis-figured the place, but it was covered by a heap of footballs, battered and dirty, each with the word Harvard or Princeton painted upon it. They were trophies which a former secretary of the association and captain of the football team had brought to this sanctum from the field. It is delightful to see this full-hearted wholeness, this apparently perfect adjust-ment between man and his environment, this buoyant faith in one's divine mission to be rich and happy. No wonder that all America loves Yale, where American traditions are vigorous, American instincts are unchecked, and young men are trained and made eager for the keen struggle of American life. [pp. 51–54]

There are other delightful, penetrating points in this article. I refer to this article because Santayana saw fit to try to explain to himself and the Harvard community why they saw themselves and Yale as they did (i.e., to account for attitudes the origins of which Harvard people do not pursue and if they did would find difficult to put into words even though these attitudes toward self and others are part of their personality makeup). But there is a second reason: In very few pages Santayana described Harvard in ways that make Robinson's far lengthier description of Henry Murray's student days there seem old hat. Murray was born the year after Santayana's article appeared, but if you want to know what Murray would experience and do in his undergraduate years and you do not have the time to read Robinson's biography, take fifteen minutes and read Santayana's nine-page article, which is a gem of a very succinct ecological description.

There is a third reason. In a legal sense Santayana was an American. Psychologically-culturally he was Spanish-European. He was born in Spain, lived and visited there over the years and considered Avila to be his home. He never felt at home in Boston-America even though his father had been part of Boston high society. It should occasion no surprise that Santayana was a fascinated, ambivalent, penetrating observer of the American psyche. He was never in doubt that the personality of Americans was inexplicable apart from their Americanness, just as he was bothered by the unwillingness or inability of Americans to confront their distinctive worldview. He would not have been surprised that Henry Murray's theory of personality did not include ecology in general and the American one in particular.

Let us now return to the two reviews of Robinson's biography with which I started this chapter. I can understand Kazin's review. He is a highly regarded, sophisticated writer, literary critic, and literary historian. So, when he devotes much of his review to Murray's pivotal role in rescuing Herman Melville from obscurity, it should occasion no surprise. But Kazin is a distinctive observer of literary scenes, past and present, who has paid attention to the local and national ecologies of those about whom he has written. Why, then, does he say next to nothing about Henry Murray's time and role in American psychology? Why does he devote few sentences to the Harvard Psychological Clinic and even less than that to why Murray impacted on American psychology? Is he, as Kazin says, noted in psychology *only* because of his development of the Thematic Apperception Test?

The answer, in my opinion, is that Robinson's biography does not address these questions, concentrating as he does on Murray's enamoredness with Melville and his sustained, torrid, erotic, and poorly explained love affair with Christiana Morgan. Love affairs do not justify biographies unless one or both members of the affair have distinguished themselves in other more public ways. It is true that one of the ways Murray distinguished himself was his role in stimulating renewed interest in Melville. But it is no less true, perhaps more true, that Murray's contribution to psychology was mammoth and, unlike his influence in renewing interest in Melville, public. I say mammoth because of the stir *Explorations in Personality* caused when it appeared. It was seen, as it indeed was, as a systematic, explicit, conceptual rebellion and challenge to mainstream American psychology. It was in its way the first and most creative attempt to wed major strands of American and European theories of the human personality. Murray was no slavish devotee of psychoanalytic theory of the Freudian or Jungian varieties. Theories required clarity of terms, their interrelationships, and the employment of converging operations to establish the validity of theories. In this respect Murray was in the tradition of American psychology. He was imaginative and creative on the level not only of theorizing but of devising means for testing theory. If Murray was poignantly aware of the complexity of the human personality, he was no less aware that clarifying that complexity would require not one method but a variety of methods. More than that, and this has gone unnoticed, attaining that clarity cannot be achieved by *one* person studying *an* individual. That is easy to say—it is a glimpse of the obvious—but only Murray took it seriously. No one since him has taken it as seriously. It is still the case that one person "studies" another person. When Murray expresses amazement that the project (the "job") at the Harvard Psychological Clinic was brought to completion and publication, the amazement is understandable. No one before or after him has had the vision, courage, and conceptual-methodological boldness to take the obvious seriously. Before the complexity of the human personality, the single investigator is very poorly armed. Murray always worked with a team, not because he liked it that way but because the problem demanded it.

The review by Fels, a psychiatrist, betrays a lack of knowledge and history of her field and American psychology that at best is staggering and at worst utterly inexcusable. To portray Murray as a neurotic, intellectually limited and superficial, sexually perverse, unorganized individual is worse than travesty—it is stupid and sinful. I said earlier that I have to assume that neither Kazin nor Fels read *Explorations in Personality*. At least Kazin's review recognizes that Murray's relatively few publications about Melville were truly incisive and impactful, reflective of a first-rate mind. Fels's review is a "know-nothing" review, as intellectually superficial a review as one could write.

I am grateful for Robinson's biography because it contains facts and anecdotes I did not know about one of my intellectual heroes. Titles of books are not randomly chosen. Clearly, the title *Love's Story Told* tells us where Robinson's interest was, and it is understandable if so much of the book is about a love affair, the account of which I found tedious, repetitive, and unilluminating. Unfortunately, the subtitle *A Life of Henry A. Murray* promises far more than it delivers because it so inadequately conveys the origins, substance, and impact of Murray the psychologist, the American psychologist whose capacity for exploration was boundless, who was shaped as much by his America as by European giants, whose need to excel and make a difference was accompanied and modulated by a refreshing modesty, a man who took himself far less seriously than he did his ideas, a man who despite a sustained extramarital affair possessed an American sense of morality, a man who despite his ambivalence about American society and culture was never in doubt that he was American, a personality with warts no less complex than its virtues. If Robinson had been able to come to grips with what *Explorations in Personality* contained and still represents, he could have done Murray the justice he deserves. I entertain the fantasy that Murray has read the biography and sums up his assessment with these words: "If only Robinson had been able to read, understand, and take seriously what I wrote in *Explorations in Personality*."

Postscript

Several months after the publication of the Murray biography, there appeared *Translate This Darkness* (Douglas, 1993), a biography of Christiana Morgan, the woman with whom he had a love affair over several decades, an affair that Murray regarded as the most distinctive of his life experiences. What does Morgan's biography contribute to our understanding of the substance, direction, and impact of Murray's work? What the reader needs to know is that the words *love affair* obscures the fact that their relationship was also an intellectual-conceptual one stemming from another fact: both were influenced (too weak a word) by ideas and theories that gained currency early in this century, with each decade gained momentum, and reached their zeniths in the post–World War II era. From Murray's standpoint, Christiana Morgan was an intellectual-conceptual force that mightily shaped his thinking. She was a force, a goad, a colleague, a fertile source of ideas, and in some ways his conscience.

It is not my purpose here to comment on Morgan's personality or how her biography rounds out the picture of Murray as a person.

My purpose is to offer some hypotheses that, for me at least, shed light on issues that have long intrigued me and that have not received the attention they deserve.

The first of these issues is contained in the question, How do we account for the positive acceptance of psychoanalysis in the early decades of this century? That acceptance, I should hasten to add, did not take place in our universities, neither in psychology or psychiatry, nor in any other discipline. Yes, it is true that Freud and Jung had prominent places in the celebration of Clark University's twentieth anniversary. But that event signified recognition, not acceptance. The acceptance began to take hold in literary and artistic circles and, significantly, among wealthy individuals (like Murray and Morgan) knowledgeable about and supportive of the arts. In those early days, wealthy individuals looked to Europe as the major source of "culture," and touring Europe to absorb that culture and its artistic products—in many cases buying those products for their homes or museums—was by no means unusual. In the course of these travels, particularly to Paris, Vienna, and Berlin, they became aware of the "new" psychology as well as of the dramatic changes taking place in the arts, for example, cubism, expressionism, surrealism, and more. Americans had long been ambivalent about Europe. On the one hand, its history, traditions, and achievements were major sources of American society. On the other hand, Europe stood for lifestyles and movements that were inimical to and would be destructive of American society. Europe was a dangerous mixture of virtues and vices.

From the standpoint of Americans generally, psychoanalysis reflected Europe's moral cesspool. It was from among the wealthy, "old money" stratum of society, seeking "culture" and uplift from the arts in Europe, that psychoanalysis gained a following in America. That, I know, is a small part of the answer but one that has not received the study it deserves. The more I read the biographies of those who comprised Manhattan's Greenwich Village at the turn of the century, the more impressed I am with how many upper-class

Manhattanites were part of the counterculture, an aspect of which was enamoredness with Freud and Jung.

I offer the hypothesis, well illustrated in the Murray and Morgan biographies, that among the wealthy who served as conduits to America for psychoanalysis, there was a hunger both for novelty and excitement, and for life's meaning. They were people dissatisfied with American puritanism and values they saw as confining and frustrating. Psychoanalysis was a magnet, an answer, a justification for departing from tradition and conventional life styles.

That is what happened on a far larger scale after World War II; after millions of lives and families had been disrupted, an old world had, so to speak, died, and few wanted or could return to what had been conventional. Psychoanalysis left the wings and came center stage. The couch was not for resting but the vehicle for figuring out new lifestyles in which personal expression would overcome inhibitions.

4

American Psychology and the Needs for Transcendence and Community

It should occasion no surprise that centennials are sitting ducks for the psychologist as spoilsport, at least some psychologists. Centennials, like other major occasions for celebration, have conceptual kinship to Roger Barker's behavior setting: times and places that engender predictable behavior in people who are very diverse on all kinds of variables. So it is not surprising that on the occasion of its one hundredth anniversary the American Psychological Association (APA) brings us together to listen to and take satisfaction from our achievements as a science and profession; from our contributions to knowledge and to the public welfare. Centennials have a "demand characteristic": we are here to enjoy recitals of our onward and upward course over a century. Let me say at the outset that there is a great deal about which as a field we can take pride. But precisely because of some of the things we have learned well, one would expect and hope that some of us would be suspicious about the purposes of a centennial celebration. That is to say, we should not accept what is said and written about this occasion as the whole story or as giving us a perspective on our past that has no self-serving aspects. This does not mean that we are victims of a

Note: This essay originally was an invited centennial address at the annual conference of the American Psychological Association, Washington, D.C., 1992. This essay was published in the American Journal of Community Psychology, 1993, 21(2), pp. 185–202. It is reprinted here with the permission of the Plenum Press.

conspiracy to blot out some of the negative aspects of our history or to distract us from unpleasant professional controversies that mark our present and which will in part determine our future. But it does mean that we temper our justifiable pride with a justifiable dose of skepticism. And for at least two reasons.

I have already alluded to the first reason: There is everything in us as individuals and a collectivity to accentuate the positive and eliminate the negative. That, to psychologists, is reason enough for skepticism, whether in regard to an individual or the APA. When either conveys the Panglossian view that every day in every way our future will be a continuation of an unexcelled past, psychologists do not have to seek pardon for their disbelief.

The second reason is less obvious but no less valid. Put more succinctly, the membership of the APA is not a random sample of the population in terms of education, income, and social class. It is a highly selected and self-selected population. Although socialization into the profession differs from university to university, it is a process that produces a marked degree of uniformity in regard to what are considered to be important problems. It is not unfair to say that it is a socialization that produces both conformity and uniformity. The conformity is not demanded, if only because of selection and self-selection factors. We take justifiable pride in the emphasis our undergraduate and graduate programs place on critical analysis, the rules of evidence, the difference between facts and truths, and that the human mind is our greatest ally and foe. But all of this in relation to a consensus about what are *the* important problems. Put in another way, subtly and otherwise, implicitly or explicitly, by statement or silence, students are rendered insensitive to certain problem areas. They are off-limits; they are not problems worthy of our research efforts; they will not be productive of new and important knowledge; they will not shed light on how psychology can contribute to the public welfare; they are and should be the concern of others than psychologists.

One of the things we have learned extraordinarily well in our endeavor to help individuals with personal problems is to note carefully what the individual does *not* talk about or relate. That is by no means peculiar to clinicians; it is something that consultants to troubled organizations take for granted in formulating their initial diagnoses. And it is no less true in research, which is why when we read research literature we are schooled to ask what the researcher has not told us but should or might have. In these instances the omissions may be deliberate or not. The important thing is that we understand the human organism well enough, which is to say we understand ourselves well enough, to know that what people do not talk about is, for want of a better term, symptomatic. That is the way I look at centennials. What is psychology not studying? What seems to be implicitly off-limits? Are there arenas of societal problems in need of understanding and action that require that they be other than tangential to psychology? In this essay I shall discuss one such problem. Let me start with the human need for transcendence, one of the ingredients of the religious worldview.

I think I am safe in assuming that the bulk of the membership of the APA would, if asked, describe themselves as agnostic or atheistic. I am also safe in assuming that any one or all of the ingredients of the religious worldview are of neither personal nor professional interest to most psychologists. And there are more than a few psychologists who not only have difficulty identifying with any of those ingredients but who also regard adherence to any of them as a reflection of irrationality, of superstition, of an immaturity, of a neurosis. Indeed, if we learn that someone is devoutly religious or even tends in that direction, we look upon them with puzzlement, often concluding that that psychologist obviously had or has personal problems. Sigmund Freud (like Karl Marx) never concealed his contempt for religion or the religious. For Marx religion was an opiate; for Freud it was a neurotic coming to terms with the violence of the id. It is to the everlasting credit of agnostic William James that he not only did not indulge contempt but understood and described the human need for transcendence. James could not buy any form of religious-institutional orthodoxy (i.e., formal religion), but he knew the strength and ubiquity of the need for transcendence. He respected it; it was for him a fact of human existence. There are very few today who can accord such respect. I regard that as both unfortunate and egregiously defeating of our aim to understand the so-called modern person.

Our tendency immediately and unreflectively to react to a phrase like "the need for transcendence" as if it requires us to accept formal religion is part of the problem. I am reminded here of the response to Freud's explanation of the origins and vicissitudes of aggression in terms of death instinct. That explanation was correctly disparaged, but with the result that sight was lost of the phenomena Freud was trying to explain. Similarly, where you stand in regard to formal religion should not, I hope, prevent you from trying to appreciate the origins and vicissitudes of the need for transcendence (i.e., the need to feel that what one is, was, or has done will have a significance outside the boundaries of one's personal place and time). Put in another way, it is a belief that one is part of a larger scheme of things in two respects: that scheme of things impacts on you, and you somehow do or will impact on it. Whether that belief is empirically right or wrong is irrelevant. What is relevant is that you believe there is a larger scheme of things in which your life is a difference that makes or will make a difference. The sense of transcendence is most clear in those who are religious. It is more murky in those who are not.

For the past few years I have been conducting an informal, nonscientific survey of psychologists, each of whom was an agnostic or an atheist. They varied considerably on almost every other variable. The survey is subject to the criticisms of my master's thesis: every variable was uncontrolled. The lead question was "Have you ever found yourself imagining that you have died but you are still able to observe those you love (e.g., your wife, lover, children, close friends)?" Since everybody answered in the affirmative, I did not bother to do any statistical tests. The next question was "Have you ever found yourself imagining that someone whom you loved dearly and is dead still 'exists' somewhere, somehow as they did in 'real' life?" Again the answers were in the affirmative. The final question was "Have you ever found yourself hoping, and I mean really hoping, that there is a life after death?" For a fair number of people that was a troubling question because they felt guilty that they could entertain a thought that violated their scientific conscience. But, being good subjects, they had to reveal a personal truth.

There was another question: "Have you ever had the fantasy, an exciting and pleasurable one, that there is uncontrovertible evidence that human life exists somewhere in the far reaches of space?" Although the answers were again in the affirmative, about half of the respondents said that it would be stretching things to say that the fantasy was exciting or pleasurable. Interesting yes, but exciting and pleasurable no. The response of the other half was best summed up by one respondent who said, "There is something comforting about the thought that we are not the only planet with human life. I am not clear why it is comforting. I've never bothered to pursue it."

Let me now add one fact and one hypothesis. The fact is that people get quite a kick from jokes about heaven and hell. Explanations of the sources of our reaction to jokes are by no means simple or clear, but there is fair agreement that that complex reaction contains elements of anxiety and wish fulfillment. One of the definitions of *joke* given in my dictionary is that it is something we do not take seriously. Psychologically, it would be more correct to say, especially in regard to heaven and hell jokes, that we do not wish to take seriously something that we regard as quite serious: separation from the human community.

Before stating the hypothesis, I have to ask you to do some imagining. Assume we can reliably categorize jokes (e.g., about sexual intercourse, ethnicity, aging, heaven and hell). Now assume that for each of the last ten decades we are able reliably to count the frequency with which each category of jokes appears in diverse places and on social occasions. (Let us not be detained by methodological and sampling problems!) My hypothesis is that with each passing decade there would be a steady increase in the frequency of heaven and hell jokes. The subhypothesis would be that most of that increase would be found in those places and social occasions populated by educated atheists and agnostics, for example, this APA audience.

What do I make of all this? The first conclusion I draw is obvious: The terror or regret or pain that knowledge of our mortality engenders inheres in its separating us from the human community of which we are a part. The second conclusion is that that knowledge inevitably engenders, however occasional and fleeting, the need, the wish, the fantasy of transcendence. I know that as psychologists we have been schooled to be gun-shy about saying something is inevitable. In this instance I suggest that you refrain from drawing your guns of skepticism. The third conclusion is that we need to understand how differing degrees of the psychological sense of community is related to the frequency, strength, and adaptive-maladaptive features of the need for transcendence. Among atheists and agnostics, there are more than a few who secretly envy the religious individual who possesses the "crutch" of faith in a hereafter, as if that type of transcendence *alone* is sufficient to deny death its psychological toll. It is an unwarranted envy that reflects ignorance of what has happened to what we call the modern Western world that was born, so to speak, several centuries ago when the seeds of secularism were planted and that, like the California redwoods, steadily grew to dominate the scene.

That explains the fourth conclusion: Precisely because the consequences of secularism have weakened, diluted, impoverished, and frequently extinguished the psychological sense of community, the need for transcendence among many religious people no longer has the adaptive feature it once had. Put in another way, historically the place and force of the need for transcendence in a religion depended on a taken-for-granted psychological sense of earthly community, of belonging. As that sense has weakened, the need for transcendence has become for many religious people a frail reed with which to cope with the fact of mortality. That, needless to say, does not mean that the need, wish, fantasy of transcendence is given up or even weakened. But it does mean that the fracturing of the relationship between that need and the psychological sense of community has had, for many religious people, psychologically and socially disturbing consequences. It is far more than a "crisis in faith," a phrase that suggests conflict between a religious and a secular worldview. It is a crisis in large measure produced and reinforced by the felt absence of the sense of human community. It is one thing to identify oneself with a particular religion; it is quite another thing to feel a part of a religious community and all that implies about social-personal relationships, obligations, and practices. A minister put it this way: "I am a minister of a Christian congregation, not of a Christian community. I wish it were otherwise and so do many of my parishioners, not because they want to or would be more religious in the narrow sense but because they do not want to feel so alone in the world. They come to church on Sunday as much or more to commune with each other as to commune with God." How many times have you or your colleagues said, "I am a member of a psychology department, not of a psychological community"?

Anyone burdened with familiarity with my writings will not be surprised that starting as I did with the need, wish, fantasy of transcendence I quickly have related it to the real crisis of the modern world: the destructive consequences of the feeling of undue individual apartness. But I did not do so as a ploy or a conceptual gimmick. I trust that there is no psychologist who will deny that differing degrees of the sense of community are differences that make a difference in how we feel and cope with the problems of quotidian living. Nevertheless, if that assumption is warranted, the fact is that none of our regnant psychological theories of human development, past or present, have dealt either with the origins and vicissitudes of the need for transcendence or its relationship to the need for community. And matters have not been helped any by psychology's studious avoidance of or disinterest in how the religious worldview is assimilated—a socialization-developmental process that for all practical purposes has not been studied—and how it impacts on and is impacted on by social contexts: family, church, peer groups, schools, media. And, I must add, that avoidance has permitted psychology to continue to deal in the most superficial way with the values on which conceptions of what is "healthy" and "adaptive" are based. So, as I have said, secularists, which includes most psychologists, regard their need, wish, and fantasy of transcendence as irrational, a kind of momentary indulgence of human frailty. That is to say, it is not "normal," let alone healthy or adaptive. They enjoy jokes about it, but a joke is not to be taken seriously.

It is my impression that hardly a day goes by when in one of our mass media there is not a story about some fundamentalist, religious sect. That Jews have finally arrived in this respect was demonstrated when on the cover of the Sunday *New York Times* magazine section was a picture of the Lubavitcher Rebbe, and inside was an article about him and his followers in Brooklyn, other large urban centers, and Israel. What the article made clear was that the Rebbe was viewed as a fraud by several Rebbes in Brooklyn who had their own devoted followers there and elsewhere. I think I am warranted in assuming that the nonreligious reader was confirmed in the belief that fundamentalist sects, Christian and Jewish, were instances of religious fanaticism run amok. Put in another way, that reader literally finds it unimaginable that he or she could get so committed to a set of religious beliefs—what we like to call a paradigm—that denies priority to reason, logic, and evidence in daily living. Am I wrong in surmising that many, perhaps even all, such readers look upon adherents to these sects as, at best, foolish and naive and, at worst, "sick" people whose internal needs and conflicts swamped a weak, or fragile, or immature ego? If *DSM-IV* offers no basis for a formal diagnosis, that does not prevent those readers from inventing their own diagnoses. In short, the conclusion is that members of these sects depend on a set of religious beliefs to an unhealthy, maladaptive degree. And the key word is *degree*, because the secularist would never arrive at such a diagnosis for people whose religiosity was only evident on a Saturday or Sunday.

I am not aware of survey data that tell us whether there has been in recent decades an increase in the number and size of these religious groups. It is my impression that both their number, and certainly size, have increased. There are survey data suggesting that a belief in God is held by a large majority of people, despite shrinking church attendance. That speaks only to the need for transcendence. It tells us nothing about when or why that need manifests itself in some way in action (e.g., whether it has motivating, consequential features; whether it is an unrooted belief in search of purpose; whether it is a response to a perceived lack of some kind; whether it is embedded in an interpersonally or socially reinforcing context). In short, we know very little about the significances of that need for transcendence. To the secularist psychologist these are not important issues because they will not be productive to the understanding of important psychological problems or to the social world in which we live. They are religious issues, not ones that should occupy the scientific psychologist who is likely to say that of course these issues obviously bespeak of psychological content and process but that is no warrant for taking them seriously.

The significance of fundamentalist groups is obscured if we view them only in terms of religious beliefs in which a sense of transcendence with a divinity is their most obvious and common feature. What is obscured is that, the usual exceptions aside, their members live in a geographically circumscribed area for the explicit purpose of having a psychological sense of community. And in the case of the exceptions, members dearly wish they could be part of such a community. What I am suggesting is that the wish for transcendence is seamlessly part of a need for a community, a community that should and will outlive its members. It is a community in which they can count on others in predictably personal ways. They are part of a community in which interpersonal-social expectations and obligations are explicit. That, of course, does not mean that, socially-interpersonally speaking, there are no conflicts, disappointments, rivalries, or other manifestations of the human capacity to create problems in living. But it does mean that the individual has the sense of belonging to a collectivity that, by its existence, nurtures a sense of transcendence.

On what basis can the scientific, secularist psychologist fault such a style of living? That is not a question such a psychologist is in the habit of thinking about. But that is a question that very much occupies those psychologists who spend their days dealing with people no longer able to cope with their problems in living, people who may or may not believe in a divinity but the bulk of whom share one characteristic: the sense of an unwanted privacy, of a loneliness, of a lack of social embeddedness, of being one in a disconnected sea of many. You will not find that characteristic in your diagnostic manuals, and yet it is a characteristic that suffuses the modern psyche. In a vague way the secularist psychologist knows— from his or her own life; from observation of others; from what clients tell them; even from formal research bearing on loneliness, aging, and stress—that that characteristic is not only powerful and frequent but picks up steam over the lifetime. A poet once said that life takes its final meaning in chosen death. What clients tell the secularist psychologist, what subjects tell the research psychologist, is that the final meaning they had chosen is unpalatable precisely because the sense of community is absent in their lives. And in giving voice to such a feeling, these people, like the psychologists to whom they go, make the error of blaming themselves; that is, it is a characteristic of individuals, a fault in them, an object of individual repair. There is a kernel of truth in that assignment of blame, but there is far more than a kernel of truth to the conclusion that they and we are blaming the victim. When another poet said that "the center does not hold," he was referring to a modern world in and to which the individual felt disconnected, a terrorizing disconnectedness.

By their failure to take religion seriously, psychologists have been unable to grasp the implications of a momentous change that the not-so-new modern world brought about in the relationship between the need for transcendence through belief in a divinity and the need for transcendence through embeddedness in a social collectivity. There was a time when those two needs were indissolubly interconnected. It was a time when it was literally impossible for people to separate belief in a divinity from the sense of belonging to a geographically circumscribed human community. If the modern world could not and did not extinguish the need for transcendence through belief in a divinity, it went far to the impoverishment of the ties that bind one to a human community:

the family; the neighborhood; the larger but nevertheless geographically circumscribed, perceptually and socially graspable community. What the severance of those two needs revealed was that the absence or weakness of the psychological sense of an earthly community was a psychologically destructive force independent of a belief in a divinity. Put in another way, the significance of the severance inhered in what it said about what happens when people no longer possess the psychological sense of community even if they do not or cannot give up the need for transcendence through belief in a divinity.

I said earlier that there was a time when the two needs were indissolubly interconnected. That is why the fundamentalist groups of today are so important to comprehend. It would be a mistake to view them as a kind of throwback or regression to a world that no longer exists, attempts to recapture what is unrecapturable, an unreasoning and unreasonable indulgence of the irrational. Those features may be in the picture, but to emphasize them is to miss the point that these groups have gone for the jugular of the modern person. And by that I mean that they very consciously and deliberately reject a set of beliefs that will destroy their sense of community, which will set them adrift rudderless on a social sea. They know that the modern world cannot alter their particular sense of transcendence. What they fear are those forces that will erode their sense of community.

Two questions arise. The first is comparative-empirical but unstudied: What difference in permanence, growth, and success has there been between collectivities created to engender a sense of community based on a sense of transcendence with a divinity, on the one hand, and collectivities similarly created but not based on any explicit need for transcendence, on the other hand? For example, during the sixties and early seventies, we witnessed the formation of many communes that not only did not express any need for transcendence with a divinity but attracted many individuals who had recently rejected their religious beliefs. It is my impression that almost all of the communes I have heard about (obviously a fraction of those that had been created) had dissolved. Their dissolution was associated with disillusionment. That was also a time when religious communes became more frequent and also a time when a reinvigoration of religious fundamentalism, Christian and Jewish, began to be noted within and without urban centers.

Those two developments were, among other things, efforts to experience and sustain a need for community. It is my impression that the failure of the secular efforts to thrive derived, in part, from the absence of any explicit expression of the need for the sense of transcendence. More correctly, it was an inability or unwillingness to confront the implications of that ubiquitous need. They were efforts grounded in a "here and now" rationale that effectively obscured that need.

That brings up the second question: Can the sense of community be sustained absent an explicit sense of transcendence, that is, the sense that one's purposes make sense only in terms of a commitment to the present *and* future purposes of a collectivity, a future beyond the span of one's life? Can there be a secular basis for such a sense of transcendence? Can it be powerful enough truly to give meaning to how one lives and dies, a meaning that one embraces? How one answers that question is one thing; not asking it is to betray an egregious insensitivity to or misreading of the changes in the modern, western psyche.

Let me try to clarify what I mean by the need for transcendence by the thinking of two men separated in time by twenty-five hundred years. Let us start, as we frequently should, with Socrates. After he had been judged guilty of corrupting the minds of Athenian youths, and shortly before he had to drink the cup of deadly hemlock, he was visited by his friend, Crito, who tells him that some people are willing to rescue him, to get him out of the country. Let us listen to a part of Crito's plea:

Wherever you go, there are plenty of places where you will find a welcome; and if you choose to go to Thessaly, I have friends there who will make much of you and give you com-

plete protection, so that no one in Thessaly can interfere
with you.

Besides, Socrates, I don't even feel that it is right for you
to try to do what you are doing, throwing away your life when
you might save it. You are doing your best to treat yourself in
exactly the same way as your enemies would, or rather did,
when they wanted to ruin you. What is more, it seems to me
that you are letting your sons down too. You have it in your
power to finish their bringing up and education, and instead
of that you are proposing to go off and desert them, and so far
as you are concerned they will have to take their chance. And
what sort of chance are they likely to get? The sort of thing
that usually happens to orphans when they lose their parents.
Either one ought not to have children at all, or one ought to
see their upbringing and education through to the end. It
strikes me that you are taking the line of least resistance,
whereas you ought to make the choice of a good man and a
brave one, considering that you profess to have made goodness your object all through life.

There, Socrates; if you aren't careful, besides the suffering
there will be all this disgrace for you and us to bear. Come,
make up your mind. Really, it's too late for that now; you
ought to have it made up already. There is no alternative; the
whole thing must be carried through during this coming
night. If we lose any more time, it can't be done, it will be too
late. I appeal to you, Socrates, on every ground; take my
advice and please don't be unreasonable! [Plato, (386 B.C.)
1948, p. 82].

Let me now paraphrase Socrates' refusal to be rescued. "I have
many reasons to be grateful to the State and its laws. It was through
the state that my mother and father could get married and beget
me. I have no complaint whatsoever with laws that deal with marriage. And I certainly have no quarrel with laws that deal with the
upbringing and education of children. Since I was born, brought

up, and educated in accordance with the laws, as were all of my ancestors, am I not a child of and servant to those laws? If I have no quarrel with the laws—far from having a quarrel, I am immensely grateful for them—on what basis can I justify a course of action that subverts the law? What gives me the moral license to do that? Whether in war or in the law courts, or anywhere else, I must do whatever my city commands or else persuade it in accordance with universal justice, not with violence that is a sin even against parents, and a far greater sin when it is against your community."

I cannot do justice to the give-and-take between Socrates and Crito. But I cannot refrain from presenting the argument that Socrates expects from the community and with which he agrees:

"It is a fact, then," they would say, "that you are breaking covenants and undertakings made with us, although you made them under no compulsion or misunderstanding, and were not compelled to decide in a limited time; you had seventy years in which you could have left the country, if you were not satisfied with us or felt that the agreements were unfair. You did not choose Sparta or Crete—your favourite models of good government—or any other Greek or foreign state; you could not have absented yourself from the city less if you had been lame or blind or decrepit in some other way. It is quite obvious that you stand by yourself above all other Athenians in your affection for this city and for us its Laws;— who would care for a city without laws? And now, after all this, are you not going to stand by your agreement? Yes, you are, Socrates, if you will take our advice; and then you will at least escape being laughed at for leaving the city. [Plato, (386 B.C.) 1948, p. 93]

What is relevant here is the bedrock sense of transcendence Socrates felt by virtue of being a member of a particular community that antedated him and *should* continue after his death. His sense of personal identity is incomprehensible apart from his sensed embeddedness in and willing commitment to something "larger" than himself. Socrates was mortal. Athens, he hoped, was not. His argument, his logic, was in the service of an expression of a wish for or sense of transcendence. The needs, stability, purposes of the community were more important than his fate. Socrates did not have to be told about the significance of the sense of transcendence or the psychological sense of community. He knew where he belonged and why. Religion and the Athenian gods are, for all practical purposes, absent from his argument.

Living as we do at a time when doing one's own thing is sanctioned and encouraged, when individual purposes take precedence over everything else, when obligation to self is incomparably more consequential than obligation to others or a collectivity, we have trouble comprehending Socrates' sense of transcendence. We have to strain our imaginative powers to get a feel for a way of thinking and feeling that permits someone to value continued existence of a collectivity over life itself. Some, agnostic or atheist, will label Socrates as saintly, as possessing a degree of consistency and courage in the application of moral principles, come what may, lacking in lesser mortals. Others among the nonreligious will say that Socrates manifested less a sense of transcendence than smugness, arrogance, and a stance of superiority. The religious person is likely to see him as blessed by forces not of this world. Why do we have such trouble taking Socrates at his word, that the continued existence of the community was in this instance more important than life itself, that to live a life devoid of a sense of transcendence was to live in a jungle? Is it possible that our difficulty understanding Socrates derives far less from what he psychologically possessed than from what most of us lack?

I do not regard it as a lack but as an unrecognized need in all of us that requires special conditions to force its silent existence into our minds. And one of those conditions is the real possibility that someone or something you love may die. Someone said that nothing sharpens the mind more than the knowledge you will be executed tomorrow. That is no less true when the knowledge is not about your death but about someone or something else's. Either type of knowledge immediately engenders thoughts about transcendence. Let me give a personal example.

I am Jewish. I do not believe that the Old and New Testaments are other than creations of very human humans. I do not go to synagogue, and on those rare occasions when I do, I get flooded with feelings of an uncapturable childhood as well as of guilt that I am a hypocrite. I am an agnostic, not an atheist. There is too much mystery in this world for me to have an absolutely closed mind. I am proud to be a Jew although there is a part of me that stops short of pursuing the origins or merits of such pride. It may turn out to be too self-serving! It would not be far off the mark to say, as one of my students did, that I am as Jewish as matzoh. So why do I so frequently feel as if I was alone in the Sinai desert? I feel kinship with other Jews, but I do not live in a Jewish community. I envy those Orthodox Jews who cannot conceive of riding to synagogue on Saturday. The day of rest is the day of rest, no ifs, ands, or buts. So, if the synagogue is in a decaying neighborhood, they willingly live there so as to be able to walk to services on Saturday and other important holidays. If I envy them, it is not because I harbor the desire to be with or of them. I have no sense of community with them, and they have none with me. What we have in common is *knowledge* of two thousand years of persecution and that, like it or not, justified or not, we fear new chapters will have to be written to bring the encyclopedia of persecution up-to-date. In brief, I have no sense of transcendence with or through this or that part of the Jewish community. More correctly, I *had* no such sense until the first week of June in 1967.

The real possibility that Israel would be wiped off the map—in Nasser's terms, "pushed into the sea"—hit me with tornado force for which I was utterly unprepared. Almost instantly I realized that whatever my sense of personal identity had been, it silently depended on the belief that Israel would endure beyond my lifetime. In ways that I had never bothered to face, in ways that I do

not fully comprehend today, I was part of something that was physically external to me and yet in my psychological bloodstream. I
could no longer maintain the fiction that I was a discrete individual whose life had meaning only in terms of ideas, work, family, or
other interpersonal affiliations. There was more to me than the old
me I thought I knew. And that more was the history of my people
and the need, the wish that unlike me Israel would transcend my
existence, that it had an endless future.

What I have just related I observed in countless people, almost
all of whom were irreligious and almost all of whom were puzzled
by the strength of their heretofore unexpressed need to believe that
they willingly were part of something that transcended the mortality of individuals. I offer the hypothesis that the strength and content of our reactions were in no small part related to a diluted sense
of community and all that implies about face-to-face relationships
based on shared values and obligations that shape living style and
its meanings.

Let me now turn to a descendent, conceptually speaking, of
Socrates, the B. F. Skinner of *Walden Two* (1948). It is not a case of
mixing apples and oranges. Few books in psychology have stimulated as much controversy, the critics far more numerous and vehement than its supporters. On the back cover of my paperback copy
is a promotional blurb that says, "A slur upon a name, a corruption
of an impulse, such a triumph of mortmain, the dead hand, has not
been envisaged since the days of Sparta." Another blurb says,
"Alluring in a sinister way, and appalling, too." That someone as
impactful and as intellectually fertile as Skinner never received the
honor of being president of the APA is an omission of which the
membership should not be proud. It is my thesis that, as in the case
of Freud and his explanation of aggression by a death instinct, critics (and even his supporters) confused problem with explanation,
means with ends. There is much in that book to criticize, but more
important for my purposes is to bring your attention to some of the
themes and statements that have gone unnoticed. Restrictions in
time require me to be uncommendably brief.

1. Skinner (1948) is very explicit in pointing out that there are many similarities in purpose between Walden Two and religious communes (e.g., monasteries, lamaseries), the most obvious being the forging of a sense of community.

> We've borrowed some of the practices of organized religion— to inspire group loyalty and strengthen the observance of the Code. I believe I've mentioned our Sunday meetings. There's usually some sort of music, sometimes religious. And a philo- sophical, poetic, or religious work is read or acted out. We like the effect of this upon the speech of the community. It gives us a common stock of literary allusions. Then there's a brief "lesson"—of the utmost importance in maintaining an obser- vance of the Code. Usually items are chosen for discussion which deal with self-control and certain kinds of social articu- lation. [p. 199]

Skinner, of course, denies the presence or need for transcendence. "Hope for a better world in the future? We like it well enough here on earth. We don't ask to be consoled for a vale of tears by promises of heaven" (p. 200).

2. To one of the visitors, Burris, who is Frazier's (Skinner's alter ego's) most caustic critic and clearly does not like him, Frazier says "of all the people you've seen in the past four days, you're sure that I'm *one*, at least, who couldn't possibly be a genuine member of any community" (Skinner, 1948, p. 249). Following this admission, Fra- zier says something with a force and depth unmatched elsewhere in the book: "'But God damn it, Burris!' he cried, timing the 'damn' to coincide with the crash of the tile. 'Can't you see? I'm-not-a- product-of-Walden-Two!' He sat down. He looked at his empty hand, and picked up a second tile quickly, as if to conceal the evi- dence of his display of feeling" (p. 249).

3. So what keeps Frazier going? The absence of what belief makes his past, present, and future behavior inexplicable? And Fra- zier's answer is very clear: "The final social structure we are work-

ing toward must wait for those who have a full Walden Two heritage. They will come, never fear, and the rest of us will pass on to a well-deserved oblivion—the pots that were marred in making" (Skinner, 1948, p. 250). In putting those words in Frazier's mouth, Skinner is giving expression to something he earlier had denied: the need, the wish, the fantasy of transcendence. Skinner's sense of transcendence is not with a divinity but with *the future*. His sense of transcendence is not with the heaven of religion but with a no less fantasied secular heaven that, although outliving him, suffuses the thinking of his earthly days. Skinner, like Socrates, knows he is mortal, but, again like Socrates, his life takes final meaning and comfort in the wish that something larger and more important than he will survive *forever*.

I can personally attest to the fact that when *Walden Two* was published in 1948, the reaction to it from psychologists centered exclusively on Skinner's application of his behavioral principles for the purposes of social engineering. The criticisms had to do with means and very little with ends. To my knowledge no one gave special attention to the obvious point that for Skinner the absence of a psychological sense of community was among the most destabilizing, destructive, conflict-producing features of modern living, a feature making for self-defeating competitiveness, narcissism, and apartness from others. In that dramatic moment when Frazier poignantly bemoans the fact that he is and cannot be a product of

---

[1]It is impossible for me in this essay to state and examine the implications of my argument for our foreign policy. It is obvious that the United States now has to deal with countries in the Mideast in many of which there is not only no separation between the need for transcendence with a divinity and the sense of community but also little or no distinction between state and religion. We in our country simply cannot comprehend that way of seeing and living in the world, and psychology has been of no help at all. That inability to comprehend—indeed, our inability even to recognize what the problem is and will be for us—has had and will have enormous consequences for which neither we or our national policy makers are prepared. A colleague of mine, Dr. Michael Klaber of the University of Hartford, put it to me this way: "As long as Americans see our problems in the Mideast as centering around oil, they are missing the point. The problems are and have been in the most fundamental way religious and in ways utterly foreign to what we in this country ordinarily mean by religious."

Walden Two's future, he is expressing envy not only of those future generations but also of the impossibility of his ever overcoming the consequences of having a modern psyche. In the secular heaven of Walden Two, Frazier feels sadly alone and apart.

I did not know Skinner. But having many times read *Walden Two*, and especially rereading it in the light of his other autobiographical writings, I had to conclude that Skinner felt keenly the lack of the sense of community he created for others in his fictional *Walden Two*. It is not fortuitous that Skinner sees kinship between Walden Two and religious communes. And it is not fortuitous that Skinner looks on the need, wish, and fantasy of transcendence as a progress-inhibiting crutch unnecessary for coping with earthly existence. Nowhere does Skinner suggest that that need is not a universal feature that, so to speak, is built into the human organism. What he plainly believed was that that need had to be overcome and extinguished. But, as I have indicated, Skinner ends up with his own brand of transcendence: a future no less heavenly than that of the true religious believer. What he would seek to deny in others, he could not in the quiet of his nights deny in himself. I offer the hypothesis that what kept Skinner going was that need for transcendence, his crutch with which to accommodate to his lack of community.

In the May 1992 *American Psychologist*, there are two obituaries: one by Mary Ainsworth on John Bowlby and one on Skinner by James Holland, the latter being far longer than the former. I find it suggestive that Ainsworth's words describe an obviously warm, socially embraceable, community-building type of person, while Holland's words say virtually nothing about Skinner as a person. I do not intend this observation as an *argumentum ad hominem* but only as a suggestion that Skinner was quite knowledgeable about the crucial importance of the sense of community.

William James sought for the moral equivalent of war. Skinner sought for the secular equivalent of the religious need for transcendence. It is to his everlasting credit that Skinner dimly sensed that the sense of community and the need for transcendence were different but related factors.

Let me return to where I began: the significances of the frequency with which religious people seek to reunite the needs for
community and transcendence. My argument would have more
force if psychology had the interest and means to estimate whether
in fact such geographically circumscribed clusters of religious people have in fact increased in frequency. And it would also be important to know how many religious people with an explicit sense of
transcendence lack but yearn for a sense of community. It is beyond
the scope of this essay to indicate the many questions that could
and should be directed to such data. What I can say, however, is
that it would be an egregious instance of tunnel vision if we were
to look at these groups in narrow religious terms, as if the "social
glue" they seek and their need for transcendence were peculiar to
the religious worldview. What we have to understand is that what
these groups seek to enjoy (which is not to say that they do) is what
most, if not all, nonreligious people seek unsuccessfully. As I said
earlier, members of these clusters go to the jugular of the modern
person; that is, they explicitly reject a style of living they see as
lonely, divisive, driven, and pointless precisely because of the
absence of a sense of transcendence.[1] We, the atheists and agnostics, cannot see ourselves as members of such clusters. That, I must
emphasize, should not keep us from pursuing this question: Is their
diagnosis of us wrong? Skinner did not doubt they are right. I agree
with Skinner. Mainstream psychology, a psychology committed to
contributing to the public welfare, has, for all practical purposes,
steered clear of this issue.

One final point. In the course of a lifetime, when and why does
the need, wish, or fantasy of transcendence arise? What are its vicissitudes? Similarly, what are the origins and contexts that give rise
to a need for community? Those are questions that members of religious groups ask and answer. They do not in the rearing of children
leave such matters to chance. Skinner explicitly asserts that, like
him, they have in the past and the present grasped the efficacy and
force of the principles of behavior. So, I collected fifteen currently

used child development textbooks. In fourteen of them there is no entry for religion. In one there is an entry that refers the reader to a single page. That is what I mean when I say that in celebrating the centennial of the APA let us not luxuriate in the feeling that we have been and are on an upward and onward course to the understanding of the human mind.

May I end with a confession. At the end of his APA presidential address in 1894, William James expresses personal feelings in typically charming, graceful, humble, disarming words that I love to read and reread. Hilgard (1978) nicely summarized the point and significance of James's paper: "James discussed an important question in cognitive psychology: Is a complex experience—'knowing things together'—made up of separate parts or is there some initial unity in the knowing of the whole? Many of his views anticipated the later Gestalt attacks on the associationist position of how mental events appear. James here modified his position from that taken in *Principles of Psychology* and stated that mental contents can be called complex if it is recognized that mental states involve a complexity in unity" (Hilgard, 1978, p. 22).

I have long hoped that there would be an occasion when I could quote James's parting statement. At the least, I would have the satisfaction of knowing that something I had written contained worthy, memorable sentences. In listening to James's words, imagine you are in a seminar room—no Hilton or Sheraton ballroom—one of a very small audience at the third annual meeting of the APA at Princeton University.

You will agree with me that I have brought no new insight to the subject, and that I have only gossiped to while away this unlucky presidential hour to which the constellations doomed me at my birth. But since gossip we have had to have, let me make the hour more gossipy still by saying a final word about the position taken up in my own *Principles of Psychology* on the general question before us, a position which, as you doubtless remember, was so vigorously attacked by our col-

league from the University of Pennsylvania at our meeting in
New York a year ago. That position consisted in this, that I
proposed to simply eliminate from psychology "considered as
a natural science" the whole business of ascertaining *how* we
come to know things together or to know them at all. Such
considerations, I said, should fall to metaphysics.

. . . My intention was a good one, and a natural science
infinitely more complete than the psychologies we now possess could be written without abandoning its terms. Like all
authors, I have, therefore, been surprised that this child of my
genius should not be more admired by others—should, in fact,
have been generally either misunderstood or despised. But do
not fear that on this occasion I am either going to defend or
to re-explain the bantling. I am going to make things more
harmonious by simply *giving it up*. I have become convinced
since publishing that book that no conventional restrictions
can keep metaphysical and so-called epistemological inquiries
out of the psychology books. I see, moreover, better now than
then that my proposal to designate mental states merely by
their cognitive function leads to a somewhat strained way of
talking of dreams and reveries, and to quite an unnatural way
of talking of some emotional states. I am willing, conse-
quently, henceforward that mental contents should be called
complex, just as their objects are, and this even in psychology.
Not because their parts are separable, as the parts of objects
are; not because they have an eternal or quasi-eternal individual existence, like the parts of objects; for the various "contents" of which they are parts are integers, existentially, and
their parts only live as long as *they* live. Still, *in* them, we can
call parts, parts.—But when, without circumlocution or dis-
guise, I thus come over to your views, I insist that those of you
who applaud me (if any such there be) should recognize the
obligations which the new agreement imposes on yourselves.
Not till you have dropped the old phrases, so absurd or so
empty, of ideas "self-compounding" or "united by a spiritual

principle"; not till you have in your turn succeeded in some
such long inquiry into conditions as the one I have just failed
in; not till you have laid bare more of the nature of that alto-
gether unique kind of complexity in unity which mental
states involve; not till then, I say, will psychology reach any
real benefit from the conciliatory spirit of which I have done
what I can to set an example. [James, 1978, p. 49]

Has the day passed in American psychology when its parts are
just parts, its divisions just divisions, and the search for integers has
been abandoned? Is the apartness so characteristic of contemporary
psychology the consequence of the apartness so many people feel
in their own lives? Is there no center that can hold psychology
together? Must we resign ourselves to a modern psychology that is
completely a reflection of modern living? Was our fall from earthly
grace signaled when psychology labeled William James and John
Dewey as philosophers, *only* philosophers?

I could have served the purposes of this occasion better if I had,
as I initially fantasized, read you excerpts from the writings of these
two giants. I ask your pardon for uncourageously succumbing to the
demand characteristic of this occasion.

5

The American Worldview: Optimism, Superiority, Pluralism, Ahistoricalism, and Disconnectedness

The title of this essay is an invitation to misinterpretation and criticism. Do I *really* mean that there are axioms, attitudes, outlooks that most, let alone all, Americans have in common? On the face of it, some will say, that is a blatantly ridiculous assertion. Aware as we are how Americans differ in terms of region, urban-rural-suburban sites for living and working, race, religion, ethnicity, and socioeconomic status—in light of these and other differences, why should we expect to find common psychological features? Even if you could find such communalities, would they not be of such generality as to be of no practical or theoretical import?

America, we are told, is not Japan, China, Iran, or most other countries that are obviously and incomparably more homogeneous than crazy-quilt America. That is true, but it is also true that we attribute to these countries a degree of homogeneity that is completely unwarranted. That is precisely the mistake that people in these countries make when they think about America; that is, they think about and attribute to us, all of us, certain characteristics. We, like them, are victims of syllogistic reasoning: All Americans are rich; this person is an American; therefore this person is rich. We know that is false; what we do not know is that we make the same mistake in regard to them, a mistake that has had untoward consequences in many of our foreign policies (and theirs). If that mistake is not peculiarly American, it is all the more reason that we try to fathom the nature and sources of how Americans view themselves and the world. Unless, of course, you believe that there is no distinctive American worldview, which is tantamount to saying that you have not had or will not have difficulty comprehending how other nationalities think and act. That, of course, is patent nonsense, a fact that every anthropologist, past and present, has experienced when he or she has spent time in a foreign culture.

Over the decades I have had the good fortune of knowing and working with anthropologists. My collaboration and friendship with an anthropologist was a mammoth influence on getting me to see how American I was. It was Thomas Gladwin who said that the ever- present task of the anthropologist studying the Bongo-Bongos of this world was how to *unlearn* the American worldview at the same time that he or she was trying to learn the worldview of others. To Tom, who spent five years on the islands of Truk in the South Pacific, it was a fact of life, not an hypothesis, that there was an American worldview.

Freud did not discover the unconscious, but he certainly made it impossible for us to deny that much of our internal dynamics makes us unaware of a good deal of what we have thought and experienced. But, as many people have noted, Freud seemed uninterested in, indeed seemed to deny, the possibility that the substance of his theorizing was in *any* way related to the facts that he was Jewish and lived at a particular time in a distinctive Austrian-European city, distinctive in terms of its history, culture, religion and politics. That possibility says nothing about the validity of his contributions—that is another story—but it says a good deal about the belief in the acultural, virginal birth of theories of human behavior. So, for example, Freud saw an affinity between his ideas and those portrayed in the plays of his Viennese contemporary, Arthur Schnitzler. It was an affinity he did not explain as reflective of where or when these two Jews lived. It was just one of those things: they "happened" to live in the same city at the same time! It was chance. Can one doubt that, if asked, Freud would have considered it inconceivable that if Schnitzler were an American, he would have written the plays he did? Freud's negative views of America are too well known for anyone to doubt what his reply would have been. As for his own ideas, Freud would not want to recognize that what was true for Schnitzler was true for himself.

In his *History of Experimental Psychology*, Boring (1957) sensitized us to the significance of *zeitgeist*. For Boring, however, zeitgeist meant the climate of ideas, those ideas those were bruited about, how and why they were accepted or rejected or transformed, all this in terms of individuals in diverse fields and places at a particular time. The history of ideas needs no defense; indeed, such histories are too few in psychology. But if you are interested in the social-national soil from which ideas have come, intellectual history has its limitations. Unless, of course, you regard such an interest as misguided and unproductive. For the sake of argument, I will concede that if, for example, your interest is in particle physics or topological geometry, such an interest may not be worth pursuing. (If I knew more about these fields, I might argue otherwise.) But if human behavior is what interests you, it is a very different ball game because no human being lacks conceptions of why people are what they are, and those conceptions are never independent of who you are, where you are, and when you are. The origins of Freud's ideas were in his head, but it was a nineteenth-century, Jewish, Viennese, head. A John Watson, Robert Thorndike, Clark Hull, and B. F. Skinner would have been explained easily by Freud as an intellectual excrescence of superficial, mechanism worshipping, parochial America.

An example. Saul Rosenzweig was my dissertation advisor at Clark University. He had worked with Henry Murray and had done experimental studies of repression. He sent some of these studies to Freud for comment, no doubt conveying the view that experimental studies of psychoanalytic concepts were both necessary and productive. Freud's handwritten reply was framed and hanging on Rosenzweig's office wall. If that letter is of obvious value as a collector's item, its contents are no less valuable for the clarity with which Freud expressed his disdain for Rosenzweig's approach. You could say that this is an instance of disagreement between two people about what and how to study a particular phenomenon. Repression was in the international zeitgeist, and here are two people in disagreement. So what else is new? Nothing is new unless you are interested in the possibility that the intellectual disagreement also reflects two very different, nationally-culturally-socially determined conceptions of what people are and how we should understand them.

But why should we be interested in that possibility? My answer is that to the extent we pursue that possibility (and assuming as I do that it will be productive), we will have a more general, comprehensive picture of the one problem that *all* psychologists are in one or another way and degree concerned: the organism-environment transaction. No, the differences between Freud and Rosenzweig are not "only" intellectual and methodological. Those differences have to be seen in light of two organisms born, developed, and socialized in two very different environments of which each was aware but regarded as "background." Believing that is like believing that Athena sprang full-blown from the head of Zeus. It is not a conception of background that recognizes its inevitable liberating *and* imprisoning features.

Let us start with this question: How do others, let us say Europeans, see Americans? You can put it this way: How do they characterize the American worldview? It is beyond my purpose and fund of knowledge to answer the question by reference to a voluminous "foreign" literature: novels, plays, treatises, and histories of events and eras. My readings have been scattered, unsystematic, but, I think, broad. On a purely personal level I have known and interacted with hundreds of non-Americans inside and outside our borders. If at the point of a gun I had to choose one person whose writings capture the answer to my question, it would be an American expatriate, Henry James, who was drawn to England and Europe because there was so much in their perception of the American worldview with which he agreed.

But why start with how others view us? For two related reasons. The first is, as someone said, that it is hard to be completely wrong; that is, how others see us probably has some validity. The second is that there is a surprising number of common threads running through the perceptions of diverse writers and observers. There is a third reason: how others see us is a good starting point for examining ourselves, a self-examination that we, like them, are reluctant to pursue. I consider it a universal law, one a par with any law in the so-called hard sciences, that human beings will resist changing their minds and behavior, even when they articulate a desire and need to change. I will also assert that a necessary, albeit not sufficient, condition for considering changing one's mind and behavior is the perception of an inciting discrepancy between our view of ourselves and that held by others. It is not a universal law that unexamined life is not worth living, but it is a very wise caveat.

An illustrative story. It was the sizzling sixties, a time when every major institution was under attack. It is important to note that similar attacks were going on in most Western countries. It was not an American phenomenon. (James Jones's novel *The Merry Month of May* well describes those times in France.) We were hosts to a British psychologist who had already visited universities in Berkeley, Chicago, Urbana, Boston, Philadelphia, Austin, and several other sites (including Esalen). Having an interest in industrial-organizational psychology, he had also met with psychologists and others in relevant sites. For the reader who was too young, or for those in whom memory has understandably grown dim, I have to note that one of the features of that era was the explosion of the group dynamics movement. I use the word *movement* advisedly because regardless of the type of group dynamics, or T-group, or self-study employed, it had features of an ideology about what people were and how they should live together. If the purpose of the methodology and group experience was to help individuals understand themselves better, there was no mistaking the overarching purpose of exposing individuals to a style of relating to and living with others. It would be unfair to say that the phenomenon of Woodstock was an exercise in group dynamics, but it was powered by and reflected some of the obvious features of the group dynamics movement.

In our conversation, and almost as an aside, I indicated to my visitor that I was far from viewing the group dynamics explosion as an unalloyed blessing and that I was truly mystified by what a big business it had become. My casual words emboldened my visitor to "explode" with these (paraphrased) comments:

In the weeks I have been in this country I would guess that 75 percent of all people I met—and they were not all academics—had participated in more than one group dynamics session or spent their days arranging for and conducting sessions with colleagues, students, schoolteachers, high school students, this or that racial or ethnic group, policemen, and more. Indeed, I met several people who used their weekends to sample, so to speak, one or another variation of group dynamics. In fact, I came away with the fantasy that on any one day one-half of all Americans are in one of these sessions, and the other half is arranging and conducting these sessions. In England, of course, we spawned the Tavistock model, and there are more than a few Tavistock partisans who would dearly love to expose all of England and Ireland to its message. I assume you know that more than a few of these partisans spend a fair amount in the United States doing, in your vernacular, "their thing." You may not know that there is a steady stream of American visitors who come to Tavistock to learn about and experience the "real thing." [I knew.] But the spread of the movement in the two countries is like the difference between night and day.

Group dynamics was far from the purpose of our meeting, but I asked him the question of how he would explain the difference between the two countries. He was reluctant to elaborate, but I pressed him to do so.

I will not try to explain *differences*. What I can say is that what I observed is in line with conclusions I came away with when I visited the States a decade or so ago. The long and short of it is that Americans have an identity problem. Who am I, why am I living, where am I headed, what is it all about, why do I feel so disconnected with others, why is life a treadmill? All of this side by side with the belief that every day in every way I am moving to a happy future. Perhaps another way of getting at it is to say that Americans have a very strong need to be liked and accepted, and I think that is related to a feeling of individual loneliness. Americans do not particularly like to be alone with themselves; they want to feel secure with others but they do not, generally speaking, of course. I hope what I have said does not offend you. This is a wonderful and great country, but your question was not directed to its virtues, which are many.

I assured him that I took no offense. He quickly agreed with my observation that what he said has been said over the decades by countless European observers and writers. We ended that part of our talk with his saying, "Graham Greene's novel *The Quiet American* might better have been titled *The Lonely American*."

One could argue that the visitor, as well as those who came before him, was overgeneralizing from restricted experience with Americans. My visitor, an academic, obviously had social commerce with an atypical sample of Americans. To those who would so argue, I would ask how to explain why similar conclusions are so blatant in the American novel, for example, those by Sinclair Lewis, John O'Hara, William Faulkner, Saul Bellow, J. D. Salinger, Louis Auchincloss, Edith Wharton, and a host of others. And why did Arthur Miller's *Death of a Salesman* strike such a responsive chord in us? Two of the most frequent sentences in a group dynamics session were (are) "Let me tell you how you are coming across to me" and "Tell me how I am coming across to you." Those sentences are as revealing as they are frequent.

I assume that when there is a consensus by others about the phenomenology and worldview of Americans, it should not lightly be dismissed as without any validity. But you cannot dismiss a consensus of which you are unaware. American psychology has been neither interested in or aware of such a consensus in regard to the particular characteristics my British visitor identified or, for that matter, other characteristics about which there is a consensus among "foreigners" (more of that later). There are words for that: *cultural* and *intellectual parochialism*, by virtue of which the boundaries of self-examination as individuals and a society are mammothly restricted.

Assuming as I do that what my visitor said contained nuggets of phenomenological truth, it is legitimate to expect that those nuggets would be important foci occupying the attention of American social, developmental, personality, and clinical psychologists in regard to theory, research, practice, and public policies. That is far from the case. There are, of course, psychologists who are aware of and study those foci, but they not only are minuscule in number but are perceived as being far from psychology's mainstream. Imagine the situation in which the leading lights of American psychology—a fair number would deserve the label "leading"—are subpoenaed to appear before a Congressional committee and are asked these questions: Is it the goal of American psychology to arrive at explanations of human behavior applicable not only to all people on earth but to an understanding of Americans in particular as well? Would you regard it as unfair or misguided for the government to expect that American psychology should be held accountable for how well it helps us understand ourselves?

The questions are, of course, rhetorical. No psychologist would answer either question in the negative. American psychology purports to strive to arrive at theories that give rise to research illuminating *Americans*. The important point is that such an effort has never confronted the possibility that there is an American worldview that, when ignored, is akin to throwing the baby out with the bath water. And if that is an infelicitous metaphor, let me say that to begin by ignoring the possibility of an American worldview is to start by shooting oneself in the foot.

If there is anything that characterizes the view of us by others, it is that Americans are naive optimists. That is to say, if we do not believe in the perfectibility of man, we sure do believe that people can, if only they so desire, dramatically improve themselves and their society. People are essentially good, and the trick is to arrange conditions that allow goodness to flourish. Americans are allergic to the possibility that in man the strength of evil forces rivals and even subdues the forces of goodness and virtue. The word *trick* refers to the perception that Americans truly believe that one can devise "mechanisms" for overcoming in individuals and nations the destructive or self-defeating consequences of any problem, assuming, of course, as Americans do, that where there is a need there is a way.

If Americans are optimistic about self-improvement, they are no less so about the rest of the world. Absorbed as they are about improving themselves, they unreflectively assume that others do, can, and should have a similar goal. Others do not fault us for pursuing life and liberty. And they do not fault us for pursuing happiness except for our tendency to regard happiness as a good deal more than a sometime thing. We are seen as having hearts that are in the right place. Our heads are not. Unlike others, Americans are unrealistically optimistic about overcoming their pasts and those of others. It is an optimism that undergirds and sustains a mischievous disrespect for history. It is not that Americans (Henry Ford aside) consider history to be bunk but rather that they, in their optimism, vastly underestimate its strength in the present and the degree to which it governs the future.

A frequently employed instance of American optimism and ahistoricalism is what happened at Versailles after World War I when Woodrow Wilson met with other Allied leaders to decide the fate of Europe. Wilson saw himself as the vehicle—and was so regarded for a time by Europeans generally—for a once-and-for-all transformation of a Europe (more than a Europe!) from a congeries of warring nations and ethnicities to a peaceful and just family of peoples. To his Allied colleagues Wilson was the quintessential

American: uncomprehending in regard to history; naive in regard to reality; unforgivably optimistic about what Europe was, could, and should be; and possessing a childlike conception of evil in man. If Wilson saw himself as a morality-proclaiming, justice-giving Santa Claus, that was no warrant for his allies to play the role of gullible children. Wilson believed in man's goodness; his allies did not.

Still another example is President Franklin Roosevelt's belief that "basically" in his heart of hearts Joseph Stalin wanted to do "the right thing." That is, when Stalin used concepts like peace, justice, and democracy, he meant what FDR meant and would act appropriately; when Stalin spoke about a free, independent, democratic Poland, he meant what FDR meant. Churchill, with an unsurpassed understanding of European history and the dynamics of dictatorship, disagreed with FDR. So did the Poles!

Countless foreign observers have noted that Americans are mystifyingly unaware of how their unbridled optimism and devaluing of history are a reflection of their being physically separated by two oceans from most of the rest of the world, in addition to which America has been a resource-laden, young country. Americans, they have said, are different, they do see the world differently, they treasure these differences, but they cannot confront the possibility that these differences have their downside in that it has impoverished their understanding of the rest of the world. Just as Professor Henry Higgins laments, "Why can't women be like men?" Americans bemoan the failure of others to be like Americans. Too frequently they take it to be self-evident that others want to be Americans (i.e., to be other than what they are). It is this aspect of the American worldview that has played a role in some of our most unfortunate mistakes in foreign policy.

How are these aspects of the American worldview reflected in American psychology? One is a derivative of the view that in numerous ways America is a superior country in terms of its adherence to a democratic ethos, its morality (political and otherwise), its technical-scientific achievements, its internal peacefulness (save the Civil War, of course), and its contributions to the survival and sustenance of countries subject to internal and external tyrannies. America is different and superior. What other country can claim the achievements that America does? American psychology is not in doubt that it is superior in terms of its range, theories, methods, productivity, and cogency of problems studied. We are the best and the biggest. When occasionally I have challenged a psychologist about such a view, I have gotten two reactions. The first is the "of course" reaction: how can you dispute the validity of that view? That has sometimes been followed by what I can only call a reflective doubt. As one put it, "When I hear myself agreeing that American psychology is the biggest and the best, a red light comes on. It sounds so smug, self-serving, and the like. I think of myself as a psychologist, not an *American* psychologist, as if being an American has nothing to do with my conceptions of human nature. That has to be nonsense."

American psychology is quintessentially American in its "can do" approach to man and the world. No problem, individual or social, is intractable as long as there is a resolve to confront it. We did not get to the moon only because we had the requisite knowledge and technology but also because there was a national resolve at a particular time to support such a venture. And therein lies the foundation of American optimism: if there is a problem, individual and social, a way to solve it will be found if the motivation is strong enough. You can pull yourself up by the bootstraps, you can make something of yourself, but only if your resolve is strong enough. Poverty has always been with us, but that is because we never declared war on it; that is, we were not serious enough. If drug abuse is rampant, it is because we are unwilling to employ the resources to eradicate it. If millions of citizens have personal problems that make for misery and unhappiness, it is far less because we do not know how to help them than because we have been unwilling to develop personnel and agencies through which that help can be dispensed. And it is no different in the case of cancer and AIDS:

unless and until we decide on an all-out effort, these problems will be with us.

Perhaps the most egregious example was when John Watson asserted that given a child at birth he could rear that child by his behavioristic principles so that it would become the person he, John Watson, intended. No less important than his saying what he did is that many Americans greeted it, if not with pride, as an indication of the potential fruitfulness of his psychology. And if you carefully read B. F. Skinner's *Walden Two* (1948), you will find Watson's proclamation put more sophisticatedly. One should note that neither Skinner nor his publisher expected the book to have the sales and durability it had and still does. I can attest to the fact that when the book was published, far more than a few graduate students in psychology (and in other fields) enthusiastically embraced it, to the point where some strenuously sought to plan and implement their heaven on earth. To my knowledge, at least, none of these graduate students was aware that starting utopian communities is a distinctive thread in our nation's history.

American optimism, especially in psychology, is in part powered by what might be called the "engineering mentality." For example, not long after we were catapulted into World War II, President Franklin Roosevelt said we were going to build fifty thousand airplanes a year. To some presumably knowledgeable people, that goal was an example of wish drowning reality. The goal was reached, reinforcing that part of the American worldview that said that no problem was intractable as long as the resolve to confront it was strong enough literally to engineer its solution. The imagery of mechanical systems suffuses the American psyche. It is not surprising, therefore, that in regard to diverse social problems, Americans' solutions tend to be couched in mechanical and/or inanimate imagery. So, we will *deliver* services; we will *network* people, agencies, and programs; we will *build bridges* among them; we will *reform* this or that; we should view people as human *capital*; we should employ *input-output* analyses; and *flowcharts* are important means for describing how things should work. In no way am I suggesting that such imagery is without any virtue, especially when it is explicitly stated that it is used for purposes of narrow analogy. It is when, as is too frequently the case, the imagery is seen not only as a replica of reality but as a basis for changing that reality that the mischief begins. Confusing a word with its "thing" referent is a frequent error, but its adverse consequences are nothing compared to confusing social reality with mechanical imagery.

Is there an American worldview? What has to happen for aspects of that view to be exposed? Let us start with December 7, 1941. World War II was raging in Europe. Japan had for a decade been overrunning China and more. Until Pearl Harbor, it was inconceivable that American territory could and would be attacked. Protected as we were by two vast oceans, and possessing as we thought we did a large and technologically sophisticated military force, and perceived as we thought we were as impregnable, why worry about an armed attack, let alone fear invasion and defeat? It was literally inconceivable. It is hard to overestimate the shock to the American worldview. Our worldview changed. Optimism and superiority took quite a beating, for a time at least.

And how did the American psyche react when it learned that the Soviet Union had orbited the first *Sputnik*? It was a psyche in which it was axiomatic that America had no peer in scientific and technological knowledge and accomplishments. We were Hertz and the rest of the world were Avises. Who would be the first to put a satellite into outer space? Silly question. Again the American view of itself and others was jolted.

The stock market crash of 1929 and the Great Depression that followed were jolts that the history books have well described. American psychology did not see these catastrophes as illuminating of the American psyche and its distinctive worldview. I use these catastrophes to indicate another feature of the American worldview: its ahistorical nature. If any characteristic of American history is incontrovertible, it has been its yo-yo, up-down economic movements. The strength and resilience of the onward-upward worldview are well illustrated by what was said and believed after World War II: we had reached the point when we knew how to "fine- tune" the economy. Again the mechanical imagery. The orchestra called America need no longer be off-key. It is imagery compounded of arrogance and the belief that we have overcome our history. That is not an uncommon view of us by others.

When we examine the theories of human behavior and development in American psychology, we are not set to notice—our worldview prevents us from recognizing—their optimistic quality. That is to say, they seem to rest on the assumption that we know enough, or clearly are in the process of learning enough, to prevent or ameliorate the problems of individual and families. That is, we can state and arrange the conditions (the fine-tuning motif) that prevent or alleviate human misery. I assume that I do not have to elaborate on the assertion that such efforts are both laudable and necessary. That is not the point, which is the boundless optimism undergirding these efforts. Put in another way, it is as if people and their conditions are perfectible. When you say that to theorists, they will deny holding such a view. If you answer by asking if they believe that the human organism is a *problems-producing* one, and that sets drastic limits about what one can expect from such an organism and about what one can do with and for them, they are puzzled, largely because they have never truly considered it an issue for their theorizing. One of them said (paraphrased), "Of course, I know that I cannot control the world, to mold it in ways that are desirable for individuals, but that says more about the world than it does about people. My theory is, I suppose, optimistic in terms of what people potentially can be. If the world will not accommodate to the conditions my conceptions say are necessary, that is something I have to accept. I do not, cannot, give up on people. I really do not give up on the world. Changing that world is not my job."

Freud (and many other European psychologists and philosophers) could never make that kind of statement. For those psychologists who truly have read Freud, he is a blatant pessimist. To Freud the nature of the human organism had built-in forces, capacities, and dynamics guaranteeing conflict, misery, problems. When you compare the Skinner of *Walden Two* and the Freud of *Civiliza-tion and its Discontents*, the differences between the American and European worldviews are obvious. They are differences in the pre-sent, but it is a present thoroughly suffused with different pasts. I write these words at a time when the dismemberment of Yugoslavia is marked by the worst consequences of ethnic-nationalist-religious conflict that has been smoldering for centuries, a kind of time bomb that was waiting to be exploded, and it has. Americans find the conflict incomprehensible, senseless, and pointless. Europeans sigh and say, "Here we go again." Americans cannot *resign* themselves to such an attitude. There *must* be a way not only of stopping the carnage but of arranging a solution that will overcome history. To which Europeans reply, "Famous last words. To Americans, if there is a problem, it can be solved in the sense that four divided by two has a solution, now and forever."

It is not surprising that in coming to grips with Freud, Ameri-can psychology (and psychiatry) did not buy his pessimism about the onward-upward course of human affairs. When after World War II American psychology embraced psychoanalysis (and for two decades after that war it was more than an embrace), American psy-chology was "true to itself in its own fashion"; that is, psychoanalysis not only illuminated the human psyche but provided a basis for a more productive pursuit of life, liberty, and happiness. Happiness is an American pursuit, as Thomas Jefferson said in the Declaration of Independence. Such a pursuit can be found in no similar docu-ment of another country.

A more current example. On *MacNeil/Lehrer News Hour*, a seg-ment appeared on the Kansas City, Missouri, school system, which had been under the jurisdiction of a federal judge to desegregate the school system. By court order the state and city were required to spend $1 *billion* to build new schools, increase personnel, and more, much more. To say that the new facilities are impressive is to indulge understatement. But the point of that segment was that after two or three years of the new facilities and programs, their intended purposes were not in evidence. In no way do I quarrel with those intended purposes.

What has this to do with the American worldview? It is an example of the view—in principle similar to that powering Skinner's *Walden Two*—that rearranging the physical environment will overcome historically honed attitudes and relationships. It is a view that permitted the Supreme Court in 1954 to call for school desegregation with "all deliberate speed." It is a view that permitted most Americans to believe that eradicating major sources of racial prejudice and injustice was a matter of time. Five years? Ten years? At most, twenty-five years. It was inconceivable that thirty-five years later some black leaders would be calling for segregated schools. In the American worldview no identified social problem is intractable as long as there is the resolve to "solve" it, to engineer its solution. That is a uniquely American view. It is the "can do" view of the world.

We have paid, and will continue to pay, dearly for holding the American worldview. Within our borders as well as on the international scene it is a worldview that has not been an unalloyed blessing. But it has not been my purpose in this essay to connect the American worldview to practical affairs, albeit those connections are in some ultimate sense inevitable and fateful. Nor has it been my purpose to criticize American psychology for not being "relevant" to human affairs. In the sizzling sixties *relevant* was the most overworked, tyrannically employed word, the litmus test for judging the worthiness of one's role and actions. Knowledge, understanding, and wisdom were luxuries to the extent that they did not bear directly on the solution of social problems. And there were many American psychologists who advocated relevance. I am not aware that anyone has noted that only an American psychologist-philosopher, William James, could have used the term "cash value" as a criterion for judging the pragmatics of our actions. (James, of course, did not employ that term for the purpose of social relevance.) There were many people in the sixties for whom "relevance" was their way of judging the "cash value" of one's life.

The American worldview has enormous practical consequences. My criticism of American psychology is that it has left that worldview unexplored. I like to think about the substance of a worldview (any worldview) as a network of axioms that is unarticulated because it all seems so right, natural, and proper. I have discussed only a few aspects of the American worldview. There are others, such as time, space, the purposes of living, money, and the criteria for progress. Any aspect of a worldview has idiosyncratic, individual determinants. But the patterning, force, and timing of those determinants are inexplicable or woefully incomplete apart from the fact that they are reflections of a society distinctive in its history and traditions. And by reflections I mean that they are "figures" whose meanings and consequences possess a "ground" of which we may be unaware but that is a silent, powerful partner in our "psychology." If it does not possess the characteristics of Freud's concept of the unconscious, it is nevertheless a ubiquitous, unverbalized presence in our psychological bloodstream.

What I am saying is the stock-in-trade of historians who looking back at past eras flush and flesh out those unverbalized axioms undergirding our national and international history. And in reading those histories, we like to believe that we are no longer psychological prisoners of those axioms, that we have overcome them or they have been changed in desirable ways, that we have "progressed." The validity of such beliefs is very much an open question. At the very least, the historical record should school us to accept the cautious conclusion that worldviews change very slowly and subtly. American psychology has changed dramatically in its one hundred years of existence. I offer the conclusion that despite those changes in "figure," the worldview that is its "ground" has not changed all that much. American psychology is still an *American* psychology.

It would be understandable to me if some readers regard what I have said about the American worldview as negative, even harsh. I ask the reader to keep two things in mind. The first is that what I have said rests on a fact and an assumption. The fact is that foreigners have been and are in no doubt that there is a unique Amer-

ican worldview. The assumption is that since it is hard to be completely wrong, it is likely that there is some truth to how we have
been and are perceived. If we do not like that perception, that is
no basis for dismissing it. Furthermore, let us not overlook that
there have long been American observers who have agreed with
how others perceive us. They are (were) a very heterogeneous
group, and their purposes are very diverse. Novelists, artists, play-
wrights, political theorists, and others have written about the
"American Experience" in critical terms. Until World War II there
was a steady flow of expatriates intent on freeing themselves from
what they perceived as a soulless, materialistic, arrogant America. I
will not comment on their judgments or perceptions except to say
that the extremity of their feelings often (not always) said more
about their passions than it did their judiciousness. When Lincoln
Steffens visited the Soviet Union several years after its 1917 revolution, he returned to America proclaiming, "I have seen the future
and it works," one of the gems in the book of famous last words.

The axioms of which a worldview is comprised have both positive and negative effects. Depending on time and context, each
axiom can be either a self-defeating or productive force. For example, Americans like to believe that they have few or no peers in
regard to respecting the rights of individuals "to make something
of themselves," to strive to become what they want to become, "to
realize one's potential." On numerous occasions during the year
(e.g., July 4), this view is expressed in a self-congratulatory tone. I
call it a view; most people consider it a fact, a glimpse of the obvious. Foreign observers long noted the discrepancy between such
utterances and the social realities, leading them to indict a stance
of blind moral superiority. In the case of blacks, Gunnar Myrdal
called it the American dilemma, a bland way of describing a discrepancy that was as obvious as it was glossed over, that was as
immoral as the American self-view was moral and righteous. And it
was no different in the case of women.

How would one characterize what has happened in regard to
blacks and women since World War II, which in almost every
respect was the watershed between an old and new world (on the

surface, at least)? There are those who would say that what has happened exposes the fragility and deceptiveness of a long-held American worldview about what is and should be, about what is right, natural, and proper. There is more than a kernel of truth to that. But is there not truth to the assertion that the speed with which these injustices were subjects of remedial legislation was amazing? It may be the case that in no other country were these injustices so quickly given the force of remedial law. Granted that there were those who resisted and still resist those changes, the fact remains that the legitimacy and force of law continues to prevail. How to explain such legislative speed and enforcement? The answer is very complex, but one part of that answer is in that aspect of the American worldview in which it is axiomatic that once a problem has been recognized—once there is a perceived threat to the social fabric, be it moral, political, or military in nature—you must do something to solve it. The virtue of that axiom is that it quickly leads to action (e.g., the Prohibition legislation in the twenties and thirties, social security legislation in 1935, Medicare, the universal health insurance contemplated today). The downside of that axiom is that it is related to another axiom: Rhetoric and legislation expressing good intentions will remedy the targeted injustice, if not tomorrow, then soon—an axiom redolent of Wilson at Versailles.

This has been called the American Century. To Americans that label seems quite appropriate because our country became the most powerful on earth. To many foreigners, however much they have benefited from the exercise of that power, that label is viewed ambivalently because, power aside, they see the American worldview as too insular, unrealistic, unwittingly subversive of how other peoples want to remain within their own traditions and uncomprehending of how the histories of these different countries gave rise to worldviews very different from ours.

In this essay I have mentioned only several aspects of the American worldview, enough, I hope, to indicate that the failure to uncover that worldview should no longer be tolerated by those who seek to understand the determinants of behavior.

6

The Mystery of Alexander Bryan Johnson

There is a long history of fascination with individuals who manifest a prodigious skill we find hard to explain except in general terms. Child prodigies in music or chess or mathematics are compelling examples. In the case of prodigies, we can usually point to factors in the family ecology that played a role even though mystery remains about the mechanisms by which those factors were coalesced and absorbed. More infrequent are those instances where we are at sea about how to explain anything about such an individual. David Feldman's book *Nature's Gambit* (1986) presents and discusses the issues in a clear, thought-provoking way.

Although Alexander Bryan Johnson was not a child prodigy, he presents us with a similar kind of mystery in that when we learn about his life, we are completely baffled to explain how in the early nineteenth century this Utica, New York, banker wrote a book *A Treatise on Language* containing a point of view amazingly similar to what became intellectual-scientific currency a century later. Johnson's writings were serendipitously discovered and circulated shortly before World War II.

The full title of Johnson's book is *A Treatise on Language: Or the Relation Which Words Bear to Things* ([1836] 1947). And as was never done before, he subjects the relation between words and things to the most incisive, critical scrutiny. As Alexander Rynin says in his introduction to the 1947 republication of the book:

The test of Johnson's achievement is not the extent to which his insights were unanticipated but rather the imagination and scope exhibited in his development of their implications.

In his own judgment, Johnson's work on language ". . . is the elucidation of but one precept; namely to interpret language by nature . . . to make nature the expositor of words, instead of making words the expositors of nature." He is quite clear that this precept is not, in statement, at all novel. It is, he tells us, a position which "theoretically . . . may be admitted by every person, and may be deemed already known; but practically [is] violated by all men, and understood by none." [pp. 15–16]

Let us listen to Johnson's summing up of his conclusions:

1) I have shown, that many phenomena of different senses are so frequently associated, that they are designated in all languages by a single word; and hence we consider phenomena as identical, while identity exists in language only. These phenomena constitute a large class of existences, and a misunderstanding of this simple ambiguity of language has filled the world with metaphysical disquisitions. As an example of these existences, I would adduce distance, which, though a unity in language, is two distinct phenomena: a sight and a feel.

2) Secondly, I have shown that words are merely sounds, which are indebted for signification to the phenomena only that we, by custom or instruction, apply them to. This seems a very obvious characteristic of words, still we frequently employ them when confessedly there are no phenomena to which they can refer. As a gross instance of this latent sophistry of language, I will say that the air which we are inhaling, and which we deem pure and transparent, is full of scorpions. This sentence is grammatical, and possesses an apparent significance, but the word scorpions, referring to no

phenomenon, is nullified. All our learning is corrupted with
this error, though, when exhibited in so gross an example as
the above, we discover immediately the fallacy.

3) Thirdly, I have shown that as words have no inherent
significant, every word possesses as many significations as it
possesses a reference to different phenomena. We all know
that when the name George refers to Washington it is digni-
fied and venerated; when it refers to a vagabond reeling
through our streets, it has an entirely different signification.
The position when thus applied seems too obvious to need a
comment; still, when differently used, it constitutes a
sophistry which occupies a large space in speculation.

4) Fourthly, I have shown that language can effect no
more than to refer us to phenomena. To judge from the contents of any library, no truth is so little known. We should
rather infer that language can effect everything but to refer us
to phenomena. Why cannot the most elaborate disquisition,
the whole vocabulary of the most copious language, teach
some sagacious blind person the meaning of the word scarlet?
We know the attempt was once made; and when the philosopher thought he had succeeded, the blind person said that
scarlet must be like the blast of a trumpet. But why is language inefficient in this particular? Is there any peculiarity in
colours? No: the difficulty is in language, which can, in no
case, effect more than to refer us to some known phenomena.
Every person knows this truth when it relates to teaching the
blind sights, and the deaf sounds; but no person seems to
understand it, when he hears a discourse to reveal what exists
in the centre of the earth, or what is transacting in the
republics of the moon.

5) Fifthly, I have shown that the only use of argumenta-
tion is to convince us that what is sought to be established is
included in the premises. Or, in other words, we assent to the
verbal proposition that a half is less than a whole, when we
understand that the word whole implies that it is more than a

half. This plain principle also is grossly overlooked; and the oversight is continually inducing men to waste their strength in vain efforts. They disregard the acquisition of mere premises, (an acquisition which alone increases knowledge,) and strive to deduce new conclusions, though that is only varying the language in which their knowledge is clothed. By this perversion of effort we increase our knowledge no faster than a merchant would his wealth, who should close his shop, and employ himself in inventing new phrases to express the money which is lying in his till.

I have shown, next, that it is the phenomena to which words refer, that give one word the power of implying another, and that give premises power to command our assent to certain conclusions. For instance, twice two apples makes four; a half of an apple is less than a whole apple—are propositions which we assent to, because our knowledge of the phenomena to which the propositions refer compel our assent. An ignorance of the source of this compulsion, has filled the world with the most fantastic conclusions. Men suppose that their assent to such propositions has no relation to phenomena: hence they say, if a half of an apple is less than a whole, the half of an insensible atom must be less than a whole. They pursue this process, and keep halving the halves as long as fancy suggests; and they suppose that each conclusion is significant and irresistible.

This constitutes one of the most subtle errors which language has betrayed us into, and I have investigated it at an unusual length. I have shown that it governs us in the construction of theories, and that it is the principal reason of the great solicitude expressed by theorists to define the names by which they denote the objects of their speculations. If they call one of the fixed stars a sun, it decides immediately that it is the centre of some group of worlds, whose invisibility adds only to the sublimity of the speculation.

Lastly, I have shown that all which Providence has placed within our grasp, is the sights, tastes, feels, sounds, and smells that our senses reveal to us; that we cannot even ask a significant question unless it refers to these, and every answer is insignificant that has not similar reference. [pp. 16–19]

Rynin asserts that Johnson was the first thinker to grasp the truly radical significance of a "critique of language" as preparation for philosophical and scientific inquiry, and he calls attention to the many striking resemblances, both in general attitude and even occasionally in language, to Wittgenstein's writings a century later.

Johnson developed with great clarity and detail the view that lies at the heart of modern empiricism, namely, that a statement for which no method of verification is supplied is insignificant, and perhaps for the first time, more or less *clearly and systematically* distinguished between the false and the insignificant, showing, in Wittgenstein's language, that "most propositions and questions [for Johnson and his contemporaries the term *philosophical* includes what is now called *science*] are not false, but senseless. We cannot, therefore, answer questions of this kind at all, but only state their senselessness. Most questions and propositions of the philosophers result from the fact that we do not understand the logic of our language"—a most Johnsonian assertion! [p. 21]

I cannot refrain from quoting from Todd and Sonkin's (1977) biography of Johnson, *Alexander Bryan Johnson: Philosophical Banker*:

The authors will make no attempt to summarize Johnson's *Treatise* beyond what has already been written, but we would like, at this point, to pair off at least two of Johnson's "propositions" with similar statements made a full century later, by the distinguished physicist, Percy W. Bridgman.

Johnson: Proposition #24, Lecture V: A *Treatise on Language*

IMPUTING TO NATURE THE IDENTITY WHICH EXISTS IN LANGUAGE CAUSES MUCH FALLACIOUS SPECULATION.

Light *moves* from the sun to the earth, and a coach *moves* from Utica to Albany. The word *motion* is proper in both phrases; but when we deem the motions as identical in nature as in language, we are transferring to nature what is simply a property of language. The mistake is unimportant till, by virtue of the supposed identity, we attribute to the *motion* of light the concomitants of the coaches [sic] *motion*. Proceeding thus, we calculate that during one vibration of a clock's pendulum, light moves as consecutively as the coach, one hundred and sixty thousand miles.

Bridgman: *The Logic of Modern Physics* (1927):

Physically, it is of the essence of light that it is not a thing that *travels*, and in choosing to treat it as a thing that does, I do not see how we can avoid the most serious difficulties.

Johnson: Proposition #4, Lecture XIX:

OUR SENSES ALONE CAN ANSWER QUESTIONS. WORDS CAN ONLY REFER TO WHAT OUR SENSES REVEAL:

When the Lord answered from the flaming bush the inquiry of Moses by saying, "I am that I am," the answer was wonderfully expressive of the nature of language. . . . We may say to life, "What art thou?" and to death, "What art thou?" . . . but language can furnish no better answer than, I am that I am.

Bridgman: *The Intelligent Individual and Society* (N.Y. 1938):

The physicist has come to recognize that it is unpleasantly easy to put words together into formal questions which admit of no possible operational check on the correctness of the answer, and in making this recognition and in learning to avoid the *meaningless* questions he has acquired an important tool in aid of precise thinking.

Percy Bridgman knew nothing of Johnson's works or even of his existence when he wrote these words. Nor did Bertrand Russell, Ludwig Wittgenstein, Aldous Huxley, I. A. Richards, S. I. Hayakawa, and other students of philosophy of language when they began, a century after Johnson wrote his *Treatise*, to delve into the meaning of words. [pp. 238–239]

So how do we account for Johnson's contribution, for the recognition of the nearly universal tendency mischievously to confuse words with their thing referents, to fail to recognize that we use words in ways that obscure the realities of things? Things are far more complex in a psychological sense than our words for them suggest. The word *rose* is *not* a rose!

Alexander Bryan Johnson was born in Gosport, England, on May 29, 1786. After a few years his parents moved to London. His father, Bryan, was a businessman. Alexander was small for his age and described as "intellectually premature." Although he had schooling, he did not find it stimulating. But he was a voracious reader and gained access to the libraries of several people. He was an only child and early on was a solitary kind of individual. The nature of his father's business is not clear, but the fact that he had his portrait painted by the American artist, Benjamin West, who was gaining celebrity in London, suggests that he was a man of some means. In 1797 the father decided to go to America and try his fortune there. The son and mother stayed in London until the father got settled.

My father, when he went to America, would have gladly taken me with him, but I refused to go and leave my mother alone. The remittances which we received from him she employed on me without any limit but my own volition, and I never encroached on them unduly except once, in procuring a rather expensive suit of regimentals, gun and all other equipment, to join a boys voluntary military association established in our neighborhood, under the gratuitous tuition of an army officer who once a week drilled us, and though I was probably poorer than any other of the company, I was the first accoutred and always the best. [Todd and Sonkin, 1977, p. 15]

It was not until four years later in 1801 that the family was reunited in Utica where the father had a small store that, nevertheless, was apparently quite profitable. Alexander worked for his father and wielded a good deal of influence over him in business affairs and, as a result, "more money was realized in the last years of Bryan Johnson's business than in all of the former" (Todd and Sonkin, 1977, p. 37).

Alexander was not content being a storekeeper. "'I desired,' he said, 'to accumulate a sufficiency of money that we might live without business, for I nourished a notion that country shopkeeping was not an elevated employment. I probably received this impression from England, and from the romances that had constituted most of my reading, and had tinctured me with undue aspirations and expectations'" (Todd and Sonkin, 1977, p. 37).

Alexander looked forward to "the expiration of my minority" in 1807. Since his father never demanded his presence in the store, Alexander began a heavy reading schedule as well as writing literary pieces that were published anonymously in the local paper and "illustrated," Johnson said, the truth of a line he had read in the *Spectator*: "whatever contradicts my sense I hate to see, and never can believe" (Todd and Sonkin, 1977, p. 40), a statement that can be interpreted as prodromal of his later word-thing preoccupation. At that time he wrote a five-act tragedy "after the manner of Shakespeare" but was told only plays that had been successful in London would attract an American audience. He was ambitious, desirous of fame, characteristics with which he was quite aware of and at home.

In 1805 he and his father became naturalized citizens of the United States.

As a young man he suffered bouts of depression. It is not at all clear from his autobiography what brought these bouts on or what their contents were. Several factors probably were part of the picture: he felt different and apart from others; he was restlessly ambitious for some kind of literary celebrity, the attainment of which he may have seen as improbable; and he was a strange mixture of intellectual self-confidence and what may be termed as a sense of social class inferiority. By the time of his thirties, he had met and socially interacted with the major political figures of his day, from President Madison on down. It is when he describes some of these interactions that one gets the feeling that he felt that he did not "belong." He approached women, especially those he considered a possible mate, with extreme, painful diffidence, again as if his display of interest would be rejected once the young woman would come to know him.

Here is Johnson's account of his courtship of the woman who became his wife:

I passed much time in walking with my father who almost constantly accompanied me, and in one of our walks up Genesee Street we passed a school house somewhere near the present location of Grace Church. The school had just been dismissed and among the female scholars I observed one whose bright appearance, mature but slight form, and auburn hair greatly interested me. Her dress was very simple, but still sufficiently unique to denote not an ordinary personage. As we passed my father bowed to her and I asked him if he knew her. He said she was a granddaughter of President John Adams and a niece of his old friend Justus B. Smith of Hamilton, New York—some thirty miles from Utica. I knew Mr. Smith, and that one of his sisters had married Charles Adams, the son of President John Adams and the junior brother of John Quincy Adams, but I had no knowledge that any branch

of the family resided in Utica. My father said this young lady
had removed to Utica for the benefit of her education, and
that she was living on the hill with her widowed mother, Mrs.
Adams, who was keeping house with the mother's maiden sister, Miss Nancy Smith, a lady some thirty years old. I had
often heard Justus Smith in his visits to my father talk of pur-
chasing articles to carry home with him to Miss Adams, but I
supposed he alluded to the wife of his brother, Col. William
S. Smith, who I knew had married a daughter of President
John Adams while he, the Colonel, was Secretary of Legation
to Mr. Adams, then minister plenipotentiary at the Court of
St. James. The marriage of Justus Smith's sister to Charles
Adams I had never heard of, nor of the existence of the young
lady we had just met. My father judged accurately that I was
pleased with the appearance of Miss Adams, and he proposed
that we should walk to the house, and he would introduce me
to the family. I gladly assented, and we proceeded onwards up
Genesee Street till we came to the residence. It was a white-
painted snug cottage house, with a garden and a small orchard
attached, and including some six acres of land. We knocked
at the door and were admitted into a parlor genteelly furnished, and we found in it Miss Smith to whom my father
introduced me, and who received us very kindly, knowing the
intimacy that existed between my father and her brother. We
failed in seeing either Mrs. Adams or her daughter, and after
remaining some time we took our leave and departed.

The next evening I returned alone to the Adams household. The young lady seemed to be engaged in some needle
work, not suspecting that my visit related in any way to her,
and I am not sure that I addressed any conversation to her or
she to me. I made several such evening visits, and as frequently as I thought could be proper, and eventually I came to
address some conversation to the young lady. My conversation was always of a grave character, and as little adapted to
the taste of a young lady as can be imagined, and I deemed

the thought preposterous of assuming the character of a lover
to one whom I thought much my superior. Besides, the aunt
remarked to some remark of mine that Miss Adams had left at
Quincy a very dear friend, and that she therefore felt indis-
posed to the gaiety of Utica. I inferred that this dear friend
was necessarily of the male gender and that it betokened she
was already engaged, and I hastily concluded to no longer
continuing an unavailing intercourse, and therefore told the
ladies that I intended to return shortly to New York. [Todd
and Sonkin, 1977, p. 80]

It was Leah Johnson who took the bull by the horns and told
the young woman's mother and aunt, "My son very much admires
your daughter."

Mrs. Adams was, of course, much surprised, and also Miss
Smith, as they said my conversation was always directed to
them and not to the young lady. Miss Smith at once recov-
ered from her error, and behaved the manner with great kindness. They both told my mother that they would impress the
young lady with my views, and that being acquainted with my
character they would further my suit all in their power. The
next time I went to the house I was most embarrassingly left
alone with the young lady, but I took courage to declare my
intentions, and thenceforth became a regularly accepting
lover, and after an acquaintance of some ten weeks we were
married by the Rev. Henry Dwight, the Presbyterian minister
of Utica, of whose church my bride was a communicant. I
belonged to the Episcopal Church, but in deference to the
wishes of my bride I made no objection to the Presbyterian
ceremony. We were married on the evening of the 23d of
October 1814 at the residence of my bride, and with no company present but my father and mother and Mrs. Adams and
Miss Smith. Great fees were not usual to clergymen at the
time, and I gave to Mr. Dwight $25, which sum was deemed

liberal, and I sent the same sum to my own minister of the Episcopal Church. The marriage on the side of bride and groom was purely intellectual. I had no reason to expect that the feelings of my bride were her impelling motive, but I took care that she should not take the step reluctantly from the persuasion of others, and I told her that if the act was not wholly voluntary on her part I would so arrange as to take the blame of its nonaccomplishment at any expense to my own feelings. She replied that she had no objections to the marriage except she thought herself too young. I saw that she fulfilled to the uttermost all that I ever desired in a wife, and that I could not fail to love her, and that, with her good sense as evinced by even the marriage to me under the circumstances of the case, and with the kind conduct I meant to pursue towards her, she could not fail from acquiring all the affection that a wife ought to feel towards a husband. Eventually no two people ever lived together with greater mutual affection and domestic happiness than we experienced. At the time of the marriage she was sixteen years, one month, and fifteen days old, and I was twenty-eight years, four months, and twenty-four days old. Her mother had, I found subsequently, consulted Col. Benjamin Walker as to my character, and he said I possessed only one fault known to him, and that was too much fondness for money, but this Mrs. Adams deemed in my favor, as she had seen in her own family the bad consequences of an opposite character. In looking back, as I often do, at this event of my life, I feel constantly abashed at the sad diffidence with which I conducted my courtship, and which satisfies me that the embarrassment is misplaced that young men usually feel on the manner in which they shall ask the question of their acceptance or rejection, for a predetermination usually exists to accept or reject, and it will not be changed by the mode in which the proffer is made. [Todd and Sonkin, 1977, pp. 81–82]

For the purposes of this essay, it is not necessary to go into detail about Johnson's career in business and banking, except to say that he became more wealthy and a nationally known figure whose advice was sought about banking policies. Concomitant with all these activities Johnson continued to write, not only on language but on economic and other matters. *Not until a century after his death did he get recognition for clearly enunciating a view of the role of the national debt that was at the core of Keynesian economic theory,* which adds to the mystery of this Utica "philosophical banker." It should also be noted that he became a lawyer but really did not practice. Writing was always first on his life's agenda.

Johnson's first two wives died, and toward the end of his days, he married a woman who survived him. He died in 1867. Here are his valedictory remarks:

All speculative philosophies precedent of mine are like tunes which skillful musicians play on a pianoforte. Each philosopher plays with words such a tune as he deems best; but my philosophy plays no tune, but refers every tuneful note to the internal machinery of the piano from which the tuneful note proceeds. I am the first philosopher that has gone deeper than language, and has sought to discover the meaning of words in man's internal organism, a meaning that is not words. The verbal systems of speculative philosophy are as interminable as the different tunes that can be formed out of the notes of a piano, and realizing how barren such philosophies have ever been for the settlement of the questions for which such philosophies are employed, I have essayed the new system as an ultimate and fixed limit of all speculative knowledge, and which will in time, I fondly trust, cause an abandonment of the old and endless speculations of the verbal philosopher. [Todd and Sonkin, 1977, p. 354]

It took a century for the world to catch up with Johnson.

So how do we begin to explain Johnson's contribution to language? Nothing in what he or anyone else has said provides a starting point. There was nothing in the Utica intellectual ambiance that contributes to our understanding. Nor is there anything in his family contexts that is helpful. He had read Locke, Hume, Berkeley, and others, and although some of their writings contained hints similar to what Johnson later elaborated, they are very faint hints. His autobiography, which is quite lengthy, has never been published.

Ideas, let alone systematic exposition of those ideas, do not have virginal births. They do have contexts of origins that reflect past experiences. If in Johnson's case those contexts are unclear, to say the least, we can at least say that he was truly obsessed with the relations between words and things. I use the word *obsessed* in order to suggest that the problem had very personal meaning for him. In one way or another the problem stood for and illuminated his perception of himself; that is, it had direct meaning for his self-definition. He wrote about the issues impersonally, but in keeping with his conceptual position, one is justified in saying that the words he used had meanings not contained in those words. Words, he obsessively reiterated, should never be confused with the complex realities of their thing referents. It is no great leap to suggest that it is as if Johnson would say, "Whatever words you use to label and describe me do not capture what I am, the realities of my phenomenology. What you call me is a fraction of what I call myself. I am *and* am not what you think I am. My identity is not contained in the identity implied between your labels for me and the one that I know. You assume an identity that is mischievous, confusing, and wrong. Whatever words you use to label Alexander Bryan Johnson prevent you from knowing the fullness of me. You think you know me, but you do not."

Let me now add to the mystery in a way that illuminates but one aspect of it. What I shall offer is *not* an explanation but a pointing to one fact about Johnson I find both fascinating and startling.

I start with the foreword that Alex Haley of *Roots* fame wrote for the Todd and Sonkin (1977) biography:

> This is the story of Alexander Bryan Johnson, who came to America as a boy not long after my ancestor, Kunta Kinte, but under somewhat different circumstances. He settled in the Mohawk Valley of New York State, grew rich, married the granddaughter of President John Adams, and until 1812 owned a black slave named Frank. He also, in 1828, wrote a unique book on language, undiscovered for a century, which showed how words are used as whips, and can distort our view of reality. How differently, he pointed out, in 1828, white Americans view the word *black* when it refers to the color of night on the one hand, and on the other, to the color of a man's skin. The questions he raised about language and reality are still being asked by philosophers today.
>
> Alexander Bryan Johnson had roots, but he kept them hidden from his friends and his Adams relatives—and often from himself. His ancestors were distinguished rabbis in Europe, and his father had changed his name voluntarily, unlike Kunta Kinte. There was a *griot* in his family, however, his Cousin Rachel in London, who wouldn't let him forget, and he censored her letters with ink and scissors, though not carefully enough. Charles Todd and Robert Sonkin, after ten years of digging through the voluminous papers of this strange and brilliant man, have told the story, which began in 1787 and ended shortly after the Civil War. It is part and parcel of the American dream—and the American tragedy. [p. vii]

Although Johnson's father had become an Episcopalian before coming to America, there is no doubt that his son knew of his Jewish origins. Why his father converted is not clear, nor does Johnson tell us in his autobiography how he viewed the conversion, although in his voluminous autobiography he goes into great detail about his experiences and thoughts before and after coming here.

There are more than a dozen places in the biography where the Johnsons' relations with their European relatives are described. I shall briefly mention a few.

1. Bryan came to the states in 1797, his son in 1801. Upon their arrivals they wrote their relatives that they arrived safely. Four-teen years passed before Bryan, who had retired from the business and was advancing in his years, wrote to his older brother, William, whose last name had become Jones. In the few letters that ensued we learn that Alexander's first name was *Zalick*, which is a phonetic rendition of the German *selig*, meaning blessed. According to Rachel (his cousin), Alexander's name was *Solomon*, the Hebrew word for peace. It should be kept in mind that Alexander's relationship to his father was inordinately close. It is far from wild speculation to assume that their Jewishness was not a rare topic of discussion.

2. Following the death of his father, Alexander began a volu-minous correspondence—"privately, perhaps even clandestinely for a while" (Todd and Sonkin, 1977, p. 133)—with his relatives, espe-cially Rachel, who minced no words about her utter disapproval of his rejection of his Jewish origins. Given her criticisms one might have predicted that Alexander would cease corresponding with her, but he did not. It is as if he somehow agreed with her criticisms.

3. Following the death of his first wife, Alexander resumed his correspondence with Rachel. Abigail's death brought on a serious depression that was of great concern to Alexander's family. In regard to Abigail, Johnson said, "My moral education had been as poor as my intellectual, and I had not attempted to cultivate it as I had attempted to cultivate my intellect. She impressed me with religious belief and social improvement. . . . Her social position had been much superior to mine, and I admired her for her youth, her beauty, her wisdom and discretion. She was essentially and peculiarly the help that was meet for me" (Todd and Sonkin, 1977, p. 234).

4. Following the death of his son, John, from typhoid fever, Johnson again writes to Rachel, who wrote back:

Our situation is not the most agreeable, nor are we at all in the sphere suitable to our tastes or feelings. I wish my girls were well married, though I see no prospect of the kind, for with our religious principles there are no suitable matches for them: with low Israelites they would of course not unite, and with the higher class, the circumstances of their births would prove an obstacle. Indeed, I often think of the promise in one of the commandments of "visiting upon the third and fourth generation," and that the sin which I committed in wandering (for I have only *wandered*) from my religion, will be visited by my children not being permitted to be reproduced in their posterity. Our fathers were, you know, of the tribe of Aaron, called among us *Cohens*, and for a daughter of that tribe to err subjected the offender to the punishment of death. . . . Perhaps you believe this bigotry—yet no, you cannot, for you believe in revealed religion, though you have diverged from the common stock. You are the only being with whom I commune on subjects like these, and to you (though seas roll between us and though most likely we shall never again behold each other) I write in the fullness of my heart, for here I have no congenial mind to commune with. [Todd and Sonkin, 1977, p. 254]

5. Following the tragic death of his second wife, Johnson and his family feared for his sanity. Fearing that his "intellect would give way under the shock, and to save my reason and perhaps my life," Johnson quickly arranged a trip to Europe. "[U]ppermost in his mind was a reunion with Rachel and her brother Solomon" (Todd and Sonkin, 1977, p. 312). The reunion took place, although his son, Charles, who had accompanied him on the trip, was excluded.

6. In 1857 Johnson wrote an article that appeared in *Hunt's Merchant Magazine*. The title was "The Almighty Dollar; or Money as a Motive for Action." In it he says:

The Jews of Europe exemplify some of the results that the money motive is eliciting here. Being debarred by law or prejudice from obtaining titular honors, they seek riches . . . and naturally subordinate thereto much that the honorary motive prefers. What a loss to the world has been their eighteen centuries of debasement, if, as is affirmed, they are more intellectually acute than any other race; an affirmation which they have, however, not verified here where they suffer no legal disabilities, and are continually vanquished at their own game of pecuniary accumulation; though probably, time enough has not elapsed to wean them from the petty traffic to which oppression originally crushed them, and to give their aspirations a higher aim. [Todd and Sonkin, 1977, p. 332]

I think I have presented enough about Johnson to justify the conclusion that the secret of his origins was ever present in his psychological bloodstream. But what does that have to do with the thrust of his *Treatise on Language*, that which he regarded as his major achievement and that, he asserted, the world would sometime recognize and praise? I feel justified in raising that question for two reasons. The first is that Johnson wrote about an aspect of the human mind in a literally unprecedented way. He did not write about atoms, stars, or inanimate objects. In writing about the relationship between words and things, it was, I assume, impossible to do so without using himself and his experience as "data." Johnson was the epitome of the self-directed, introspective, even brooding individual. He was a solitary person. And when you peruse articles and books he wrote on a truly wide range of topics, you have to be impressed with how each of them, except for the treatise, is the fruit of personal experience and observation. Johnson always used himself!

The second reason is that Johnson's "secret" is as clear an example as one can find of how words-labels should never be confused with their thing referents. In his daily life—in letters to him, how people described him, the identifying labels people pinned on him (e.g., businessman, banker, church member)—Johnson knew full well that the one "thing" he was was not signified by those labels.

It is obvious that I think that the secret of his Jewish origins and the writing of the treatise were not in separate psychological realms. That, I should hasten to say, is not to suggest that the former is a "cause" of the latter. We simply do not have the evidence to draw such a conclusion. That the two were psychologically intertwined I have no doubt. In his treatise Johnson frequently uses the word *identity* in regard to the tendency to confuse a word with its thing referent. That word cuts to the core of that most unusual Utica banker.

Johnson remains a mystery. He also represents a challenge to anyone interested in unusual creativity, especially, as in this case, when there is no intellectual-historical context to which that creativity can be related, from which it sprung, so to speak. A *Treatise on Language* cannot be explained by genes. What that book does is give force to the concept of *coincidence*, a concept Feldman employs in his studies of child prodigies. What that concept suggests is that creativity is not explainable by a list of psychological characteristics but rather by a coincidence of factors that, when they coalesce, *may* lead to unusual creativity. That is to say, Johnson's creativity was not predictable on the grounds that he was bright, lived in the world of ideas, was intellectually curious, had unusually supportive parents, had the leisure to think and write, was very ambitious for intellectual and literary fame, and had intellectual self-confidence to a mammoth degree. He had all that and more. So did and do a lot of people whose creativity we do not celebrate. It is the fortuitous coming together of these factors—their strength, timing, and external support—that starts the unusual developmental process.

But, I would argue, what is unusual about the Johnsons of history is not the process but rather the product. Coincidence is no less a factor in the development of any human being whose uniqueness we seek to explain. What do we mean when we say that every person is unique? To that assertion Johnson would say that when we say *unique*, when that word is a premise in our thinking, we inevitably will end up with a mystery incapable of anything resembling a persuasive explanation. In explaining Johnson I have been no more persuasive than if I attempted to explain my closest friend. The human personality is and will always be a mystery, if only because coincidences are unpredictable and unseeable. Of course, we have identified processes, contents, and relationships that we are certain play a role in personality development. But they do not help us explain uniqueness. This is not to say they explain nothing. It is to say they do not explain uniqueness. In regard to uniqueness it is the case that the more you know (or think you know) the more you need to know.

Was it Churchill who said that the Soviet Union was a puzzle wrapped in an enigma encased in a mystery? Churchill was knowledgeable about the Soviet Union, knowledgeable and honest enough to expose his ignorance. That is the stance we should take in regard to understanding human uniqueness. And, like Churchill, it is a stance that should in no way prevent us from doing our best to understand what I consider to be an impossible task. The pursuit of such understanding is interesting, exciting, and useful at the same time it is humbling. Unfortunately, theorists of personality have not been—in public, at least—humble people.

7

Explaining the Sixties

You can place psychologists into four categories. The first would contain those whose primary interest is to develop generalizations applicable to all people regardless of place, culture, or even time. They are very heterogeneous in terms of the substance of the problem they are studying: visual and auditory perception, problem solving, the nature and structure of abilities, and so forth. However the problems differ, it is the intent of the researcher-theoretician to seek laws, principles, generalizations, call them what you will, of people anywhere. The oedipal complex, the *Sturm und Drang* of adolescence, the origins of morality, the nature and course of learning, frustration and aggression—these are a few examples. For any of them there are different points of view and, therefore, heated controversy. Is the oedipal drama universal? Is adolescence inevitably conflictful? Is aggression always preceded by frustration? Do all children pass through the same stages of cognitive development? Does deprivation in infancy and childhood always have untoward consequences? These and other questions are powered less (but nevertheless powered) by a search for differences among people than by the goal of establishing communalities among all people. If you peruse a random sample of introductory texts, it is hard to avoid the impression that the overarching aim of the writers is to get the reader to understand that there are universal principles without which human behavior anywhere is either incomprehensible or leads one to glaringly incomplete explanations.

The second category is much larger, containing as it does psychologists interested in individual differences: their origins, development, consequences, and the implications of these for practical actions (e.g., planning, placement, treatment, policy). This category is large because in it I place all those psychologists whose stock-in-trade are tests or therapies of one kind or another. Some of these psychologists are primarily researchers seeking new knowledge about problems of practical, social significance. They are interested in exploring the practical, social policy implications of their research but less so than in attaining new knowledge and reconceptualizations. This group aside, most psychologists in this category spend their time determining and dealing with individual differences. Psychological universals may be of interest to them, but these are usually unrelated to their focus on understanding and dealing with individual differences. Clinicians, of course, make up the bulk of this group.

The third category is for those I will call "group psychologists." Included here are those who study behavior in dyadic relationships, families, therapeutic groups, parent groups, classrooms, and all sorts of meetings having different purposes (e.g., conflict resolution, planning, decision making, simulated juries, focus groups). It would be more correct to say that these psychologists are interested in *small* groups that tend to be relatively homogeneous in some respect. Some of these psychologists may be interested in reaching generalizations about the "natural history" of groups: how and why they are formed, who becomes leader and how, changes in mode of interaction, changes in language, emotional expression, atmosphere, and cohesion. But in the work of these psychologists, as in most others in this category, there is an emphasis on individuals and their behavioral differences in the small group.

Before going on to the fourth category, I want to suggest that there is a communality, not an identity, among the first three categories: on the level of theory, research, and practice, their psychology tends to be about individual organisms. They derive their data from individuals (even when in a group) and employ an individual psychology to interpret their data. Freud's writings on group psychology are a most clear example. No less clear (to me, at least) is the way learning theorists, past and present, rivet on the single organism, rat or human. They aggregated their data, they offered generalizations, but when you read their discussion sections, you find it hard to avoid the impression that they are projecting onto their subjects a psychology of the individual organism. Was it Tolman who asked how he would think and what he would do if he were a rat in the maze? Is it not a universal law that you cannot explain another human or other animal independent of your individual psychology? The answer is, as Roger Barker's ecological studies indicate, no. You can explain (to an important degree) *and* predict the behavior of people without special studies of them as individuals. His explication, criteria for, and studies of *behavior settings*, and how these settings demand and elicit behavioral regularities among widely different people whom you may never know, are truly a seminal contribution to psychology. Barker's focus was not on individuals but on the structure of the ecologies in which they live. Clinicians, personality theorists and researchers, and most other psychologists interested in "psyches" do not find Barker's ecological psychology of help or even of interest. Barker is far away from mainstream psychology. He has been influential only on community psychologists, and even in that small field on a few of its members.

Let me illustrate this point with some personal history. When I came to Yale in 1945 (Lincoln had just been shot!) the department had one secretary, Sue Henry, in a room adjoining that of the chairperson. In the hallway outside their offices were the mailboxes. It made no difference who or what you were in the department; several times in that day you were in that circumscribed space, and you saw and very likely interacted with Sue Henry. Sue was an important person in the department because she, even more than the chairperson, could answer almost any question you posed about this or that. And if you needed a paper or a letter typed, you, of course, gave it to Sue. When you were in that circumscribed space, you were likely to meet and talk with others: faculty, students, the person in charge of the workshop for instrument and maze construction, and so forth. It was a meeting place. It is important to note that in Yale's Institute of Human Relations, the hallways were long and narrow and the doors opened outward so that if two opposite doors were open, you had to be thin and agile to maneuver passage. That meant that doors were kept shut, making perception of and interaction with others impossible. If the "Sue Henry–chairperson" space was small and circumscribed, it was still "open" space, one in which in the course of the week you would see, meet, and interact with almost everyone. We took Sue and that space for granted. They were fixtures in our lives in much the same way that the lighting was.

Then came growth and another secretary, the no less legendary Jane O., was added in an office next to Sue's, although for the first year or two she may well have been in Sue's office. But nothing essentially changed in terms of greeting, talking, meeting behavior. It was space that elicited and sustained rather predictable behavior that more often than not may be called superficial but by no means always.

Then came the increase in the number of students and faculty and, because of research grants, secretaries housed nearer the faculty with grants. Slowly and unnoticed two things started to happen. The first was that the "Sue Henry—chairperson—mailbox" space began to lose the features of Barker's "behavior setting." The second was that the frequency and quality of social interaction changed. There was no longer one such setting but a variety of settings. To someone like me who quickly became an "old timer," this dispersion was obvious as I became aware that there were students and new faculty I rarely saw or knew. I had my "show" on another floor. There were many such shows, each on a different stage. To Sue Henry, Jane O., and some old timers like me, something valuable was slipping away, and this in a most civil department not noted for the depth or frequency of social interactions. If we, inchoately, mourned the good old days, that was not the case for younger faculty among whom one heard choate complaints about how easy it was to feel alone and isolated, feelings they explained wholly in terms of individual personalities and not at all in terms of a changed ecology. Explanations in terms of individual person-alities is second (first?) nature to psychologists. *Such explanations were by no means invalid; they contained a large kernel of truth.* But they were incomplete, and that is the point.

The department moved to a building near the center of the campus. (Yale is in the Broadway and Forty-Second Street of New Haven; the word *campus* arouses the wrong imagery.) Let me now describe what you encounter when you enter the building. You walk up several steps and you see a large, glass enclosed office in which are four desks for four secretaries. When you begin to enter the glass enclosed office and look right, you see more offices, and if you meander left there are still more. There are approximately ten to twelve staff people in those offices. All women. I do not have to do a study to buttress several conclusions. Using the early Sue Henry–Jane O. era as a baseline, there is very little interaction between those behind the glass wall and everyone else in the department. Indeed, the bulk of students and faculty would be unable to give the names of three or more of the staff there, and each of the staff has a nameplate on his or her desk. With very few exceptions (e.g., the business manager and a couple of others) the staff has rarely, if ever, had anything like a personal conversation with a faculty member or student. From the standpoint of the staff they exist in a world apart, and to everyone else that glass wall is another world. That world, very definitely a behavior setting, is a *community*, which is far more than you can say about the rest of the building.

Several years ago Yale came to national attention when it was unionized and a long strike began. The background for that long and bitter strike is complicated indeed, but two aspects of it are rel-evant here. The first is that what had happened in our department was by no means atypical in the university, particularly in the medical school–hospital complex. The behavioral regularities in the relationships between faculty and staff were like those between people on top of the mountain in Kafka's *Castle* and the mass at the foot of the mountain. The second aspect was in the complete failure of Yale planners, faculty, and administration to comprehend the consequences of two things: the changing demography-ecology of New Haven and the ways in which the women's liberation movement was dramatically altering the racial, social class composition of the ever-growing size of staff. The story is more complicated than our everyday explanations would suggest. Nevertheless, the point is warranted that our explanations and understandings of individual behavior are egregiously incomplete precisely because we are schooled to ignore the ecologies within ecologies. The psyche is figure; all else is ground: a globby, unstructured, ignored ground.

The fourth category is the smallest because it contains psychologists whose major interest is very secondarily the individual. They are interested in what may be termed sociological, epidemiological, cultural, political, social policy, "mass movement" questions. It is noteworthy that these labels are not the usual ones we employ to identify psychologists. They are not the "social" psychological questions that are the focus of American social psychology that concerns itself with interindividual behavior in dyads and small groups (i.e., with interpersonal cognitive and personality variables).

How do we explain the sources, strength, and consequences of gender, racial, ethnic prejudices? How do we explain marked changes in or the spread of personal, familial lifestyles? Why are our major societal institutions (educational, religious, political) so resistant to change? How do we account for the "sexual revolution" and intergenerational gulfs and their consequences? What are or will be the societal consequences of the space age, computers, TV? Despite billions of dollars we have budgeted, and despite the millions of pages contained in thousands of commission–task force reports, why do the outcomes of our educational system remain inadequate or become more so?

These and similar questions are the *primary* interest of few psychologists. Indeed, many psychologists would say they are not psychological questions but rather "sociological" or philosophical. That is to say, they are questions that do not and cannot derive from extant psychological theories; they imply or require "variables" or kinds of data these theories were not intended to gather or confront. No one, I assume, would deny that these are important questions in terms of the here, now, and future, that their implications for the lives of people are not great, that how as a society we understand and deal with them will be fateful indeed—granted that the questions are important and deserve study, discussion, and social action, it does not follow that the conceptual-theoretical-research strengths of psychology should be changed or diverted so that these questions are more in the center of the field's concerns. This is a stance that permitted the field to say that William James was once a psychologist who "became" a philosopher, and John Dewey was a psychologist who "became" a philosopher and educator. Psychology is psychology. It cannot cover the waterfront of important problems. You play to your strengths, and the indisputable strength of psychology is its quest to understand the individual psyche. It makes sense, incomplete sense.

Imagine the situation in which psychology paid little attention to human sexuality. It would not be because sexuality was considered unimportant or off limits but rather that the study of sexuality was not where the field could and should makes its best contributions. The fact is that what I ask you to imagine was true for psychology before World War II. Very few psychologists (like Frank Beach) spent their careers studying the mysteries of sexuality. So, we can ask another of those questions: How do we explain the dramatic change in this respect before and after World War II? How was that change related to "larger" societal changes? What do those changes say about America *and* American psychology?

I said that there are very few psychologists in this category. That is true only if you pigeonhole psychologists in light of what occupies them in their working days. If, however, you go by the phenomenology of these psychologists when they are not doing their professional things, then the sample questions I raised earlier are far from secondary interest to them. Every one of them is concerned with these questions, and I use the word *concerned* in its affective connotations. From this standpoint, this category is by far the largest of the four.

So how do we explain the sixties? Why are the sixties regarded, validly or invalidly, as a societal watershed, in much the same way that World War II was a watershed? How did it come about that every major societal institution came under attack, especially from younger people? No one witnessed this period in a neutral manner. Something was happening that was stirring, exciting, and refreshing to some people, that to others was upsetting, mindless, and unexplainable. Few were in doubt that their "psychology" and that of others were changing. It would be more correct to say that no one doubted that the psychology of many people *had* already changed. The plaguing questions were how this came about and where it was all leading. In the case of psychology there were many who offered explanations: intergenerational conflict; a heightened sensitivity to moral-ethical issues (racial-ethnic inequities, gender discrimination); disillusion with the bitter fruits of World War II (the cold war, atomic bomb); Vietnam and a rejection of American imperialism; and the reaction of individuals to being imprisoned in large, impersonal bureaucratic institutions engendering or exacerbating feelings of loneliness, impotence, and hopelessness. Each of these explanations, alone or in combination, were psychologically salient in that they pointed to problems about which there was strong feeling. They were psychological explanations that required no change in the substance of psychological theory. If you were partisan to psychoanalytic theory, your explanation faced no special difficulties. If you adhered to a social constructivist or social interactionist view of personality, there was much grist for that theoretical mill. If you were a child developmentalist, the intergenerational gulf and war seemed tailor-made for your theories. And if you were an organizational psychologist interested in how life is lived in large public or private institutions, the social scene of the sixties was not all that difficult to understand.

In no way do I regard these explanations as invalid, if only because their starting point was what so many individuals were saying, thinking, and acting in accord with. That is to say, they started with the behavior, overt or covert, of individuals in this or that setting, age, or racial-ethnic group. They sought to explain here and now behavior and that often meant pursuing life-history events, processes, relationships.

My purpose in this essay is to suggest that conventional psychological explanations of the sixties are woefully incomplete in one important respect: they permit us to ignore or gloss over ecological variables and their vicissitudes that set, so to speak, the stage for the sizzling sixties. And when I term them ecological variables, I mean that they have no psychological content. They impact on individual psyches, but the impact is so general and comprehensive that it becomes figure, and individuals and their differences become ground. These are not variables like aggression, fantasy, ambition, ability, love, hate, shame, or guilt. They are variables external to individuals but not concerned with the reactions of individuals. Henry Murray introduced the concept of "press" to refer to an external force impinging on the individual, and his list of discrete presses was long indeed. The variables I shall be discussing are of a different order. It is like comparing a reading of one and eight on the Richter scale for size and consequences of earthquakes. When these variables come into play, it is as if everyone and everything changes. And that is their hallmark: the "impersonal" way in which they alter individuals, groups, institutions. Accustomed social regularities go by the board, and irreversibly so. The world has changed, and there is no turning back. Individuals are aware of changes within them. With few exceptions, they cannot grasp the societal dimensions of the change, let alone how the course of the society will be different than the past.

Let me illustrate what these variables are *not*. No one would dispute that when the first human being walked on the moon, it was a dramatic, momentous occasion, one that the civilized world knew was a dividing point between past and future. It is a glimpse of the obvious to say that it was impactful, regardless of individual psychological differences. But in one crucial respect it lacked the hallmark of the kind of ecological variable I am attempting to identify: its impact was transient; individuals, groups, institutions, and relationships were not altered; *the regularities of daily living did not change.* In some abstract way people knew that sometime in the future it would be apparent that the human psyche had changed. But in the here and now *and* in the foreseeable future, life would be as before. No changes were *required.* It could be argued, and validly, that putting a person on the moon was but a point in a past, continuous stream of scientific-technological advances that had already altered human "psychology" and daily living in slow, subtle, but potent ways. In that sense it was science-technology that could be called an ecological variable, not putting a person on the moon—an impersonal science-technology that, for all practical purposes, was unconcerned about psychological variables, on the assumption that its impacts would be benign or desirable.

It could also be argued that if putting a person on the moon was not in itself an ecological variable, *seeing* it was because it stunningly made people aware that henceforth they could be witness to any event. Television existed before a person walked on the moon, but that event dramatically and realistically enlarged the universe of possibilities and expectations.

I am indifferent as to what label you give to science-technology as a variable, as long as you recognize that its impacts are subtle and, relatively speaking, slow to be recognized, and unpredictable as to how it will change lives. Like the economists' conception of markets, science-technology is an impersonal variable with enormous psychological consequences. You might say that it is a kind of impersonal intellectual market that, intended or not, influences and regulates human behavior in ways (good and bad) of which most people are unaware until events force their recognition.

In regard to explaining the sixties, science-technology pales in comparison to the role of an ecological variable that was sudden in time and revolutionary in its immediate and long-term consequences: our entry into World War II. The words *World War II* have no specific, concrete, psychological referents. They are words we use to signify the coalescence of a mass of events and processes, a coalescence that separates present from past and will have predictable and unpredictable, nonreversible consequences for everyone and everything. It signifies cataclysm and catastrophe. If it is not in any conventional linguistic or psychological sense a psychological variable, its impact on psyches cannot be overestimated. If it impacts differentially on individual psyches, it is also the case that individuals cannot or do not grasp the dimensions and consequences of the cataclysm (i.e., unseeable dimensions and consequences that will be no less salient, or that will become salient, for their lives). Ecological variables are not *seeable*; they have to be conceptualized, imagined. They are not things or people. They are, initially at least, a cloud chamber of correlated and uncorrelated, impersonal goings-on.

It is fair to say that on Sunday, December 7, 1941, every adult American, regardless of individual differences, was asking four questions: How did this come about? What does it mean? What does it portend? How should I think about it? If you had asked individuals what they meant by *it*, they would have been unable to answer the question because *it* is a word intended to have a concrete referent, an impersonal referent, and in that sense each person knew that World War II was not an "it." We are not schooled to think about an "it" we cannot see except by giving it meaning in terms of our individual lives, which thereby hugely constricts our understanding of the dimensions and consequences of the "it." It is an understandable form of trivialization, excusable in individuals but not in those who seek to understand how the "out theres" of people influence their "in heres," how ecological variables influence—silently, subtly, inevitably—psyches, independent of individual differences.

Let me start with the predictable consequences of World War II. The most obvious is that millions of people would no longer be doing what they had been doing or had hoped to do. In a population somewhat over a hundred fifty million people, seventeen million became part of the armed services. It is not playing loose with words or concepts to say that that represented a form of mammoth, unsought emigration.[1] You do not have to be a psychologist to say that such a disruption in lives would have consequences not only for those who entered military service but for those they left behind (e.g., parents, wives, lovers, children, friends). For each person World War II was personalized in a circumscribed way. Practically no one saw "it" as having differential effects on identifiable *groups* in the society (e.g., blacks, women, diverse professional groups, those living in rural areas). No one said about these identifiable groups, "People in these groups will change in ways that will alter their view of themselves in relation to the larger society, alterations that are both predictable and unpredictable, intended and unintended. These alterations will be inevitable and irreversible. Their dynamics, course, and pace initially will not be visible, but at some point they will be and in ways that will be psychologically salient for everyone. We will not understand any of this by looking at individuals unless we look at individuals from the standpoint of the place their group has in the larger society. If the impact on these groups will be discernibly and markedly different, it is highly likely that those differences will have similar consequences for the larger society."

[1]It is important to note that there were other "transfers of populations" as a result of World War II, among the most important of which was the mass movement of people from rural to urban areas that were manufacturing-industrial centers. Anyone familiar with the history of transfers of population, forced or unforced, could have predicted in a general way the disruptive consequences World War II would have in the present (and future) of those transferring and those "receiving" them. It could be argued that World Was II came up on us so suddenly that it is asking too much to expect that attention would be given to the consequences of these transfers. One instructive exception: very soon after December 7, 1941, it was recognized that medical-psychological casualties would be of such a scale as to overwhelm existing facilities. That is, the "lesson" from World War I had been learned; the predictable consequences were clear. Planning began, the fruits of which were changes that altered the character of the relationship between universities and the larger society. That kind of recognition and planning did not extend to other no less predictable influences on individuals and groups.

It is far beyond my purposes to describe the differential impacts of World War II on major societal groups. Scores of books have been written about how that war affected women, racial-ethnic minorities, professions, and those in the military. It is my purpose to suggest that, however different the impact, in each group it engendered some common "themes." A better way to put it is to say that in each group an altered worldview was emerging inchoate and hardly articulated. It was an emerging worldview reflecting new axioms about what life is and should be. That these themes were embedded in what on the surface were very different phenome- nologies made them difficult to be discerned from the standpoint of psychologies in which ecological variables have no formal role and a concept like worldview has no standing. There were several such themes.

1. This is a stupid, immoral world in which the individual is akin to a snowflake in a storm. If this is the way things have been, then things have to change. This is the "never again" theme, a rejection of old rhetoric and stances, a willing, indeed eager, embracing of "fundamental" change. This has to be seen in relation to an ecological variable preceding World War II: the Great Depres- sion.

2. What we want and expect out of life we want *now*, not in a distant future. Life is short and unpredictable. My travel agent's logo was "See the world before you leave it." This theme is "Experience the world before you leave it, and the quicker the better." Time per- spectives were changing. Delayed gratification of desires, goals, and status was not congenial to this changing time perspective.

3. "We" deserve, need, and expect a new lease on life, an expanded lease, a lease that is not a gift but a right. We (especially the military and blacks) have paid our dues and we expect some- thing in return. And for those (e.g., women) for whom the war had given a new lease, not only was that lease renewable, but it would have to be expanded. This is the "expectation" or "rights" theme.

4. This theme is a composite of interrelated themes: "I want to go home again. I should want to go home again. I do not want to go home again. You can't go home again." Many who were adults during the war years had read Thomas Wolfe's novels and identified with his ever-present central character's longings, loneliness, and search for intimacy. What the war years did was enormously exacerbate the saliency of his portraits in that the need for intimacy, the need to break out from the prison of unwanted privacy, *and the willingness to do so* took on a force that heretofore it lacked. The search for meaning was the search for intimacy, and if that search required unconventional actions, so be it.

5. We are morally obliged to prevent our children from experiencing what we have experienced and continue to experience. They must not be what we are. They deserve a new world, not our old one. They must not live slotted, pigeonholed, frustrated lives. Our world was a screwed-up, unhappy one and that should not be their world. This is the "pursuit of happiness and fulfillment" theme for the coming generations.

I have labeled these themes, but that implies a degree of clarity and articulation I do not intend. They were stirrings in what may be called a readiness to depart from the past. If you peruse the social science literature about the war years, including clinical psychological-psychiatric journals, these stirrings are hardly noted. What you get are descriptions and explanations of disruptions in lives in terms of extant theories of individual development and adaptation. We learn a great deal about individual differences, how differences in pasts produced differences in presents. You will find little about these stirrings, all of which concerned the *future*. And for two reasons. The first is, as I have said, that these stirrings were inchoate. The second is that our psychologies in no way sensitized us to these stirrings reflective of changes in worldview far more than they are reflective of what we ordinarily mean by personality dynamics. The barometers of individual change are not those of changes in worldview.

In stating these themes, I in no way intend value judgments. Nor am I suggesting that they inevitably led to the sixties. What I am suggesting is that in different groups with very different phenomenologies and pasts, these stirrings were, so to speak, in the air. That these stirrings had and would have *individual* consequences is a given. Whether the stirrings in these groups would have a *societal* impact would depend on whether postwar events would serve to coalesce the stirrings in the different groups. The present is not pregnant with *a* future; it is pregnant with many futures. And that is what I am saying about the stirrings aroused by World War II.

This is an essay, not a book. I cannot do justice to all, or even most, of the events in the post–World War II period that served to reinforce and coalesce these stirrings, that is, to put them into clear words and with a force that could not be glossed over.

The first of these is a congeries I label as "The Return" or "The Emigrants Return." When in early 1944 it became clear that the tides of war were in our favor, few people did not indulge fantasies about the joys of victory and peace. (Except, of course, those who had been injured, those who had lost a loved one, and those whose changed existence during the war would be *negatively* affected by the ending of the war. This was a heterogeneous but by no means a small number of people.) There were some individuals in officialdom who looked at the ending of the war with foreboding, but primarily in economic terms. How could the economy absorb millions of soldiers, and how could we go from a war to a peace economy without social disruption? If these forebodings were primarily economic, they were powered by a fear of social unrest, by threat of political upheaval. The approach of World War II ended the Great Depression. Would the end of the war bring about another social economic catastrophe?

Undergirding these forebodings was a very realistic, albeit intuitive, understanding of the pervasive social and psychological consequences of peace. I say intuitive because that understanding did not rest on any clear set of ideas about how cessation of the war might have different *and* similar impacts on different groups. Of course, the war's end would not have the same economic impact on millions of veterans, but all veterans would confront the "you can't go home again" problem. The veterans had changed; their families and friends had changed; and to many veterans the physical appearance of home, neighborhood, and town-city-village had changed. The point that deserves emphasis is that everyone had changed and in ways they had neither expected or fantasized. These were changes that affected self-attitudes, style and depth of relating, sexual activity, and a lot more. It was not what people had bargained for. Much of what I am saying here is portrayed well in the film *The Best Years of Our Lives*, which came out shortly after the war and had poignant meaning for almost everyone. It was a best-selling film. Among its themes were these: You cannot go home again. You can go home again. The pre–World War II world is over; we will make a new world in which equity and justice will prevail. If the ending of the film is typically Hollywood in its upbeat note about family cohesion and social justice, it said more about hope than it did about social realities.

Much has been written about the problems of transition for veterans, blacks, and women. What has gone relatively undiscussed are the transition problems encountered by thousands of professionals and other highly educated people whose careers had been disrupted, or who were no longer current in their fields, or who were no longer interested in what they had done in the prewar years and sought a career change, or who were simply at sea about what they wanted to do and where. Cutting across group lines was the fact that many veterans had achieved a status and degree of authority in the military they had not previously had and would not have in the foreseeable future. And for many who had little or no status in the military, there was a large number intent on forging a future of higher status.

There was another transition problem that almost all veterans experienced in different degrees: however difficult, frustrating, scary, and crazy living in the military was, it had order, direction, and community. You were not alone; you were part of something; you lived in a kind of iron social cage but one in which there was a kind of freedom of personal expression different from that in civilian living. M*A*S*H was about the Korean War, but what it depicted was no less characteristic about the World War II years.

The point of all this is not that transition from war to peace would be predictably difficult for everyone in or out of the armed forces. That is a glimpse of the obvious. The point is that the transition gave articulation to the themes I described earlier and that I now put under the heading "Rejecting the Past and Fearing the Future." At the same time that the end of the war engendered joy, relief, and hope, individually and collectively, it was accompanied by three "of course" axioms: the world had to be changed; that world would have to satisfy—it had the *obligation* to satisfy—the hopes and ambitions of people regardless of past status or custom or tradition; and respect for civil authority would be determined by how well that authority discharged its obligation. What I am suggesting here is that in different ways in different individuals and groups, a militant dissatisfaction was brewing, a dissatisfaction with self and the world, a dissatisfaction that however vaguely expressed was, so to speak, in the psychological wings waiting upon events for its role to become clear.

I am having a problem with language here. It reminds me of the time my wife and I visited our daughter who was a college freshman. On her desk I noticed a paper she had written for her introductory psychology class. She had received a grade of C, which crushed her. In that paper Julie had written a paragraph in which she said that for what she was trying to describe or explain language was an inadequate instrument. In the margin of the page the instructor castigated her and wrote, "Language is the best means of expression," underlining his words. I quite agree with Julie. When I use words like *theories*, *stirrings*, and *worldview*, I know that readers will find them fuzzy, lacking the specificity that we think words like *hate*, *love*, *work*, and *ambition* have. The reader will have noticed that I have used the word *inchoate* several times. In using that word, I am trying to avoid conveying the impression that stirrings are "ideas" or identifiable feelings. A stirring has elements of both but not the direction or consequences of either; it is more fleeting and unformed, a droplet in the stream of consciousness, a droplet of possibilities.

I was not in the armed services in World War II, but I knew and talked with scores of people who were. It was from these discussions that I got the sense of stirring, a sense that each of these individuals had changed and was changing in unverbalized ways. Unverbalized by them and unverbalizable by me, the sense of "never again," that "the world had better change *or else.*" However, putting it that way gives stirring a clarity it rarely had. Stirrings are poorly sensed "possibilities."

No one who is an adult today and lived through the war years will deny that people today, in contrast to people in the prewar years, think and act differently. Values have changed, styles of living have changed, expectations have changed, and more, much more. Some view these changes as unmitigated disaster, others view them as a desirable release from suffocating tradition, and an equal number are puzzled. But when those holding these different views explain the changes, they employ an ahistorical, individual psychology that is at its core asocial in that it ignores the *continuous* presence and force of social ecology. In a "legal" or formal historical sense World War II is over. In terms of explaining people today, World War II is far from over; it unleashed possibilities for thinking and acting with which we are still dealing. I am not saying that World War II was a "cause" of what we are dealing with today; I am saying that the psychological changes initiated or exacerbated by the ecology of World War II are in a dynamic sense in our present, not superseded but transformed.

I cannot go into all the major post–World War II happenings that gave strength and direction to the stirrings, a plethora of happenings, national and international, that coalesced them. There was one, however, that well suits illustrative purposes because by its very substance it was relevant to any psychology. It was the 1948 publication on male sexuality by Kinsey and his colleagues (Kinsey and others, 1948). As one might have expected, psychologists and almost everyone else were interested in what Kinsey would report. It is not unfair to say that this interest was an individual one in the sense that people sought answers to two questions: What do males think and do in the sexual sphere? How do I (or my husband, lover) compare to others? Rarely have so many people been so curious about themselves and others. If all that is quite understandable, it nevertheless ignored what I consider to be the larger significance of that interest.

Consider three associated aspects of the Kinsey report. The first has to do with the several months before the report was made public. Begin, say, with the first day of the first of the three months before publication, and plot daily the frequency and lengths of articles on the coming Kinsey report in all of the mass media. What you will find is that your plots follow an ever-ascending line, culminating in a thundering crescendo requiring a new graph. It was like a Rossini overture: it starts slowly, the entire orchestra is not involved, the pace and decibel level pick up steam, and at its end players and audience seem unable to contain themselves.

It was as if an astronomer had located a huge comet that seemed on a collision course with earth, and the day of collision was predictable. How do we explain this prepublication excitement? The ready explanation was that everyone is interested in sexuality, especially in "puritanical" America. That explanation, of course, has a large kernel of truth. But coming as the report did a few short years after World War II ended, was that excited interest unrelated to the changes wrought in people's outlooks? Was that excitement powered only by curiosity? I would argue that in addition to curiosity, there was the hope that the report would serve as a basis to justify a freedom to think and act in new ways. The fruits of peace had not been very edible. Dreams for a new world were not being realized. The shackles of custom and tradition had not loosened. The usual ties that bind one to family, friends, and work were confining and frustrating. Expectations were illusions. Life was too short and iffy to justify postponing exploration of avenues of personal expressions, of lifestyles holding out promise of personal gratification.

To researchers in the field of human sexuality, Kinsey's report was no occasion for great surprise. What distinguished his report from previous ones was the size and stratifications of his sample. One of these researchers said to me that Kinsey was the right man at the right time with the right data. I did not find that explanation persuasive, although I did not then have a better one. Why was this the right time? My question went unanswered.

Let us now turn to what happened in the professional communities: psychology, medicine, psychiatry, social science. What happened at Yale was, I assume, representative of what happened elsewhere. There were meetings, special seminars, debates—a plethora of them. Some of them were devoted to critiquing Kinsey's methodology. Some were devoted to what the report meant—the challenges it posed—to psychological theories, especially of the psychoanalytic variety. And some, I think most, were about what the report meant. What did it tell us about American society? How would it be interpreted by different groups? What did it portend? What *should* it portend? A frequent thread running through these discussions was what I will call "freedom from stifling constraints" or "changing criteria of normality." That is to say, society's moral *and* legal restraints on certain sexual practices and marital relationships were wrong, or self-defeating, or neurosis producing, or all of these. Society did not free people in these respects; it imprisoned them in ways and to a degree that undercut personal and family happiness. To those who so argued, the Kinsey report was a breath of fresh air. If you want to get an idea of what I am describing, read the letters-to-the-editor page in leading newspapers and weekly news magazines for at least a month after the book was published. If in the prepublication phase the report stirred the social pot, that pot boiled over after publication. I should point out that despite the fact the book was written in a most dry and impersonal style, containing scores of graphs and tables, discussions the opposite of polemical, and a selling price that was not small for its day, the book had a sale in the hundreds of thousands, perhaps more. If the book was intrinsically interesting, it was not intrinsically readable.

My memory is undoubtedly selective, but I cannot recall anyone who connected the uproar the report engendered to the changes in worldview wrought by World War II. Bear in mind that the report came out at a time when the war was still very much in the national psyche. Indeed, almost everyone who contributed to the discussions had, directly or indirectly, been part of the war effort. And let us not overlook that the professional-scientific discussions were taking place in colleges and universities in which millions of veterans were students. That point deserves some elaboration because it concerns an ecological variable of immense importance that, nevertheless, has gone scandalously unstudied. I refer to the GI Bill of Rights. Again, the GI Bill was a piece of legislation (just as our declaration of war was). That, of course, does not justify the label ecological. What does justify it is that the legislation reflected, so to speak, outcroppings and convergence of a variety of ideas, interests, values, and outlooks held in varying degrees by diverse groups. It was not intended to be a gathering storm that would dramatically change the social scene and some of its major institutions. I say "gathering storm" because no one fathomed (or could fathom?) the unintended consequences of the legislation, the ways in which it began to have percolating effects.

That legislation implicitly conveyed a message: "A grateful society will give you an opportunity to be other than what you were before the war. Regardless of your past status, you can move in new directions. We will provide you the opportunity to explore, to learn new things, to become a new person in a new world." That millions of veterans bought the message may not seem to require explanation. But it does, and for the same reasons that the response to the Kinsey report requires other than a simple explanation. For one thing, what was being bought was not only the possibility of a new future but (for many) a rejection of a past, a past of ideas, values, and custom they regarded as outmoded. The possibility of a new future was not only a feature of the outlook of the millions of veterans who flocked to our campuses. It was also a feature of faculty who had left these campuses to enter the military and whose outlooks had been mightily changed by their experiences.

It is hard to exaggerate how the physical and social psychological ecology of our colleges and universities changed in the years immediately following World War II, largely because of the GI Bill. They grew in size. They were overcrowded. New disciplines were created, old ones changed their substance and direction. The demographics of the student population changed: students were older; many were married; and many came from religious, ethnic, socioeconomic backgrounds minimally represented on campuses in the prewar days. It is fair to say that to a literally unprecedented degree, millions of students willingly found themselves in a world of ideas, possibilities, and great expectations.

To people like me who started their teaching careers when the war ended, or who returned to their faculty roles, those were the "good old days." And by that two things are meant. The first was the maturity, drive, and outlook of the students. (In my case the age differential between me and the students was near nil.) They were not wet behind the ears, newly minted high school or college graduates, and those that were stood in awe of them. The second thing meant by the "good old days" was the sense of new, that as individuals and collectivities we were *obliged* to consider nothing sacrosanct. It was as if everything was up for grabs. Not only ideas, theories, methods, but lifestyles as well.

Literally, as I was writing these words an article appeared in a Yale campus monthly titled "GI Blues" (Lewinnek, 1993). Because that article is so relevant to what I have tried to describe and that journal would be unavailable to almost all readers of this essay, I reprint it here in its entirety.

Discussion of changes at Yale often gravitates toward the 60s, with images of hippie students and tenured radicals. But by the late 1940s, post-war realities had already begun to alter 250 years of Yale elitism, as ex-soldiers in fatigues sat in class next to navy-blazered prep school graduates. The freshman class of 1946 was the largest in Yale's history, included more public-school graduates than the university had ever had, and began a lasting liberalization of Yale.

Behind Yale's post-war transformation was the GI Bill of Rights, part of the Serviceman's Readjustment Act. With this legislation, the U.S. Government agreed to pay for four years of college for all returning soldiers. Yale patriotically accepted as many of the ex-soldiers it could squeeze in, even housing some students on cots in Payne Whitney Gymnasium and in specially built huts around New Haven.

Congress passed the GI Bill in 1944 to ease the country's shift into peace time. Instead of having thousands of unemployed soldiers trying to find work all at once, Uncle Sam sent the servicemen to college. American universities faced a sudden flood of students. Yale's enrollment increased by 60 percent. In 1945, there were 257 people in the freshman class at Yale. In 1946, the freshman class burgeoned to an astounding 1,767 students.

These statistics may be misleading, since during the confusion of World War II, Yalies often switched classes. For example, Reverend Harry Adams, now the master of Trumbull College, entered Yale in the summer of 1942 expecting to graduate in 1945 through Yale's accelerated year-round war programs. Adams was called into service in February 1943, returned to Yale with some of the first released soldiers in October 1945, and finally graduated in January 1948. His case was not unusual.

"By the spring of '43, there were almost no civilians left at Yale," Adams recalled. He estimated that 90 percent of his class left for active duty in the war. The army and navy stationed training programs at Yale, housing soldiers on Old

Campus and in all but three of the residential colleges. After the war, Yale's policy was to "accept anyone who had been here under any program," Adams said. The classes entering in 1945 and 1946 included not only many students new to the Ivy League, but also five years' worth of backlogged Yale students and those who had come here for army and navy training. "It began to be a very complex and diverse place," Adams said.

The aftermath of World War II shaped the Yale that students know today. Before the war, a three-room suite held two people. After 1946, the same suite, now with army-style bunkbeds, held four. "Yale has never gone back to the space it had before," Adams said.

College dining halls typified the changing Yale. Before the war, students wore ties and jackets to dinner, sat at tables with linen table-cloths, ordered from printed menus, and were served by waiters and waitresses. After the war, the new crowds forced dining halls to change "from restaurant-style to army-style," according to Larry Schafer. Students waited in long cafeteria lines and ate from metal trays identical to the ones they had used in the army. "Jackets became customary rather than obligatory," said Harold Parritz.

The revolution in dress code was not confined to the dining halls. "Some of the returning soldiers still wore their GI-issue clothes, at least for the first year," Schafer said. "They often were too poor to buy new clothes. There was something of a clothing shortage after the war, and army clothes were good clothes."

But Yale had more pressing concerns than dinner dress to worry about. To house roughly 200 married Yale students and their families, Yale built special quonset huts—half-dome structures with a living room, kitchen, and bedroom, near the Yale Bowl and at the present site of the Pierson-Sage garage. Other married students (25 percent of the class of 1950) found off-campus housing. George Bush, for instance, lived with his wife Barbara and 40 other people in crowded quarters at 37 Hillhouse Avenue.

As the average age of graduating seniors rose from 21 to 23, marriage became only one index of maturity. "Many of those men had three or four years of violence behind them," said Bradford Wright. Some of the returning soldiers suffered from battle fatigue, Schafer said, but few manifested overt problems. People before 1946 referred to students as "Yale boys." With the battle-forged class that entered in 1946, people began to speak of "Yale men."

The ex-GIs generally earned higher GPAs than the younger students, according to a 1946 *Yale Daily News*. "Having had experiences outside of academics, we were clearer, more focused," Adams said. Older and sometimes less privileged than typical Yalies, many GIs were also more conscious of the need to find a job after graduation. John Blum said the veterans "brought a more serious approach to college than there had been in the past. Gut courses didn't attract the vets. They were interested in learning, trying to get as much as they could out of college."

Schafer, who first entered Yale in 1938, disagreed, despite the statistics. "Some of those boys who got in on the GI Bill might have been good men, great soldiers and all that, but they were less academically inclined. I think on the whole the returning GI had a poorer high-school education than most Yale students before the war. Yale became more democratic as a result of the GI Bill, and I don't think that was entirely a good thing. There was some loss of academic standards. Yale stopped looking so much like an ivy-covered academic institution and more like a boot camp."

Many veterans did protest having to submit to what they considered unnecessary authority. To avoid taking the swimming test required to graduate, Blum convinced the administration that he was allergic to chlorine. He said, "We were there for an education and the other stuff wasn't important.

We had been out in the world, we weren't wet behind the ears, and we felt, 'Yale's not a prep school, it's a university. Don't tell us about discipline.'"

Many Yalies in the 1940s, like students before them, spent their free time watching football games, participating in intra-mural sports, and road-tripping to Vassar, Mt. Holyoke, or Smith. But the older GIs were less interested in typical college activities. In particular, married students living off campus tended to shy away from the college party scene. The returning soldiers brought a more adult social life, Adams said. "Heavy drinking and partying didn't hold the novelty for returning GIs that it had for some students straight out of prep school," he said. "My memory of the social life is mostly sitting around talking with friends."

Fraternity influence gradually waned in those years, though some of the decline had begun with the institution of the residential college system in the mid-1930s. The *Yale Banner* of 1948 reported that 52 percent of Yale students believed fraternities "don't justify their existence." According to Blum, "Nobody was out to break the frats, none of the change was belligerent, but it just didn't occur to me to join a fraternity." Instead, Blum was active in the Labor Party of the Political Union and in the American Veterans Committee, a liberal political organization that in 1946 was the largest political student group at Yale. "That sort of political activism was new," he said.

"The administration was open to us. They wanted ideas on how to handle a whole new population," Blum said. "It was not business as usual." America's transition to peace had unleashed forces of change in the nation as a whole. At Yale, Adams said, "Every month new people were flowing in. It seems chaotic now as I look back on it." The administration, in its support of the GI Bill, welcomed a more diverse student body. Many at the time may not have been aware of the long-term consequences for Old Yale.

Forties non-conformists like Blum foreshadowed the political unrest of the 1960s. "Political activism came along with the liberal wing of the GIs, but it was pretty mild stuff," said Blum. "We never confronted the administration; there was no militancy."

But Blum pointed out that the late 1940s represented a transitional period at Yale. "The impact of the GIs was to gradually start momentum toward the kind of changes that came later, such as admitting women," said Blum. "It began a change in tone that continued with the liberal presidencies of A. Whitney Griswold and Kingman Brewster." The GI Bill made "Yale boys" into "Yale men" and helped lead to the evolution of a new species, the Yale woman. [pp. 7–10]

Let me now briefly give two examples that were barometers or heralds of what was brewing in many American psyches.

It was, I think, two years before the publication of the first Kinsey report. Kinsey visited Yale to enlist people as interviewees. He gave a talk to our department and others in the medical school. Kinsey was an evangelist against the sin of ignorance and for the freeing virtues of the scientific study of sexual behavior. The truth shall set you free, and nowhere was this more necessary than in the arena of sexual behavior. In that respect he was a moral evangelist. But he was not an evangelist in the sense of desiring to convert people to any particular life style. Let us ascertain the facts about sexual thoughts and practices and then deal with the truths they suggest. More in private conversation (I had a lengthy one with him thanks to Frank Beach) than in anything he wrote, Kinsey had long been appalled by the neurosis-producing attitudes of American society toward sexual behavior deemed to be deviant.

In his talk to our department, Kinsey made two points. The first was that in order to enhance the scientific status of his data he needed 100 percent samples of representative social groups. The second point was that we should feel *obliged* to sign up to be interviewed—no ifs, ands, or buts. If Kinsey was an evangelist, he was talking to people who wanted to be evangelized. He was talking to the converted. And that is the point: at Yale and elsewhere Kinsey's message of knowledge and freedom was welcomed; it fitted in with an emerging worldview about the shackles of the past and a liberated future. Prewar puritanical America was and should be no more. Never again.

The second example is Skinner's *Walden Two* (1948), probably written during the same year Kinsey came to Yale. In the opening pages of that book, you will find an explicit, succinct critique of a misguided problem-producing, self-defeating, imprisoning society. Pollution, gender discrimination, prejudice, alienation, tradition-bound lifestyles, and more are excoriated by Skinner. Unlike Kinsey, Skinner's moral evangelism was quite public. And, of course, the utopia he describes in that book represents a nearly wholesale rejection of the underpinnings of American society. *Walden Two* is a moral treatise, a plea that the America that was is the America that should not be in the future. Less important here than *his* answers is his moral indictment of things as they were.

What surprised me when the book was published was the interest it engendered in students. In fact, some of our students met many times to discuss and plan for the creation of a Walden Two, and they sought to enlist students in other universities. Initially, the book did not have much of a sale, but within a few years it became a best-seller, exciting interest and controversy and a few attempts to organize a setting consistent with Skinnerian principles. The commune movement of the sixties was by no means unrelated to what Skinner had indicted and proposed. There were many matches that lit the fires of the sixties. Skinner was but one of them, but an amazingly prodromal one.

Kinsey and Skinner were individuals, but they spoke and gave voice to many groups, each of which in its own way sought freedom from the past. And all of this in the context of national (e.g., the 1954 desegregation decisions, the emerging civil rights movement) and international (e.g., the Berlin blockade, atomic explosions,

Soviet imperialism) events that made a mockery of peace. If the end of the war was greeted with both joy and great expectations, on the one hand, and a subdued anxiety, on the other hand, the next decade was experienced with puzzlement and disillusionment. If American optimism was not extinguished, it was subject to challenge.

What I have been suggesting is that the conceptual problem is not how to explain the sixties but rather how to explain and integrate what was happening to people in the two decades before the sixties. Americans had changed; their "psychology" had been altered; the American worldview had undergone some changes. It is not my position that World War II "explains" the sixties, that it caused the sixties. I do not subscribe to the Marxist-like view of inevitability. What World War II did was to begin to unleash people's identification with their pasts. What the war did was to initiate what I like to call the era of *personal redefinition*. Blacks, women, gays, religious people (e.g., Catholics and their church), nurses, artists (e.g., abstract expressionists), and youth began to redefine who they were. And that was also the case for psychologists of the clinical variety who, like nurses, sought independence from medical imperialism and who in two decades became the largest group in the field of psychology. Yes, there were distinctively different groups, but they had one thing in common: they did not want their future to be like their past. They sought liberation, they rejected significant features of their pasts, and that included styles of living.

It was a gathering storm. Storms are chaotic but not to meteorologists, who place storms in the wider spatial context from which they emerge, a context containing the storm's origins and its predictable and unpredictable directions. Storms do not have a single cause; they have many "triggers" that when they coalesce produce the storm. Meteorologists are literally schooled to attend to these triggers long before the storm is a reality or possibility. If their ability to track the direction of a storm is far from perfect, their ability to predict that a storm is brewing has dramatically increased. They are not surprised the way so many people were in the turbulent sixties.

I do not think it unfair to ask why psychology was so utterly unprepared for the sixties. A lot of fields were surprised and unprepared. But not all fields have as their raison d'être the aim of understanding what people are and how and why they change in significant ways. If you were to ask psychologists why on earth so many of them study families, they will look at you with staring disbelief. How can you claim to understand any individual apart from his or her family? You cannot. But is it not also true that everyone in that family bears the stamp of happenings outside family, happenings containing "messages" to which they are never neutral, messages about what is right and wrong, how life should be lived, how we should regard our individual and collective parts, how we should approach our futures, whether we should accept or reject the way things are? Everyone in an American family has an *American* worldview, not a German or Japanese or Yugoslavian worldview. Worldviews contain unarticulated axioms. They have an "of course" quality, so right, natural, and proper that they do not require articulation. Until. Until what I have called an ecological variable challenges those axioms because it compels us to change how we see ourselves and the world.

When I was teaching, I would ask the class this question: What axiom does each of us possess without which this class makes absolutely no sense? No one, but no one, ever said that axiom is that we will be alive tomorrow. Of course, we will be alive tomorrow!

The bombing of Pearl Harbor on December 7, 1941, came as a clap of thunder to the American psyche. The world we knew, the world we thought we knew, the world we wanted to know was no more. Tomorrow was a tomorrow our American worldview could not assimilate. The axiom that America could defeat any foe could legitimately be challenged. It was a new ball game, a new world in which American optimism received a narcissistic wound.

There was nothing in the substance and theories of psychology that directed us to identify the American worldview and how that view might be challenged *and* changed by what had happened and would happen. No less than any other type of citizen, psychologists became concerned with how they could aid the war effort. Having lived through those days, I could justly be regarded as egregiously stupid to expect that psychologists would, even if they could, start delving into the vagaries of worldviews. But it is not stupid to note and emphasize the fact that neither then nor later (including the decade and a half after the war) was psychology sensitive to the significance and possible changes in the American worldview. It lacked the concepts and methodological barometers by which to track what soon became a gathering, crazy-quilt social storm in which people's "psychology" was subtly changing.

We have learned a great deal about intrapsychic structure and dynamics in relation to very circumscribed interpersonal contexts. We accept as a given that each of us is governed by internal dynamics, much of which we are unaware. We loosely call them unconscious or subconscious personality dynamics or variables. That we also possess an equally "unconscious" worldview no less governing our lives is unrecognized in psychological theory. That lack of recognition is of no great practical, social significance in a world or society that changes slowly or is relatively exempt from encompassing ecological happenings. We have not lived in that kind of society for a long time, and the history of the modern era, however defined or demarcated, is one in which those kinds of happenings have wrought dramatic changes in worldview. If psychology cannot change the world, that is no warrant for ignoring how worldviews change in relation to social ecologies, the effects of which are the opposite of trivial. No psychology riveted on the individual psyche can deal with that problem.

What I have said in this essay is far from a comprehensive explanation of the sixties. My goal was to suggest that the origins of what we call the sixties well antedate that decade. If I were writing a book on the subject (too daunting an affair), there would be several points I would emphasize:

1. For the first time in history people could *see* what was going on in the society. I refer, of course, to the introduction of TV in the late forties, and we need to be reminded that in those days there were few channels, and, given the novelty of the medium, everyone tended to see the same things. Among the happenings they could see were the civil rights clashes and demonstrations, the dead bodies of civil rights activists, the National Guard in Little Rock, leaders in Louisiana parishes hurling the most egregious vituperations at black citizens, the awesome power of atom and hydrogen bombs being tested, the McCarthy hearings, the Berlin Blockade, and more, much more. The fifties could be labeled as silent only by those who could not see or hear.

2. What is absolutely crucial about these happenings is that they were witnessed by young people who came to maturity in the sixties. When in recent months I have interrogated a fair number of them, some were quick to point that they were aware then of the discrepancy (some said hypocrisy) between the "real" world and TV programs like *Father Knows Best* and *Ozzie and Harriet*. A few were able to say that the picture of family life portrayed in these sitcoms was obviously different from what they experienced in their family and those of others. As one of them said to me, "My cynicism about morality in America began way back on TV."

3. Nowhere was the rebellion against or rejection of custom and tradition more clear and sharp than in popular music. (It is interesting how many of those I interviewed recalled their reaction to seeing [first] Elvis and [second] the Beatles on the Ed Sullivan show.) It seems (today) that almost overnight the romantic "June-moon" songs took a very back seat to rock and roll and its variants. The Hollywood musicals disappeared. The new popular music to which young people were drawn was distinctive for its contents: protests against an immoral, crazy world and uncomprehending older generations.

4. Rejection of the past was, unlike that of youth in the thirties, moral, not political. Quite the contrary, it was as if the underlying theme was "Stop the world—we want to get off." Timothy Leary's advice to "turn on, tune in, drop out" was taken by many young people who figuratively and literally went "on the roads" of the American wasteland with Kerouac and Cassady who, in the fifties, started at Columbia's Morningside Heights and ended at San Francisco's Haight-Ashbury. It needs to be stressed that the rejection and rebellion were moral, individualistic, and apolitical. There was no "program" for political action, which was perceived as inherently corrupting.

5. Moral fervor aside, the protests were against impersonal bureaucracies, public or private, cipherdom, and the loss of a sense of intimacy and community. It is noteworthy that when today I ask the "veterans" of the sixties, "Can you point to one or two things that captures *your* phenomenology at that time?" the frequent response (Woodstock aside) was a movie (e.g., *Easy Rider, Five Easy Pieces, The Graduate, Carnal Knowledge, Midnight Cowboy*). In my opinion, the one film that best represents aspects of the world against which the youth of the sixties were rebelling is *La Dolce Vita*, a film painfully prodromal of what was coming down the road.

6. To explain the sixties and the rise of a counterculture, one cannot overlook what happened in music and the visual arts (abstract expressionism) very soon after World War II. What happened, more in the visual arts than in music, was a very conscious, thoroughgoing rejection of the past. More correctly, the past was past, a new art was called for; the old art must not be a guide for the new art. In the sixties the proclaimed caveat was "Don't trust anyone over thirty." What happened in the visual arts and music needs scrutiny because it suggests, given when the changes occurred, that an altered view of the past was taking hold in the society; that is, a change in the American worldview was beginning to occur. That is not to suggest that what happened in the arts stands in a causal relation to the phenomena we call the turbulent sixties. But it does suggest that an altered view of the past started to pick up steam

shortly after the war, and I do assume that it was not restricted to the arts.

If I have by no means explained the sixties, I hope that what I have said persuades the reader that understanding the American outlook in the post–War II era will not be furthered by a psychology of individuals.

8

Leadership and Machiavelli

How does one account for the growth of a problem area in several disciplines at the same time? More concretely, why did the nature of leadership attract such interest in the social sciences after World War II? Putting it that way is clearly too narrow for two reasons. First, leadership, precisely because of its centrality to the national and international arena during and after World War II, was of general interest; better yet, it was a source of anxiety. The second reason, particularly in the United States, was that the necessity after Pearl Harbor to create and sustain a gargantuan military organization, and to interconnect it with thousands of civilian organizations, made it all too obvious that the nature of leadership at all levels and, therefore, the criteria for selection and promotion of leaders, had to be better understood on theoretical and practical grounds. Someone once said that the most interesting question was not why the war was won but why we did not lose it. Joseph Heller's *Catch-22* was but one of scores of war novels describing the efficiencies and inefficiencies, dilemmas and opportunities, the tragic and comic aspects of leadership. At least to the millions of veterans returning to civilian life, leaders and their authority were regarded with ambivalence and suspicion.

With the war's end, it was expected that the prewar, bitter, and often bloody conflicts between labor and management would reappear, and they did. No one saw these problems more clearly than

Joe Scanlon, an ex-boxer, a cost accountant, a steel worker, a union leader, and after the war an MIT lecturer. Indeed, MIT became a most intellectually fertile center for the study of groups, group relations, and leadership. Before his premature death, Kurt Lewin had spearheaded those kinds of studies at MIT. Albeit few in number, there were private-sector executives who accepted the fact that the way things had been was the opposite of the needs of the future. The dramatic growth of the field of organizational development and behavior is to a significant degree explainable by what had been developed at MIT, from which its graduates radiated to other universities or set up their own consulting firms. The University of Michigan was another such center. It needs to be noted that a very large majority of those who led or were part of these efforts were veterans mightily influenced by their war experience.

For my purposes here I wish to note several themes, or goals, or values, or outlooks undergirding these developments. Some were explicit; others were not. Their interconnectedness was taken for granted, an interconnectedness reflective of a changing worldview of the nature and obligations of mutuality in the workplace and elsewhere. One way of characterizing this interconnectedness is to say that it was a wholesale repudiation of the "robber baron" mentality and era. A kind of togetherness would replace adversarialism; cipherdom and alienation would be replaced by a sense of mutuality and belongingness; authoritarian and arbitrary leadership would give way to a democratic style and ethos. As one eminent proponent of the new view said to me, "We didn't fight the war only to defeat *military* dictatorships that looked upon people as expendable fodder. The lesson we learned, or should have learned, is that people in an organization do not exist only to help their leaders achieve goals they define according to their self-interests." That was not said by someone who saw utopia on the horizon. He did not underestimate the battles ahead, the resistance that would be encountered both from leaders and followers. What he was articulating was a vision, themes, an antidote against the virus of arbitrariness, a virus containing the seeds of social unrest and upheaval. He spent his days conveying his message and methodologies to new generations of leaders. Let me briefly state the themes.

1. The behavior of an individual is incomprehensible apart from his or her work group in the organization, regardless of where in the hierarchy that group is. That is a glimpse of the obvious, but who takes the obvious seriously? Whose responsibility is it to confront the obvious in ways that expose and resolve problems and conflicts that make for inefficiencies? Furthermore, what is true within a group is no less true for intergroup relations. Traditionally, these issues either have been ignored or handled in ways that exacerbate problems for the individuals and groups. Unless and until leaders (at all levels of the organization) gain more understanding of and more skills relevant to these issues, smoldering resentment will do its work. Leaders who "command" followers win battles and lose wars.

2. Every individual has needs to feel worthy, respected, and listened to. And "listened to" means that the person is seen as having *assets* in regard to how the organization is or should be functioning. When these needs are ignored, it not only negatively affects the individual but sets the stage for intraorganizational and intragroup conflict and inefficiency. To dilute or avoid such untoward effects requires that leaders possess, and sincerely so, one overarching value: the needs of the individual are also *rights*—he or she should *expect* to be listened to. The individual has obligations to the organization, but so does the latter to the former.

3. Conflict within the organization, regardless of its nature and source, is inevitable, a fact of human life leaders have difficulty accepting, holding dearly to the myth that there must be a way to avoid conflicts and that once a conflict is "resolved" it never has to be solved again. What is required is a new type of leader better and more realistically prepared to cope with the needs and rights of individuals, the conflicts that arise, and the organizational goal of surviving and prospering. That is a very tall order but one that cannot be avoided living as we do in an increasingly complex, competitive,

dangerous world in which the democratic ethos is far from domi-
nant. What is required is not simply leadership but creative leadership that empowers people, that gives them a stake, a responsibility
in the health of the organization. Arbitrary, power-aggrandizing,
insensitive, adversary-producing leadership is counterproductive for
the individual, the organization, and the society. As one person
once put it, "The 'screw you' era of leadership is over."

In 1994 these three themes do not seem radical. In the immediate post–World War II years they were because organizational
leaders of the day (with the usual exceptions, of course) were not
brought up, so to speak, to regard "followers" as having needs and
rights—not only economic needs and rights but psychological ones
as well. When Winston Churchill said that he was not made prime
minister to preside over the dissolution of the British empire, he
was articulating values and traditions identical to those held by
most nonpolitical leaders, namely, that they did not become leaders to dilute their powers, let alone to give them away.

But this stance revealed a blind spot: these leaders vastly underestimated the changes in worldview that the war had wrought, not
the least of which was a rejection of passive acceptance of leadership. The "followers" after the war were a different breed than those
before the war. They had expectations and perceived rights that
could not be met by resignation to being a cog in an impersonal
wheel. World War II put this new breed on a collision course with
traditional styles of leadership. Initially, the sounds of the collisions
were muted. They became ear deafening in the sixties. If the sounds
have muted somewhat, it is only somewhat.

How is this to be explained? Obviously, anything resembling a
comprehensive explanation would be horribly difficult and complex, and even if I felt, as I do not, that I could offer such an explanation, it would be far beyond my present purposes. What is my
purpose is to examine certain aspects of the changed view of leadership in the postwar era. I do not undertake this as a practical matter in the sense that what I have to say is intended to be relevant

to the selection and role of leaders. My purpose is more narrow in that I shall argue that the pictures of leadership, ideal or otherwise, we have been given are woefully incomplete and ahistorical. This, I must emphasize, does not mean these pictures are wrong. Far from it. They are incomplete in a way that oversimplifies the phenomenology of leadership and the cultural-societal context from which leaders emerge.

You could easily fill a very large, empty library with articles and books on leadership written in the postwar era. Beginning in the forties and fifties, publications about leadership steadily increased. Beginning in the sixties, the steady, narrow stream of writings became a torrent. A significant fraction of this literature deals with the characteristics of successful and unsuccessful leaders. The criteria for such judgments are many, of which the following are the most frequent:

1. The organizational climate created and the depth and quality of the willing commitment and cooperation elicited and sustained

2. Innovativeness, boldness, staying ahead of the field, not being allergic to new ideas

3. Articulating a clear vision about where the organization is and where it should be in the future

4. The degree to which the needs and abilities of others are respected and utilized

5. Confronting and handling conflicts in non-self-defeating ways

6. The ability to be flexible in regard to organizational structure and individual roles (i.e., altering both in light of changing conditions internal or external to the organization)

7. Profitability in regard to two "bottom lines": financial and psychological or personal. Either profitability is shared throughout the organization; it is not restricted to a few people. It derives from consideration of equity and from recogni-

tion of personal needs and expectations not extracted under pressure but given on moral grounds (i.e., "investment" deserves a return, be it financial or psychological or both).

Another large fraction of the literature has to do with the selection, training, development, and education of leaders. Included here are the activities and goals of business schools, especially those that explicitly state that their primary goal is to select and prepare future leaders. These self-consciously elite schools make a distinction (at least they seek to make a distinction) between preparing leaders and managers. Managers are important, leaders are crucial, and these programs aim to select and prepare future leaders. But not all graduates of these programs take leadership roles or even seek to do so. Many join consulting firms whose main function is to consult with leaders about problems in their organization. It is from these consulting firms that we get articles and books about organizational problems in general and leadership issues in particular. The consulting industry is not small; it is big business. So big and influential, in fact, as to suggest that the quality of leadership is, to say the least, nothing to write home about. Indeed, the preparation of leaders has been criticized for its failure to select and realistically orient future leaders. What has gone unnoticed or unremarked is that a significant number of consultants to leaders have never been in leadership roles. That is not to suggest that lack of such experience ipso facto disqualifies you from consulting to leaders. But it certainly does not constitute a credential to do so.

A relevant story. Years ago I ran into Warren Bennis in New Haven, where he had given an invited address. "How goes it with you at MIT?" I asked. To which Warren replied that he was leaving MIT to take a leadership role at a major university. I was surprised and asked him to explain; his answer was characteristically direct and provocative. His reply went like this: "I am considered quite an organizational theorist. I have consulted to heads of some of our largest corporations. But I have never been in a leadership role, and

I decided that I should and needed to test my ideas in the crucible of personal experience and organizational realities."

A year later I visited that university, and when I met Warren my first question was "Tell me how it has been." It was a stupid question to ask because it was a large social occasion not conducive to serious discussion. But Warren indicated that his experience had been both enlightening and intellectually and morally upsetting. So, I invited him to come down to our clinic to tell us what he had learned, and I promised him complete confidentiality. He visited, and for three hours he described his phenomenology as a leader. Everyone at that meeting agreed that that discussion was one of the most thought-provoking experiences we had had at our clinic. It is fair to say that Warren made clear how misleading extant theories of leadership were, how the phenomenology of the leader makes a mockery of much that was in the literature. As he put it, "I found myself thinking and doing things I would not in a million years have recommended to any CEO to whom I consulted." His later experience as a university president did not, of course, cause him to change his mind.

The point of this story is threefold. First, what Warren presented was in every respect similar to my experience as head of a clinic with a staff of more than twenty people. Second, although almost everyone (really everyone) else at the clinic firmly believed that leaders should be morally and interpersonally impeccable—a model for what their colleagues should be, a model of fairness, openness, and consistency—they had to conclude that the personal examples Warren described not only challenged their beliefs but required them to rethink their conceptions of means-ends dilemmas. Leadership was a morally messy affair, especially for people with galactic superegos.

The third point of the anecdote is that it allows me to discuss Machiavelli, who is considered the father of political science because he was the first person to examine and discuss the nature and uses of power. And he did this with a candor, specificity, and clarity yet to be exceeded. And if the world has not forgiven him, if the adjective *Machiavellian* is used as a pejorative, the fact is that scholars of Machiavelli and his times are not part of that world. Just as the world has not forgiven Freud for his theory and descriptions of sexuality in infants and young children, it has not forgiven Machiavelli for exposing what a moral leader encounters in an immoral world. That, of course, is a central theme in Shakespeare's tragedies, but we do not use *Shakespearean* as a pejorative. Although in one of his plays the Stratford bard refers unkindly to Machiavelli, he seeks to elicit our sympathy for his heroes who so often act in accord with Machiavellian principles for action. We do not write Shakespeare off because of his portrayal of Shylock. We should not write Machiavelli off because some of his principles offend our sensibilities.

Let us turn to what is so important about Machiavelli for the way we look at or for the expectations we are taught to have about leaders. Initially, I restrict myself to a few points Machiavelli makes that deserve emphasis because he makes them almost in passing, as if they are so self-evident as not to require elaboration.

The first is that how you achieve power determines how you should think and act to utilize and sustain your power. The different ways you achieve power have very different significances in regard to friends and enemies, those you can count on for support and those who will seek to subvert or supplant you. The process of achieving power is the opposite of neutral in the feelings and attitudes it engenders from different individuals and groups. To deny this, to gloss over it, to accept people at their word, to downplay the relation between status and self-interest is to expose your ignorance about human behavior. Realistic leaders not only have to identify their "enemies" but also have to neutralize and/or get rid of them, and *quickly*. Too much is at stake to allow you to assume that time heals all wounds. It does not; it likely causes the leader to be wounded. Leaders who temporize are vulnerable. Leaders who are incapable of quick and decisive use of their power or who are unduly plagued by what their actions mean for their enemies will not long be leaders.

The second point is that leaders whose goal is self-aggrandizement are abominations. Power should be achieved and utilized for an overarching purpose having meaning for leaders and followers. It is a goal that forges unity and community. And to Machiavelli in his times that meant fulfilling the obligations of national destiny (i.e., getting rid of foreign armies from Italian soil). In writing to the new Florentine prince, Machiavelli beseeched him never to forget what his major goal was: the unification of Italy and the welfare of his subjects, not what in modern parlance would be called an "ego trip."

The third point is that leaders have obligations to followers, not the least of which is inculcating in them a sense of self-respect, worthiness, pride, and mission. In gaining the trust of their followers, leaders must do it in ways that do not violate their traditions, families, and morals. Precisely because leaders need the trust of their followers, they must avoid being hated by them. In the best of all circumstances, leaders should be both loved and feared by their people. But if push comes to shove and a choice has to be made, it is more important to be feared. If love is desirable, and it is, there are times when leadership requires playing the cards of fear rather than those of love.

Machiavelli understood well the significances of liberty.

And whoever becomes the ruler of a free city and does not destroy it, can expect to be destroyed by it, for it can always find a motive for rebellion in the name of liberty and of its ancient usages, which are forgotten neither by lapse of time nor by benefits received; and whatever one does or provides, so long as the inhabitants are not separated or dispersed, they do not forget that name and those usages, but appeal to them at once in every emergency, as did Pisa after so many years held in servitude by the Florentines. But when cities or provinces have been accustomed to live under a prince, and the family of that prince is extinguished, being on the one hand used to obey, and on the other not having their old prince, they cannot unite in choosing one from among themselves, and they do not know how to live in freedom, so that they are slower to take arms, and a prince can win them over with greater facility and establish himself securely. But in republics there is greater life, greater hatred, and more desire for vengeance; they do not and cannot cast aside the memory of their ancient liberty, so that the surest way is either to lay them waste or reside in them. [Machiavelli, 1952, p. 51]

The last sentence in this quotation is a good example of why Machiavelli has been considered immoral. At the same time that he sincerely proclaims the virtues of liberty, he tells his prince that if he were to take over a free city, he is asking for trouble because the people's memory of their past liberties will be a constant source of rebellion and threat. So, either lay waste to the city, which to the modern mind is immoral or unthinkable (but not during *our* civil war), or reside in it, as the Romans always did, and seek to gain the respect, fear, and love of its people. To Machiavelli, leaders who are not seeable or knowable to the populace do not understand human behavior and are begging for trouble. The difficult task of leaders is to be apart from the populace at the same time they must be seen as one of them. Familiarity does not breed contempt if a leader does not lose sight of the overarching goal.

Let us listen to Machiavelli ([1532] 1952) on the "reform process."

Those who by the exercise of abilities such as these become princes, obtain their dominions with difficulty but retain them easily, and the difficulties which they have in acquiring their dominions arise in part from the new rules and regulations that they have to introduce in order to establish their position securely. It must be considered that there is nothing more difficult to carry out, not more doubtful of success, nor more dangerous to handle, than to initiate a new order of things. For the reformer has enemies in all those who profit by the old order, and only lukewarm defenders in all those who would profit by the new order, this lukewarmness arising partly from fear of their adversaries, who have the laws in their favour; and partly from the incredulity of mankind, who do not truly believe in anything new until they have had actual experience of it. Thus it arises that on every opportunity for attacking the reformer, his opponents do so with the zeal of partisans, the others only defend him half-heartedly, so that between them he runs great danger. It is necessary, however, in order to investigate thoroughly this question, to examine whether they depend upon others, that is to say, whether in order to carry out their designs they have to entreat or are able to compel. In the first case they invariably succeed ill, and accomplish nothing; but when they can depend on their own strength and are able to use force, they rarely fail. Thus it comes about that all armed prophets have conquered and unarmed ones failed; for besides what has been already said, the character of peoples varies, and it is easy to persuade them of a thing, but difficult to keep them in that persuasion. And so it is necessary to order things so that when they no longer believe, they can be made to believe by force. Moses, Cyrus, Theseus, and Romulus would not have been able to keep their constitutions observed for so long had they been disarmed, as happened in our own time with Fra Girolamo Savonarola, who failed entirely in his new rules when the multitude began to disbelieve in him, and he had no means of holding fast those who had believed nor of compelling the unbelievers to believe. [p. 54]

That is as succinct and incisive a statement of how reform leaders should think and act, of the psychological context that transfers of power engender, as you will find. One can sum up what

Machiavelli is saying in this way: Gaining or losing power has psychological-interpersonal consequences that, if ignored or indecisively handled, will defeat your purposes. You deal with the context as it is, not as you would like it to be. You did not become a leader to fail or to be disarmed. You became a leader for purposes beyond yourself, and if, in forgetting those purposes, you are led to ignore what gaining or losing power does to people, you court disaster. Things may be otherwise in heaven, but you gain or lose power on earth.

Machiavelli was perfectly capable of distinguishing between moral and immoral leaders. But in the case of immoral leaders, he was able to identify and appreciate personal characteristics leaders should possess: courage and decisiveness. Machiavelli was a moralist, but that did not prevent him from saying, "He was an immoral leader, but, nevertheless, let us not ignore that he possessed *some* of the characteristics a leader needs to possess." For example, he discusses the exploits and accomplishments of Agathocles, a Sicilian who rose from the lowest and most abject position to be King of Syracuse.

It cannot be called virtue to kill one's fellow-citizens, betray one's friends, be without faith, without pity, and without religion; by these methods one may indeed gain power, but not glory. For if the virtues of Agathocles in braving and overcoming perils, and his greatness of soul in supporting and surmounting obstacles be considered, one sees no reason for holding him inferior to any of the most renowned captains. Nevertheless his barbarous cruelty and inhumanity, together with his countless atrocities, do not permit of his being named among the most famous men. We cannot attribute to fortune or virtue that which he achieved without either. [Machiavelli, (1532) 1952, p. 66]

One more excerpt, one most salient to my purposes:

It now remains to be seen what are the methods and rules for a prince as regards his subjects and friends. And as I know that many have written of this, I fear that my writing about it may be deemed presumptuous, differing as I do, especially in this matter, from the opinion of others. But my intention being to write something of use to those who understand, it appears to me more proper to go to the real truth of the matter than to its imagination; and many have imagined republics and principalities which have never been seen or known to exist in reality; for how we live is so far removed from how we ought to live, that he who abandons what is done for what ought to be done, will rather learn to bring about his own ruin than his preservation. A man who wishes to make a profession of goodness in everything must necessarily come to grief among so many who are not good. Therefore it is necessary for a prince, who wishes to maintain himself, to learn how not to be good, and to use this knowledge and not use it, according to the necessity of the case.

Leaving on one side, then, those things which concern only an imaginary prince, and speaking of those that are real, I state that all men, and especially princes, who are placed at a greater height, are reputed for certain qualities which bring them either praise or blame. Thus one is considered liberal, another *misero* or miserly (using a Tuscan term, seeing that *avaro* with us still means one who is rapaciously acquisitive and *misero* one who makes grudging use of his own); one a free giver, another rapacious; one cruel, another merciful; one a breaker of his word, another trustworthy; one effeminate and pusillanimous, another fierce and high-spirited; one humane, another haughty; one lascivious, another chaste; one frank, another astute; one hard, another easy; one serious, another frivolous; one religious, another an unbeliever, and so on. I know that every one will admit that it would be highly praiseworthy in a prince to possess all the above-named

qualities that are reputed good, but as they cannot all be possessed or observed, human conditions not permitting of it, it
is necessary that he should be prudent enough to avoid the
scandal of those vices which would lose him the state, and
guard himself if possible against those which will not lose it
him, but if not able to, he can indulge them with less scruple.
And yet he must not mind incurring the scandal of those
vices, without which it would be difficult to save the state, for
if one considers well, it will be found that some things which
seem virtues would, if followed, lead to one's ruin, and some
others which appear vices result in one's greater security and
well-being. [Machiavelli, (1532) 1952, p. 92]

Can a leader be consistently moral, if by moral you mean adher-
ing to agreed-upon principles governing how people should regard
and treat each other? Lying, spreading rumors, withholding the
truth, deceit, undercutting friends, violating trusts, destroying (figuratively) or impoverishing enemies (competitors)—can a leader
be impeccably moral? Machiavelli gives three answers. The first is
that the question must be preceded by this crucial question: Why
do you seek power? Is it because you are enamored by power, you
seek to indulge and enjoy the prerequisites of power, your words
about vision and mission are empty and ritualistic, you are insensitive to the consequences of assuming power, and you have no deep
sense of what people need and want from you and for themselves?
In reading Machiavelli, one must never forget that he was giving
voice to a desperateness about the plight of Italy, an Italy with a glo-
rious past that foreign invaders were intent on erasing from the Italian psyche. To change that unenviable situation did not require
power or force in the abstract but leadership sophisticated in the
uses and misuses of power and in the knowledge that history
will judge harshly those who seek or use power for personal aggrandizement.
    Machiavelli was not proposing a general theory of leadership
from which his advice for action derived. He was proposing how a

political leader should think and act in the Italy of his day. And his proposals did not stem from armchair musings but from long personal experience in the political arena and from a most scholarly knowledge of political history. He understood as no one before him did the phenomenology of political leaders: the strength of the seeking of power; the social-familial origins of that seeking; the concrete contexts within which power is sought, gained, and utilized; the inevitable conflicts between the personal and overarching purposes of power; the multiplicity of factors a leader confronts; the ease with which that complexity can be ignored or underestimated; the obstacles to using history productively—for Machiavelli all of these factors came with the territory of leadership. And it was a seductive and corrupting territory to the degree to which the political leader lacked the overarching purpose of welding a people, a nation, with pride and self-respect, an end always informing means. Means were moral to the degree to which they furthered that end. Means, any means, do not justify an end unless it serves the overarching purpose. And in choosing means, the leader must never forget that he will be judged by history. The leader ignorant of history is the leader likely to be judged most harshly by history.

Means and ends. When we use *Machiavellian* as a pejorative in regard to leaders we mean one thing explicitly and one thing implicitly. The explicit judgment is that the person or action is deceitful, cunning, and immorally self-serving. For Machiavelli the *self*-serving leader is a fool. The implicit judgment is that it is (or should be) possible for political leaders never to engage in what is considered an immoral or unethical act. That, for Machiavelli, is an inexcusable indulgence of fantasy and hope having no basis whatsoever in human experience. It is not that Machiavelli was unaware of the human capacity for heroic, virtuous action but rather that whenever power becomes a factor in human relationships, ordinary considerations of morality and ethics may have to go by the boards. In the case of political leaders, the word *may* is inappropriate—it often does and has to go by the boards because of overarching, not personal, purposes.

It cannot be overemphasized that Machiavelli was writing to and about a political leader. There is nothing to suggest that in regard to human relationships outside the political arena he justified any of the gory actions the political leader sometimes has to employ. The world has not forgiven, and probably never will forgive, his analysis and description of the realities of the political arena. At best he is regarded by the world as a misguided immoralist who wrote at a time when, so to speak, anything goes (went). At worst he is regarded as the incarnation of evil, a "primitive" in regard both to morals and grasp of human psychology, a person irrelevant to the modern world. *To those who hold such a view, I have to point out that in the post–World War II period there is not an action contained in Machiavelli's writings that has not been undertaken by political leaders in America, either on the domestic or international level, and that includes sanctioning killings of foreign leaders.* I am not passing judgment on any of these actions. (I trust that I need not present a dirty laundry list of domestic scandals.) What I am saying is that, far from being irrelevant, Machiavelli is all too relevant, especially in regard to his warnings about leaders who do not possess other than a desire for personal aggrandizement or who lack the courage and decisiveness without which overarching purposes are empty of meaning.

The twentieth century is drawing to a close. No previous century contains, unfortunately, as much evidence confirming Machiavelli's analyses, and at least in two ways. The first has to do with the Hitlers, Stalins, Mussolinis, Maos, and Husseins of this era. More correctly, the inability of Western leaders to comprehend that they could not afford for their national self-interests, for their overarching national purposes, to accommodate to, temporize with, or seek to seduce leaders possessing unbridled power willing and able to sacrifice their own people on the alters of personal power. Far from being courageous and decisive, or realistically sensitive to these external threats, they could not take preventive actions (which did not necessarily entail declarations of war). They committed what to Machiavelli was a cardinal sin: not comprehending how your "enemies" regard you or, worse yet, taking what your enemies say at face value, or both. Machiavelli was the last person who needed to be told that we live in a political world where our choices for action are between lesser or greater evils. But he also did not need to be told that leaders should not assume that their intentions to abide by Marquess of Queensbury rules of power exchanges are those of their adversaries. Machiavelli did not believe there were Santa Clauses in the political world.

Perhaps the most egregious example of this point is when, not long after Hitler obtained power, he marched in and reclaimed the Saar. Western leaders did nothing, literally nothing. Worse yet, in the following years, they essentially sought to appease him even though in his book *Mein Kampf* he said in crystal-clear language that reclaiming the Saar was only one step to achieving his grandiose ambitions. (It was later learned that if the West had threatened to retaliate, Hitler would have retreated because his war machine was still in its infancy.) The Western leaders made the un-Machiavellian mistake of believing that their adversary could be trusted to be consistent with his proclamations of peaceful inten-tions. So did Stalin when he signed the Hitler-Stalin pact of nonag-gression *and* collaboration! I entertain the fantasy that Machiavelli witnessed all of these goings-on and sadly had to conclude that he, like Santayana, would never be taken seriously in regard to using the past as one of the guides for actions in the present. The fantasy ends with Machiavelli sighing, "Apparently, reading has gone out of style, a victim of wish fulfillment and the denial of the realities."

I have not discussed Machiavelli to make the point that he has given us a bible, a kind of "how-to" manual, that contains unvar-nished truths we should uncritically accept. Bibles are about heaven, earth, and hell. Machiavelli believed in heaven and hell. That did not prevent him from confronting and describing earthly realities. And that is the point: Machiavelli asks us, at the least, that we recognize those realities, that we neither ignore or oversimplify them, that we be clear about overarching purposes, that personal aggrandizement is evil, that the verdict of history will be a moral one in that a judgment will be rendered about the consequences of actions for the welfare of the people whom the leader led. Machiavelli would have recognized that Hitler had *some of* the necessary characteristics of great leaders, as he also would have about the Japanese leaders who planned the attack on Pearl Harbor. But, like the verdict history has rendered, he would say they made the egregious mistake of allowing unrealistic ambitions to overestimate their power and underestimate the power and resolve of their adversaries, with the result of visiting catastrophe on their peoples.

But what if Hitler and the Japanese had been successful? What would Machiavelli have said? He would have said what he did in the excerpt about Agathocles: "his barbarious cruelty and inhumanity, together with his countless atrocities, do not permit of his being named among the most famous men. We cannot attribute to fortune or virtue that which he achieved without either" (Machiavelli, [1532] 1952, p. 66). Those are not the words of an immoralist. Nor are his words about the dangers of taking over peoples who were used to liberty.

The genius of Machiavelli inhered in his ability to state and describe the phenomenology of the leader in regard to crucial practical and moral issues. The modern sensibility recoils from some of the things he either approves or recommends. To such recoiling it is appropriate to thank God for big favors. However, the fact remains that neither in Machiavelli's days nor *ours* are the *problems* he raised on a back burner. Given the history of the twentieth century—perhaps the most gory of centuries in human history—we should plead to God to give us more Machiavellis to help us confront the realities of power in the modern world. If those realities are unpleasant (to indulge understatement), if the universe of action alternatives are morally messy (to indulge understatement again), if there are no cookbook answers, they are no warrant for allowing the human need for hope to overwhelm the perception of what the modern world is. I write these words at a time when the Balkans have again exploded around issues, the very same, concrete issues that caused the initial explosion in the Balkans in Machiavelli's era. I hear

Machiavelli again sighing and saying, "So tell me, what else is new?"

What is new is that, unlike in Machiavelli's days, our concerns about leadership are by no means restricted to the political arena. We live in an era of a myriad of organizations, large and small, national and international, varying in their relationships to and impact upon their members and their societies. For the bulk of Western people, how they experience their lives in these organizations suffuses and shapes how they think, feel, and act. It is no exaggeration to say that, family of origin aside, the psyche of people—their view of themselves; their approach to their future; the frequency, strength, and contents of their affective ups and downs—is incomprehensible apart from that psyche's "work" context. The industrial revolution was made possible by, among other things, scientific-technological advances that brought in their wake the general problem of leadership: what is or should be the relationship between workers and leaders? Whatever judgment you pass on Karl Marx and Friedrich Engels, it is to their everlasting credit that they articulated the moral issue of the obligations of leaders to their "people" (i.e., their workers). What were the overarching purposes of the industrial enterprise? Did workers exist only to satisfy the leader's need for money and power? How does one justify treating workers as "things," devoid of needs, quite expendable, not possessing pride and self-respect?

For at least a couple of centuries after the industrial revolution, industrial leaders made the mistake about which Machiavelli cautioned the political leader: forgetting that one's people, one's ultimate constituency and source of power, had to feel pride, self-respect, and, therefore, a willing commitment to the leader and the enterprise. A sullen, angry, alienated constituency means the leader is vulnerable. The history of industrial relations is the history of personal aggrandizements. Indeed, when one reads that history and then reads Machiavelli, it becomes obvious that those industrial barons totally lacked his understanding of the moral complexity of the relationship between leaders and followers. Machiavelli did not have an elevated view of followers. He was not a forerunner of modern liberalism. He was no moral angel who knew all the questions and all the answers. But he was a person who understood that leaders without overarching moral purposes, but with unbridled quests for personal power, would be negatively judged by history.

A new conception of leadership has taken hold in the modern Western world in the post–World War II era. At the risk of oversimplification, that conception asserts that the task of leadership is to recognize that followers, far from being ciphers, have assets, needs, hopes, and ambitions that in diverse ways the leader should seek not only to recognize but to gratify (i.e., a recognition and seeking that should inhibit or control the evils of purely personal gain). Leaders lead, but they also serve in accord with some overarching moral commitment. It is a conception informed and suffused by a democratic ethos.

Is Machiavelli relevant to this conception? I have had occasion to put that question to leaders of small and large, public and private organizations. If my sample is relatively small and nonrandom, these are limitations that do not explain why *none* of these leaders had ever read Machiavelli and why *all* of them seemed to regard the question either as stupid, at worst, or mystifying, at best. As in the popular mind, for them the adjective *Machiavellian* meets all of the criteria of a pejorative. But how did they answer this question: Can you give me examples of times when you felt justified in lying, undercutting, acting ruthlessly, or in one or another way doing something that violated your moral code? I can recall only a handful of these leaders who were not taken aback and obviously reluctant, even unable, to respond. From their facial expressions, stammering, and long pauses it was obvious that many were unwilling to give examples. Among the handful who responded quickly and forthrightly, one put it this way: "Are you serious? Are you implying that sitting at the top, having *the* [his emphasis] responsibility for the health of the organization, you never have to do something that will cause you guilt or a sleepless night? But in the examples I will give I had to do what I did for the organization, not for my personal needs."

I am in no position to pass judgment on what these leaders described. The purpose of the anecdote was again to call attention to points implicit and explicit in Machiavelli's writing. These points are beautifully and dramatically illustrated in a play by Ignazio Silone, who in his life and writings sought to expose Stalinist barbarism. The title of the play is *The Story of a Humble Christian* (Silone, 1970), a drama based on recorded historical people and events in pre-Machiavelli Italy. Briefly, it is about a time when a new pope had to be chosen and the two most powerful factions could not agree on a choice. Each wanted a pope they could control. Finally, someone suggested that there was a hermit known and revered for his piety and who, if pope, would not upset the existing balance of political power; that is, his otherworldliness would keep him from intruding into earthly matters. They visit him in his isolated mountainous retreat and offer him the papacy. He refuses, but he is made to change his mind by the argument that he cannot, should not, ignore God's calling him to lead God's church. He becomes pope, but after several months he resigns because he has concluded that it is impossible to be pope and absolutely moral. (Pope Celestine V is the only pope to have resigned that role.) He refused to allow himself to be corrupted. When it is too hot in the moral kitchen, you get out!

We are used to hearing that power corrupts and absolute power corrupts absolutely. As I read Machiavelli, I think he would have been puzzled by that maxim. For Machiavelli moral corruption meant seeking, attaining, and exercising power for personal aggrandizement, not for an overarching purpose that took into account the welfare, pride, and self-respect of those for whom the leader is responsible.

What if Machiavelli were alive today and avidly read the accounts in our mass media of leaders in all walks of life in whom personal greed and power are "what it is all about," leaders lacking moral vision and purpose? Machiavelli wrote to the new prince of the Florentine republic. What would he write to the princes of today? What if he sat in on the thousands of courses, workshops, and seminars on leadership that are given each year? If my limited experience with such occasions is at all typical, I have to conclude that he would criticize them on several grounds. First, they deal superficially with the phenomenology of seeking, attaining, and exercising power; the process is a *transforming* one. Second, they oversimplify and gloss over the realities of the power arena, an arena that always is and always should be morally demanding and messy. Third, the inevitable and seductive conflict between personal and overarching purposes cannot be learned through sermons. Fourth, they are egregiously deficient in considering the history of theories of power. History is not a museum of relics we go to, if we go at all, on a rainy Sunday. To be ignorant of the history of power is inexcusable precisely because that ignorance makes it all too easy to put the moral issues out of awareness.

I close this essay with what I regard, as Machiavelli would have, as one of the most heroic events of this century precisely because of what it says about overarching purpose. It concerned President Harry Truman and General Douglas MacArthur, who at the time was a far more revered icon in American life than Truman. The long and short of it was that MacArthur, informally and formally, sought to subvert or get around the president's policy and orders. To Truman—the most historically minded president since the country's founders—MacArthur represented a challenge to constitutional authority. Truman knew that if he did what he should do, fire the general, he would be criticized, vilified, hanged in effigy, and more. Personally Truman could not win; politically he could only lose. He could try to ride out the challenge or temporize or compromise in some way. But Truman concluded that given the overarching purposes of his office he had no choice. He fired MacArthur, and all hell broke loose. History vindicated Truman. Few presidents would have had the guts to take that course of action. If he had served the people the way they desired in regard to the general, it would have been a different story. But it was a time to lead, not to serve. Leaders who serve only on the basis of public opinion polls are not leaders. Neither are those whose conception of leadership centers around personal pride and power and to hell with anyone else. Machiavelli wrote to the prince of his day. The princes of today would do well to rediscover Machiavelli the realist, moralist, and scholar. At the very least they may conclude that history is not bunk, that the more things change the more they remain the same or, as this century suggests, get worse.

I began this essay by noting that shortly after World War II, the nature of leadership increasingly became a central concern of theoreticians, researchers, and university educators. One of the most important features of that concern was the emphasis on values inherent in leadership informed by a democratic and participatory ethos. If you peruse the literature on leadership, it is hard to avoid concluding that the task of leaders had been made more difficult in contrast to earlier times. Consistent with a democratic-participatory ethos, leaders were now required to take the feelings, attitudes, and interests of all groups in the organization into account, requirements that had two obvious related consequences: inhibiting the tendency of the leaders to act quickly and/or arbitrarily, and adopting a much longer time perspective in regard to organizational change than that of the "old" leadership style. However stirring, necessary, and justified the democratic ethos, it requires time-consuming processes that test the patience and efficiency of everyone, especially leaders whose seeking a leadership role always is accompanied by diverse motives, not all of which are compatible with a democratic ethos. What that ethos requires is control of those incompatible motives, and that is asking a lot.

What I find noteworthy in the literature on democratic leadership is its emphasis on how leaders *should* act. The shoulds and the oughts are always made clear, and there is an abundance of case presentations illustrating how leaders should initiate or react to the initiatives of others. I have no quarrel with that emphasis. What is missing and bothers me is how little there is on the phenomenology of leaders, that is, the psychological transformations experienced in their roles, how the nature of the role engenders conflicts about what one should do, how one should do it, and how to justify what one wants to do or actually does when what one does is a violation of the democratic ethos or one's personal moral codes or even the obligations of courtesy. This is but another way of saying that departing from the democratic ethos should be expected. It is, so to speak, in the nature of things. These departures have to be judged by the goals they are supposed to achieve, the degree to which they reflect narrowly personal goals in contrast to overarching organizational goals. What I am saying is that these departures are not only to be expected but they are sometimes justified.

I write these words during the days when Boris Yeltsin arbitrarily and unconstitutionally dissolved the Russian Parliament and then felt compelled to attack the building at a cost of many lives. It is interesting that President Clinton and other Western leaders supported this action on the grounds that the action furthered the overarching goal of bringing about a more democratic political order. And in so doing they were agreeing with Machiavelli that there are times when a leader is justified in departure from a conventional morality. Many people criticized and denounced Yeltsin's actions on moral, political, and historical grounds. Posterity, the cruelest of critics, will be the ultimate arbiter, just as posterity has passed judgment on the American colonies' decision unilaterally to rebel against the longstanding prerogatives of the British crown.

As I have said earlier, I have no quarrel whatsoever with the democratic-participatory ethos for leadership, be that leadership in the public or private sectors of our society. But to proclaim that ethos without coming to grips with the moral dilemmas of leadership is both unjustified and mischievous in its consequences precisely because the picture we are given is woefully incomplete. And that conclusion has been supported by every biography of a leader I have ever read.

I trust that that conclusion is interpreted as saying not that in principle I support these departures but rather they should be expected in an imperfect world populated by imperfect people. At the time of these departures you take a stand. Posterity will provide its own answer to their occurrence and justification.

9

The Failure of Presidential Leadership in Educational Reform

Beginning in the late sixties, and with increasing explicitness in the years after, I said that whatever was being done in the name of educational reform was not, could not, have intended outcomes. That stance was not mine alone. Yes, it was based on extensive observations derived from my roles as consultant, researcher, and workshop participant. But it also reflected what countless, and I do mean countless, teachers and educational administrators told me in conversation, the contents of which they could not bring themselves to make public. Teachers and administrators rarely write for publication, and most are fearful of expressing their views in public forums. They suffer inwardly, trying to grasp at straws in order to stay afloat in a cascade of waves of reform nostrums. Generally speaking, they know they are not highly regarded by the general public; they feel under pressure to appear innovative and on top of things, basically pessimistic that their efforts are other than Band-Aids, very unsure that they know what the problems or the answers are.

What I have just described is true in spades for our urban schools where problems of race, poverty, drugs, guns, and more are daily fare. If these problems are less frequent in our suburban schools, those sites confront, especially in middle and high schools, students whose motivation for learning is superficial, who regard schooling as a form of harassment by parents and school personnel, and who distinguish the real world "out there" (in film and on TV) as incomparably more interesting than what they experience in the encapsulated classroom in the encapsulated school. What urban and suburban schools have in common is less the question of how to get children to learn and meet grade norms but rather how to engender that kind of satisfaction or gratification from learning that reinforces the desire to continue to learn. As one suburban high school teacher said to me, "Most of my students are bright. They are at or above grade level. But it is the rare student from whom I get the feeling that they enjoy, really enjoy, the struggles of and outcomes from learning. Most of them are going through the motions, but their hearts are not in them. They do what they are told to do, not what they want to do, and I have to be honest and say that I am not sure I know what they want to do."

Two factors have mightily fed the pessimism of educational personnel. The first is truly new and momentous: in the quiet of their nights they do not believe that the problem is one which increasing budgets will help, except minimally. The second, and by no means new, is that schools have to deal with consequences of external conditions that set limits to what schools can be expected to achieve. Unfortunately, too frequently school personnel use this second factor as a kind of defense mechanism against criticism and bypass the question of what schools can and should do to dilute the consequences of those external conditions. It is one thing to point to "invading" conditions; it is another thing to determine how, so to speak, to capitalize on them for learning in school. To say there are limits is not to say that one is without options. To say there are options is to say that schools can and should change. But, as I shall be emphasizing, resistance to change is a bedrock law in human behavior. Death and taxes are, we are told, inevitable. So is resistance to change.

No one denies that the inadequacies of our schools are a national problem that has percolating negative effects in all arenas of the society. That some of these effects are obvious goes without saying. If what is obvious is troubling, it is the vague feeling, hard to articulate, that these effects are prodromal of worse to come which cause, to say the least, unease. And this unease is heightened by the brute fact that efforts at reform provide no reassurance that a general improvement is in the societal cards. If past and present diagnoses of the problem are either incomplete or faulty or both, if national leadership for moving in new directions is absent, what do we do?

During the Vietnam War, a Vermont senator advised that we proclaim victory and leave. That is not an option available to us in regard to education. We cannot avoid two questions: Where are our diagnoses inadequate, and even if we stumble on a more adequate diagnosis, how can our national leadership get public support to act in accord with an altered view? We do not have a national educational system. We have thousands of autonomous school districts. So, if a more adequate diagnosis comes to the fore, it will require of national leadership the task of making that diagnosis understandable to the general public, understandable in a way that will gain national support because, one can assume, a lot of changes in individuals and institutions will become necessary. Without appropriate national leadership we resign ourselves to "victories" in schools A, B, and C while the bulk of schools remain as they are. To concretize what I am saying, let me turn to two past comparable national problems and how they were diagnosed, communicated, and dealt with.

The catastrophe called the Great Depression required explanation and action. President Hoover and his advisors had no ready explanation and were reluctant to take decisive actions. It is interesting that in the presidential campaign of 1932, President Franklin D. Roosevelt called for a balanced budget, exposing his lack of understanding of what had happened and why. When he took office, he began to see the dimensions of the problem, which is not to say he had a diagnosis on the basis of which the roots of the problem could be attacked. But he took decisive actions, most of which were Band-Aids or turned out to be ineffective or unconstitutional. It has to be recalled that the Great Depression continued, indeed increased in severity, during his first two terms. The government tried this and that, certainly not in a random fashion but, equally certain, not on a basis of a valid diagnosis. Recognizing that something is radically wrong is not a diagnosis, just as pointing to symptoms without in some way interrelating them is not a diagnosis. The purpose of a diagnosis is that it serves as a basis for action, to restore normal function, to ameliorate the condition, or to prevent further deterioration. When actions fail of their purposes, both the validity of the diagnosis and the appropriateness of the actions are called into question. Roosevelt's New Deal programs were called into question on the basis of faulty diagnosis and actions, just as in the post–World War II era the variety of efforts of educational reform have been called into question.

Of the few pieces of New Deal legislation exempt from the negative verdict of history, the Social Security Act of 1935 and the Unemployment Compensation Act are the most notable exceptions. Undergirding such legislation was a diagnosis as obviously valid as it was compelling: the need to prevent the harsh psychological realities of dependency in old age and the morale-killing effects of unemployment. The diagnosis was not only economic in nature but psychological as well. And that is the point: the consequences of undue dependency threatened the social fabric, and *preventive* actions were necessary. But if that diagnosis was obvious and compelling, it required a dramatic change in the role of government, which is why that legislation met strong opposition in and out of congress.

Why did the legislation pass? There were two related reasons. The first is that FDR—his words, style, fireside chats, and previous actions—had convinced most of the citizenry that he understood what they were thinking and experiencing. What he said was congruent with their plight. His words had the ring of truth. His diagnosis of the shattering effects of dependency required no confirmation, and his proposals were appropriate to the diagnosis. Many readers of this essay may be puzzled that the diagnosis and the actions met with opposition. After all, how more obviously valid and simple could a diagnosis be? I have to remind the reader that the validity and simplicity of the diagnosis meant a change in tradition, practice, and the conventional wisdom. By the time the legislation came to a vote, FDR had prepared the country for what needed to be done, and he did that in the most concrete terms. A rich, patrician president convinced the people that he understood the guts of the problem. He did not depend on abstractions, sloganeering, and expressions of pious intent. He was concrete. He was persuasive. The passage of the legislation is incomprehensible apart from FDR's leadership. It is not, I think, wild speculation that his crippled condition due to polio played a role in his desire to introduce national health insurance; he *knew* what a major illness involved, financially, psychologically, and socially. He was dissuaded from such a proposal because it would endanger passage of the Social Security Act. More than a half-century later we appear to be accepting the principle of national health insurance but with nothing like the implementation simplicity of the Social Security and Unemployment Compensation Acts.

The second example is the Medicare legislation of 1965. The story here is similar to the first example but more complicated because it was based on a valid but incomplete, misleading diagnosis. What was valid in the diagnosis—its emphasis on the repair *and* prevention of illness in old age—requires no elaboration here. Where the diagnosis was incomplete and even wrong was in the assumption that most children responsible for their aging parents wanted to place them in nursing homes, that sons and daughters were being adversely affected, financially and psychologically, by the burden of caring for their parents. There was, of course, truth to that conclusion, but it was incomplete and faulty in one respect: it overlooked the possibility that there were more than a few children who did not want to place parents in a nursing home but had no viable alternative. That is to say, their parents could remain in the community if appropriate programs and services existed, but they did not. The initial Medicare legislation said little about such programs and services; what the legislation contained were essentially financial incentives to facilitate a nursing home placement. It was only in later years that programs and services were developed making such placements unnecessary or postponed in many instances.

The Medicare legislation met vehement opposition, but President Johnson, as activist a president we have ever had and who had idolized FDR, exerted leadership in convincing the general public and a majority of congress that the legislation had to be enacted. The point here is that he understood (he grew up during the Great Depression) what financial dependency brought in its wake. What he and others did not grasp, and was therefore absent in the diagnosis, was that some children of aging, sick, or frail parents sought nursing home placement because there were no viable alternatives to help them keep parents in the community. Put in another way, the psychological dynamics, motivation, and hopes in some families went unnoticed. FDR came from an aristocratic background, but he came to understand what poverty did to people. President Johnson's understanding of families was on an abstract level, not derived from concrete experience or intuitive understanding. He understood well the fear of financial dependency but not the strength of the need to be psychologically independent. Nevertheless, it was his leadership that made passage of the legislation possible, and it was truly landmark legislation. If it was in part flawed, the fact remains that President Johnson posed the general issue in ways people understood.

In the course of writing this essay I began to read Nathan Miller's (1992) biography of Theodore Roosevelt. I never understood why that Oyster Bay, Harvard-educated, Rough Rider spearheaded so many societal reform efforts ranging from endorsing environmental conservation to making it illegal for garment manufacturers to dole out piecework to be done in the tenement apartments (read hovels) of very poor people (read immigrants). In regard to piecework, Roosevelt initially fought the legislation, but he was persuaded "to see for himself." He did, he was aghast, and he became the most articulate proponent of the legislation. Roosevelt had the refreshing capacity "to see for himself," not to remain on the level of abstraction but to test his ideas by personal observation and experience. I emphasize this point because as I now turn to efforts at school reform, the failure of national leaders to use personal experience, or to seek to gain firsthand experience, has prevented them from grasping what I consider to be the basic issues that, being ignored, guarantee that what they do propose will have no or minuscule positive effects.

Let us start with the fact, confirmed in research and not disputed by any knowledgeable person, that, generally speaking, classrooms are boring, uninteresting, go-through-the-motions places for students. Put in another way, for the bulk of students, there are two worlds: the uninteresting world of the school and the fascinating world "out there." Indeed, much of the effort at school reform in the post–World War II era has sought, in diverse ways, intellectually to enliven for students their school experience. Although these well-intentioned efforts should not be peremptorily dismissed or derogated, it is the case that the fruits of these efforts are very far from encouraging, and in my opinion that is a charitable assessment if only because those efforts distract attention away from some truly basic questions.

Over the years in the course of discussions with teachers, individually and in groups, I have asked this question: When you review *your* experiences as a student, what were the characteristics of those instances when you felt a sense of insight, or of growth, or what may be called productive learning—the feeling that you have learned something causing you to see yourself and the world differently, be that difference personal or intellectual or both? The initial response was *almost* always one of puzzled silence, usually a very prolonged silence. It is fair to say that it was obvious that the teachers had never given thought to the question, to using personal experience illuminating productive learning. Those silences were sometimes so long (and painful for me and them) that I would say, "Think of *any* instance *outside* of your school experience illustrative of a productive learning experience." That suggestion was a kind of ice breaker facilitating instances and their characteristics.

Those characteristics were several. The first was a state of puzzlement or curiosity or sheer interest in what the person had read, or observed, or was told, something that had aroused questions whose answers were not readily at hand. The second was a feeling, usually but not always vague, that the question and the answer had personal significance in that the answer would be illuminating both of that person's internal and external world. Frequently, the question or problem brought up past questions that had not been answered. The third characteristic was being able to go to someone who they felt could be helpful, a person they had reason to believe would be knowledgeable, patient, and supportive. The fourth characteristic was that as a result of getting a clarifying answer, they were stimulated to learn more about that class of problems associated with which was the sense that one's horizons had been enlarged. It was not always the case that another person played a part in the illustrative instance. Sometimes the person persevered on his or her own, but even after such personally initiated clarification of the problem, it was important to get recognition of the accomplishment from others.

Following these discussions I always reserved time for this question: Why do students have such difficulty coming up with examples of what have been described as the characteristics of productive learning? Why do all but a few experience school as uninteresting, unstimulating, and personally irrelevant? To those questions, the answers pour out and with a great deal of emotion. The answers fall into two categories, those that point to external factors like changing family constellations, societal breakdown, racial conflict, TV, drugs, gangs, poverty, and more, and those that indicate internal factors like a predetermined curriculum, lack of time for the individual student, the pressure to make sure that achievement test scores meet norms, the lack of supportive services, insensitive or unsupportive or unimaginative leadership, and unmotivated students. *No teacher ever said that the situation was overblown, or denied that the characteristics of productive learning were rare in occurrence, or said or implied that the root problem being ignored was that they and almost everybody else did not take seriously what their personal experience said about productive learning.* Granted that each of the internal and external factors they identified had a kernel of truth, but that does not account for why classrooms are so often intellectually stultifying affairs, viewed by too many students as a legally sanctioned form of harassment. I never had the courage to ask teachers why *they* had such inordinate difficulty coming up with examples of productive learning in *their* years of schooling.

In several of my recent books, I have elaborated on these issues, and I shall not attempt here to summarize those discussions. But it is possible to state in relatively few words the bedrock basis of those arguments. *From its earliest days, the human organism is a question-asking, questing one, aware of and responsive to novelty, features that in its transactions with its environs feed its ever-present curiosity about its internal and external world. To the extent that these features are recognized, nurtured, and supported, its question-asking, answer-seeking characteristics make for new, productive learning experiences. To the extent that they are ignored or blunted, as they so frequently are in classrooms, those characteristics are not extinguished but, so to speak, go underground and/or attach to goals that frequently are individually and socially self-defeating.* Let me now state it in terms of the classroom: If we do not recognize and start with what children are and where they psychologically are—their questions about self, others, and the world, their need to feel competence and growth and to experience the obstacles to the mastery of problems, and all of this in relation to their personal experience—if you do not start with such a stance, you have reduced the possibility of productive learning nearly to zero.

All of this has been said before, countless times. It is a glimpse of the obvious. But it is the polar opposite of what undergirds teaching in our schools where *we* decide what students will learn, *we* decide what is of interest to them, *we* isolate content from personal experience, *we* assume that meeting grade norms on an achieve-ment test means that subject matter has been productively assimi-lated and will be productively used for new learning, and *we* assume that being able to read means that children *want* to read outside of the situation where they are required to read.

I have learned from experience that I must disabuse some read-ers of the conclusion that I am advocating that we teach children only what they want to learn and know. To advocate that is both mindless and irresponsible. What I advocate is that we start with "what and where the child is" and capitalize on that understanding in order to enlarge the person's personal and intellectual horizons, to feed and reinforce his or her question-asking, answer-seeking pro-clivities so that he or she gets productively directed to realms of knowledge, problems, and skills of which the child has been unaware.

In a conversation with an unmotivated, recalcitrant high school student from the inner city, he asked me, "Why should I learn geometry?" I was nonplussed; I did not know how to answer him. One part of me wanted to say that he needed geometry like he needed a hole in the head. But, I decided, that would be grist for his mill in regard to the irrelevance of schooling, all schooling. For reasons not clear to me, except that I had to say something, I asked him, "Why do you think the school thinks you should learn geom-etry? Do you really think you are asked to learn geometry for the hell of it, that it has absolutely nothing to do with you and the world you live in, that it is an empty exercise that has no meaning for understanding the world you see?" He looked at me with a mix-ture of puzzlement and contempt and said, "No one ever told me *why* I should learn geometry. The only thing I was told was that I *had* to take it." It was that reply that caused me for the rest of that day to review my experience learning algebra, geometry, chemistry, and more. It also forced me in subsequent years to sit in classrooms the first two or three days of the school year to find out how teach-ers explained the "why" question. No one "handled" or raised it. The teachers were absolutely certain about what the students needed to learn. Why they should learn it, what significance it had in their personal experience, what it could mean for their intellectual development and for possible vocational choices, the roles these subject matters played and play in the development of the society, how the daily life of everyone is incomprehensible apart from understanding the contributions of these subject matters— none of this was ever taken up. Some might argue that it was self-evident to students that these subject matters were important. I concluded that it was self-evident to the teacher that it was important, but it was equally self-evident to the student that they did not know why it was important, why it should be important to them.

All that I have said is obvious, painfully so, and I feel obliged to apologize for reiterating it here. But the gulf between the obvious and conventional practice is so huge as to require reiteration. It is a gulf that must be bridged, at least start to be bridged, if our society is to become what we want it to become.

So I wrote a book, *Letters to a Serious Education President* (1993), for several related reasons. The first was to tell the president that he should look into his school experience in regard to what were productive and unproductive learning experiences. Precisely because he had ultimate responsibility for federal educational policies, programs, and expenditures, should he not use personal experience as some sort of guide, just as he uses it in foreign and economic and political policy? And I suggested that if he were not secure in the conclusions he was coming to, he should take the time to observe in schools. Time is precious in the life of a president, but does not the educational debacle he publicly says should no longer be tolerated warrant some of that time? Does not the failure of past and expensive reform efforts require him to use himself to gain new experience and ideas? Can he continue to be content with supporting policies that in no way reflect his experience? Is that personal experience utterly devoid of significance? Is it not incumbent on a leader to know a problem in a way that allows him to convince the general public that what they are hearing has the ring of truth, that it fits in with *their* experience? Does the president know that a large part of that general public has concluded that nothing can be done to improve schools?

The second reason I wrote the book is that I believe that *only* the president—in the style of a Theodore Roosevelt, an FDR, a Lyndon Johnson—can persuade the citizenry to depart from traditional educational policies *that that citizenry already knows are unproductive*. No one else can play that role. The educational community is a fragmented one containing groups intent on protecting their vested professional interests and incapable of reaching the public. And that is the point: whatever kernels of truth are contained in their positions (and there are kernels if only because it is hard to be completely wrong), *they do not address the root problem that classrooms today are organized on the basis of a wrong conception of productive learning*. If they do not address it forthrightly, it is not because they are ignorant of the invalidity of that conception. Strange to say, I have never met any leader of these groups who, in private conversation, disagreed with my criticism, a criticism, I must emphasize, that has been articulated by countless writers, theorists, and researchers long before I was forced to confront the obvious. My plea to the president was to use and accrue personal experience to be able to proclaim convincingly that the time has come to take the obvious seriously, a proclaiming that many in the general public will find to have the ring of truth.

The third reason is more complicated because it raises the question, So what do we do? To a question like that, there is not one, and only one, course of action available to us. On the justifiable assumption that we have to decide among alternatives—we do not live in a world in which we can simultaneously act on all fronts—where should we put our marbles? My answer to the president was that we should radically seek to transform the preparation of educators, a suggestion I elaborate in detail in *The Case for Change: Rethinking the Preparation of Educators* (1993). That suggestion was in principle identical to the rationale informing Abraham Flexner's report in 1910 on medical education. Few people are aware that the quality of medical practice and education at the turn of the century was discernibly poorer than it is today in education. History has confirmed the wisdom of Flexner's analyses and recommendations. Flexner was the right man at the right time with the right diagnosis. No one comparable to him exists in the educational arena today, save for a John Goodlad or Larry Cuban, to whom few seem to listen. If the president *understood* what Goodlad and Cuban understand, his resort to empty rhetoric and nostrums that have been tried again and again in the past would be replaced by a concrete, truth-ringing diagnosis that would change the substance of the debate. As someone of stature in the field said to me, "If the president truly understood your letters and presented your proposal, all hell would break loose in the field." Indeed it would, which brings me to the final reason I wrote the letters book.

To transform radically the preparation of educators understandably would not be greeted with enthusiasm by the hundreds of existing programs in our colleges and universities. No one greets the need for change warmly, which is one reason past reform efforts have steered clear of preparatory programs, except in piddling, window-dressing ways. I do not advocate a frontal assault but rather the development of incentives to facilitate change. Even so, one has to expect strong resistance. But incentives to do what? Put most succinctly, incentives to take seriously what we have long known about the characteristics of and contexts in which productive learning stands a chance of being realized.

But it is not enough for the president to state the correct diagnoses and actions appropriate to it, because the sought-for transformation is the polar opposite of the quick fix; it will take time, a *minimum of two decades* before we begin to see a general improvement. Used as we are to quick fixes and hoping as we do that there are quick fixes, the president's message will not be seen as politically sexy. And that is why it is only a secure, courageous, *and* personally knowledgeable president who can begin to give currency to the need to move in new directions. Someone said that the best national debates "change the substance of the conversation." In the case of educational reform, that is the obligation of the president.

No one else has, in Theodore Roosevelt's words, such a "bully pulpit." I have no doubt whatsoever that most people are ready to hear, because of their personal experience, the diagnosis.

Crucial in the president's message would be the unambiguous theme that there are no villains in the story. *No one willed the present situation.* We have all been victims of a past that inculcated in us a picture of the modal classroom that seemed right, natural, and proper, just as that past told us that "separate but equal" was right, natural and proper, and just as it told us what was right, natural, and proper about the role of women, and just as it told us in the pre–Great Depression days that the role of government should never intrude into matters of individual health, employment, *and* education. As one sage said, "It is a societal law that change does not come about until we have been hit over the head time and again, until national leadership emerges that has the courage to say that the emperor is not only naked but has a terminal disease and that new leadership is necessary."

We are told that the first step on the road to recovery for an alcoholic is to say out loud, "I am an alcoholic." In regard to educational reform, the first step is to say, "Whatever we have tried has not worked, and coming up with carbon copies of past efforts speaks volumes about our ahistorical stance." If we could say that and mean it, and if we go the route I have suggested, the next step involves several interrelated questions: Are we prepared for the institutional upheavals that route takes us? Will we have the vision, patience, and courage to act consistently with a relatively long-term perspective preventive at its core? Will we have the national leadership without which we will live through eras in which the more things change the more they remain the same? Will we continue to do what we know how to do and not what in the quiet of our nights we know we need to do?

I conclude with a story told to me by a colleague, Samuel Brownell, about an experience he had as commissioner for education in the early Eisenhower years. Brownell was among the first to see the implications of the "urban crisis": escalating juvenile delinquency; underfunded educational systems overwhelmed by escalating school populations; cities near bankruptcy; and an increasing number of people, largely black, mired in poverty. He met with President Eisenhower, who had been president of Columbia University where he helped create and support an institute that, among other things, had demonstrated through an analysis of World War II recruits the pervasive personal and monetary costs of a scandalously large number of poorly educated and/or illiterate people. Brownell proposed that the federal government should enter the picture, a proposal he knew would require a dramatic break with a tradition that believed that education was a family, local, or state responsibility, a tradition reflected in the fact that our constitution does not contain the word *education*. Eisenhower agreed there was a real problem, but, in light of tradition, he wanted the advice of his cabinet and arranged for Brownell to make a presentation to that group.

Following the presentation, the president asked each member of the cabinet to express an opinion. With no exception they (including the likes of John Foster Dulles and Ezra Taft Benson) counseled against breaking with long-standing tradition, although a few did so with reluctance. The president then turned to Vice President Nixon, who in unambiguous language explained why not breaking with tradition would be ultimately socially destabilizing and self-defeating. Following that the president said that he agreed with the vice president and that Brownell (not a member of the cabinet) should start drafting legislation. A new era began. Eisenhower knew the opposition such legislation would engender and, I assume, that his personal experience in World War II with the quality of recruits and, by deduction, the schools from which they came gave him an understanding of the implications of the problem. And, it is safe to assume, he was quite knowledgeable about the armed services' displeasure (to say the least) with a similar problem in World War I. In any event, President Eisenhower had the vision and courage not only to depart from tradition but to use his bully pulpit to gain a national constituency that hardly needed convincing. Opposition in congress was strong, but it was overcome.

That legislation was no less tradition shattering than that which brought about the social security, unemployment, and Medicare legislation. That legislation was based on a diagnosis, in large measure correct, that the problem was monetary and required some kind of monetary solution. Unfortunately, that diagnosis continued to be made and acted upon long after its inappropriateness should have been apparent, a blindness to the obvious that continues to this day and will continue until God, Lady Luck, or both give us a president who can use his or her experience to come up with a truly new or more adequate diagnosis that takes seriously what we have known about productive learning.

10

The Failure of the Deinstitutionalization Policy Makers

My first professional job after leaving graduate school in June 1942 was in a new state institution for mentally retarded and/or epileptic individuals. I lived and worked there for four years, after which I continued in one or another way to be connected with "training schools" and also state hospitals for those with psychotic disorders. In short, I have lived through the revolution we call deinstitutionalization, a revolution that in recent years has been blamed for most of the socially upsetting phenomena associated with homelessness. To someone like me, that assignment of blame is possible by those whose capacity to oversimplify is matched only by their ignorance of history. Mencken said that for every problem there is a simple answer that is wrong. Nowhere is this more true than in current discussions of the sources of the failures of deinstitutionalization.

I can understand and even semiexcuse the ignorance of politicians who are required to say or do something about the scores of thousands of troubled and troubling people who wander and live on our urban streets. I, at least, do not expect public figures to be historically minded. But I do expect that those professions that are most related to and have been and still are administratively responsible for the care of these "deviant," dependent people would be allergic to simple explanations. I refer specifically to psychiatry, medicine in general, and psychology. This is not to say that I blame them for their historical role as gatekeepers, administrators, and

214 ESSAYS ON PSYCHOLOGY

caretakers. If I did, I would be subject to the Mencken criticism. But I do expect that highly educated and trained professionals would know something about the history of their professions, at least the history of the past fifty years. That is not asking a lot. But as I look over the current education of these professionals, it is asking a lot because they are exposed not at all to the intellectual *and* social history of their fields, to how regnant theories and practices reflected and in turn impacted on public policy about "deviant" people.

What I shall attempt in this essay is to describe certain aspects of the predeinstitutionalization era: public attitudes, professional outlooks and practices, and the organization and quality of "humane" institutions. Deinstitutionalization and its consequences are utterly incomprehensible apart from, among other things, these aspects. There are no villains in this story, unless ignorance, denial of reality, and the law of unintended consequences justify the judgment of villainy. In the confessional booth, as on the psychoanalytic couch, to understand all is to forgive all. That is very hard to do in the realm of public policy and action where whatever is said or done forever changes the lives of people, too often in negative ways. If I draw on personal-professional experience in this chapter, it is with the conviction that what I experienced was by no means atypical. I should tell you at the outset that what I learned required me to *unlearn* an indoctrination, a worldview, that was upsetting and humbling. And it took years. Unimprisoning one's self from so-called conventional wisdom is as painful as it is liberating.

There is one fact about those days with which one has to start: with few exceptions state institutions (and private ones as well) were built in the middle of nowhere. That, of course, spoke volumes about the "out of sight, out of mind" stance. There were two beliefs undergirding this stance. The first was that residents needed and would benefit from an environment protecting them from the pressures of community living; that is, they would be not only safe but cared for by people who would understand, educate, or rehabilitate them. The second belief was more explicit in regard to mentally retarded than to psychotic individuals: such individuals should be with "their own kind," on the unverbalized assumption that misery is diluted by company. No one said publicly that these institutions existed to protect communities from troubled and troubling people, as in the case of criminals. The rationale, as their charters and enabling legislation clearly stated, was in terms of the "best interests" of those requiring an institutional environment. Nothing confirmed more the validity of this altruistic rationale in the public mind than another belief: the problems of these individuals were basically biological and, therefore, these institutions had to be administered by physicians and allied personnel. The psychotic individual needed to be in a state *hospital.* Institutions for the mentally retarded were called training schools, but by practice and law they were administered by medical personnel.

A relevant story. The training school in which I worked after leaving graduate school was the product of a state commission to make recommendations about the need for a second training school in the southern part of Connecticut. They recommended building what became the Southbury Training School, which opened in the fall of 1941 several months before I arrived. The commission made another recommendation: the governor should appoint Mr. Roselle as superintendent. The medical community was up in arms. How could you appoint an educator to head up an institution whose population required medical oversight? Nowhere in the United States was such an institution not administered by a physician. The commission knew exactly what it was recommending: a redefinition based on visits to other institutions in the country and the conclusion that they were warehouses. Southbury, they said, would have revolving doors. It would have a philosophy and programs maximizing the chances that those who came in would have opportunity to return to home and community.

The opposition to the appointment was so strong that when it appeared that the governor would not appoint Mr. Roselle, the commission threatened to resign en masse. It needs to be said that in terms of insight and foresight, that commission deserves more than a footnote in the history of public institutions. Although they were responsible for building another institution, they had seen and identified almost all the factors and conditions that years later gave ammunition to those advocating deinstitutionalization. Mr. Roselle was appointed. It needs also to be said that his appointment would not have been made were it not that two of the commission members were Stanley Davies, a recognized sociologist quite sophisticated about the field, and Dr. Grover Powers, chairman of Yale's department of pediatrics, who had no peer in matters of caring and compassion for children and families.

More about Southbury later. What deserves emphasis at this point is that there is a similarity between the rationale for these institutions and that for racial segregation, more correctly, between the legal rationales of these two types of segregation. That is to say, going to a racially segregated school and being sent to an institution for mentally retarded or psychotic people had the force of law. But there was one difference that should not be overlooked. A child in a racially segregated school did not have the state as legal guardian but rather his or her parents. In the case of institutionalized mentally retarded or psychotic individuals, the state, not parents or family, was the legal guardian. You entered or left these institutions only by permission of the state, even if you left for a day.

In both instances of segregation, the attitudes, legalisms aside, powering the stance of "separate but equal" were remarkably similar. It all seemed right, natural, and proper. The commission (established in the mid thirties) did not challenge the separate-but-equal policy. What it did challenge was the morality of the political system in sanctioning institutions that made a mockery of the concept of "humane institutions." As a member of that commission said to me (he was a retired executive of the Standard Oil Company), "Every state institution is as far from family and community living as you can get. Calling them schools or hospitals is not only a travesty on language but a deceit to make people feel less guilt or pain." Another member, a retired executive of a large Hartford insurance company, told me, "Visiting institutions around the country may not have been the most appalling, upsetting experience of my life, but at the moment I can't think of a worse experience."

I could not truly appreciate what these and other members were telling me. This despite the fact that for a year before I came to Southbury, I had interned at the Worcester State Hospital, which had the reputation of being *the* outstanding public institution for psychotic individuals. From the standpoint of research and attracting psychiatric, medical, and psychological personnel of the highest caliber, it deserved its reputation. To a fledgling psychologist like me, it was the most dispiriting, frightening, soulless place in which I had ever been or that my imagination could conjure up. Not that the professional staff were insensitive, uncaring people. That was not the case. Architecturally, the state hospital was straight out of a Charles Addams cartoon. It would be incorrect to say that patients lived in poorly lit, aesthetically revolting locked wards. It would be more correct to say that they existed or languished there. They were objects, or things, or "cases."

Given that experience, why did I not appreciate what these commission members (later the board of trustees) described to me? It was certainly not because I doubted their descriptions: people herded in large congregate buildings, insufficient budgets, personnel most of whom were poorly educated and lacked any knowledge about the kinds of people for whose care they were responsible, professional personnel not distinguished by the quality of their expertise or intellectual curiosity or sense of mission or even courage to change that which they knew needed to be changed. For the most part, professional staff spent their time "administering," the chief aim of which was to avoid disruptions to institutional law and order that could bring criticism from the public or the central office of the department of mental health in the state capital.

When I say that I did not appreciate what these commission members described to me, I use the word *appreciate* in the sense of gaining *increased* valuable knowledge. On the basis of my limited experiences in public "humane institutions" (in college and graduate school), I had no reason to doubt the validity of their descriptions. To the extent that they confirmed conclusions I had come to on the basis of limited experience, my knowledge did "appreciate." But in one momentously important respect that increased knowledge had the effect of preventing me from thinking, let alone examining, the logic of the conclusions they had drawn from their observations. To explain that, I need briefly to describe the Southbury Training School.

The first time I saw the school I could not believe my eyes. The administration building had a Monticello-like quality, perched as it was on a hill overlooking a valley. The school building was tastefully colonial. And dotting the surrounding sloping hills were "cottages" that would not be out of place in the wealthiest sections of a community. Each cottage had its own kitchen, a spacious dining room containing enough tables to accommodate twenty to thirty residents, with dormitory beds on the second floor. Each cottage had its own cook and a house "mother and father." The school did not have anything resembling a large congregate-living building. Southbury was more than an architectural gem, pleasing only to the eye. It was a most creative effort to design structures that took family living seriously. Mr. Roselle, the superintendent, had formal credentials in education, but he really was a frustrated architect. In the years he served as chief consultant-planner to the commission, he was able to give full expression to his artistic interests. So, for example, Southbury had quite a greenhouse to ensure that every building contained a display of flowers. In terms of its architecture and conceptual rationale, Southbury almost instantly attracted the attention of people with an interest in or responsibility for public institutions.

Southbury was one of three state institutions that had offered me a position. First, I was interviewed by the psychiatrist-superintendent of the old state training school. The second interview was for a position in a state hospital. The third interview was at Southbury with Mr. Roselle. There was no doubt in my mind that beautiful, eye-arresting Southbury was for me. No contest. For two years

I luxuriated in the feeling that I worked in a state institution that uniquely challenged the conventional ways in which people who needed institutionalization were cared for. I was a lucky guy.

It took two years for me to begin to put into words a conclusion that allowed me to reexamine the significance of the contrast between Southbury and similar institutions and state hospitals: aside from its dramatic architecture and educational-living rationale, on what basis should one expect Southbury to outperform the traditional state institutions? Was the self-congratulatory stance of the commission and Mr. Roselle justified? Were my expectations for Southbury a reflection of my being taken in by appearances and my lack of knowledge of life in a large organization (fourteen hundred "children," several hundred employees) embedded in a state bureaucracy? Several observations and experiences, each unconnected in my mind, got connected by the end of my second year there.

The first of these experiences had two aspects: none of the residents wanted to be at Southbury; they wanted to go home. Runaways were not rare. Given the poor, disorganized, even abusive families some of the residents came from, I (and everyone else) took their desire to be home to reflect a lack of appreciation and their mental limitations. If they could not appreciate what Southbury could do for them, and that in a most comfortable, beautiful, resource-rich setting, it was face evidence that they needed Southbury! It took me a long time to understand what it meant to them to be removed from their families, from what was familiar, however unpleasant and problem producing their families had been. To many of the residents, there was truth to the saying that the worst family is to be preferred to the best institution. If that saying is extreme, it nevertheless points to a phenomenology hard for most people to comprehend, and such a comprehension was totally lacking among Southbury's staff.

The second was a type of experience that was very frequent after the school opened. It, too, had two aspects: public schools saw Southbury as an excuse to close their special classes and send their students there. More frequently, Southbury was seen by them as a placement for retarded individuals who were behavior problems. These efforts brought me into conflict with the public schools (and with some of Southbury's professional staff) because after testing these referrals, I could not honestly say they were mentally retarded. That they were academically retarded was clear, that their IQ was well below normal was no less clear, but in terms of their intellectual potential, I could not pin the label "mentally deficient" on them. I learned what "dumping" meant, a consequence of the out of sight, out of mind attitude. Slowly but surely I began to see that Southbury's "revolving door" rationale was in trouble. Once a child was placed at Southbury, the community was not going to roll out the welcome mat for him or her. The revolving door would revolve very slowly. By the end of the first two years, it had not revolved at all!

The third type of experience had obvious and subtle aspects that made a mockery of the revolving door rationale. The obvious aspect was that in selecting heads of departments and supervisory personnel, Southbury sought those with "relevant" experience, which, with few exceptions, meant institutional experience. Indeed, the rules and regulations for personnel selection were those of the state's personnel department, and Southbury had to conform to them, which meant that individuals without relevant institutional experience would have a very hard time meeting criteria employed by the state for institutional positions. In any event, with one or two exceptions, heads of departments and supervisory personnel had previous institutional experience. Despite that fact that they, like me, knew full well Southbury's revolving door rationale, their institutional backgrounds had inculcated in them the belief that residents should be returned to the community *only* after *years* of "training."

In these first two years, there were a number of cases in which I thought the individual did not have to remain in Southbury for more than a year or so. When I brought these cases up for discussion, I was, so to speak, laughed out of court. The training-rehabilitation process, I was told, takes years! Besides, in light of the families from which many came, how could you return the child to them? In the years I was at Southbury, there may have been a handful of placements: males were placed with private farmers, females as maids in homes. Those who were placed had spent a minimum of fifteen years in the old institution from which they had been transferred to spanking new Southbury.

The fourth factor contributing to my belated enlightenment is wrapped up in a question I fleetingly began to put to myself by the end of my first six months at Southbury. Given the revolving door rationale and all that implies about returning to family, neighborhood, and community, why was Southbury built in the middle of rural nowhere? It was miles from the small and large cities in which the residents had lived. There was no public transportation, and in those days many families could not afford to own a car. Indeed, there was a fair number of employees who had no cars or lived too far from their homes to make commuting possible; they had rooms in two attractive personnel buildings from which they fled on weekends. Language is revealing here. Everyone, children and employees, used the expression "on the outside" to refer to the rest of the world, a world that the children had no opportunity to see. Southbury was "inside"; the outside was far, far away. You expect to hear such labels in prison. Phenomenologically, that is the way the children and many employees experienced Southbury.

As best as I could determine, the choice of the site of the institution was political in that it reflected the power and influence of a local state senator. But I also determined that the community saw nothing wrong with the site. That you can remove a person from family and the community, place that person in the middle of rural nowhere, keep him or her there for years, and expect that after those years the individual is prepared for family and community living—the self-defeating nature of such thinking escaped recognition by the commission that was so proud of its revolving door metaphor.

The fifth factor is an instance of the "outside" impacting on the "inside." Southbury opened two months before December 7, 1941, when our country was catapulted into World War II. The impact derived from the fact that Southbury was designed on the assumption that *at least* one-third of those sent there would be "high-grade" retardates (i.e., those who were considered most "trainable"; in those days, they were literally labeled morons). For at least two years before we entered the war, the Great Depression receded as the country began to pour millions into rearming and training a larger military force. Employment became easier. With our advent into war, jobs became plentiful; indeed, there soon was a labor shortage. That explains, in large measure, why Southbury was not being sent high-grade, trainable individuals. They could find jobs, and a not inconsiderable number were accepted into the armed forces.[1]

It took two years for these factors (and others) to force me to the conclusion that Southbury was a doomed affair: the doors did not revolve; a significant number of those for whom the institution was built seemed to be nonexistent; it was apparent that within a few years Southbury would have a waiting list comprised of the most severely, neurologically impaired individuals who could not take advantage of its multifaceted educational programs and resources; and the early enthusiasm and sense of mission of the staff gave way to a lowered morale, routinization, and resignation. By the time I left, Southbury was well on the way to having most of the characteristics of the traditional institution. Tradition won over innovation.[2]

I was not the only staff member to reach such a conclusion. To make a long story short, the state's office of mental retardation began, shortly after the war, to wrestle with the problem of how to

[1]Nationally, the number of very low IQ people who were accepted for induction into the armed forces was by no means minuscule. Their numbers, roles, and performances have been described in detail in *The Uneducated* (Ginzberg and Bray, 1953). That book never received the attention it deserved, despite the fact that it exposed the invalidity of assessing problem-solving performance and intellectual potential by using scores on an intelligence test. It is a book worth reading today.

[2]I am writing this essay in 1993. Sometime in the early eighties, the condition at Southbury had worsened to the point where it was placed under the jurisdiction of courts. At the present time, plans are under way to close Southbury. The older of the two institutions was closed several years ago.

take care of the increasing waiting lists of the state's two institutions. What emerged was the "regional center plan": small residential centers in the more populated towns and cities of the state, allowing residents to be near their families and these centers to make use of community resources. I was intimately involved in the first regional center to be built. That experience told me that the regional center stood a good chance of becoming a mini-Southbury. So, when I was asked to participate in the planning of a second regional center, I implored officialdom to consider alternative ways of placing children in the community (e.g., group homes, apartments, services that would make it easier for families to keep the child at home). Indeed, we had independently determined that many parents whose children were on the waiting list would keep their child at home if certain services were available to them, such as respite care. And these alternative ways would cost far less than building and staffing a new regional center.

My pleas fell on deaf ears. Unfortunately I was right. The regional centers became traditional mini-institutions. It was in these discussions that I came to see that officialdom, whose experience and "expertise" were in and about *institutions*, simply could not entertain, let alone understand, alternatives to some kind of residential institution. When I would mention group homes, they would react with staring disbelief and would indicate that neighborhoods and communities would never accept such a program. This despite the fact that two Yale college seniors in my community psychology course decided to develop a group home and did it in a most politically sophisticated, successful way! And they did it with practically no money. They located and exploited community individuals and resources in the most creative ways. They knew the community with a depth of which officialdom in the state capital was utterly incapable.

The regional center concept was in its way a recognition of the necessity for deinstitutionalization, and this was long before "deinstitutionalization" entered common parlance. But it substituted a mini-institution for a large one. And it did so in ways that did not

224 ESSAYS ON PSYCHOLOGY

involve communities (i.e., the regional centers were in but not of the communities). I cannot deny that the regional centers represented an advance in the care of their residents. But precisely because they were encapsulated sites having "beds," they were perceived both by their staffs and the communities as *the* place to which children should be sent.

That perception, of course, did little or nothing to alter the out of sight, out of mind community stance. For example, I tried to get officialdom to reserve at least two beds for respite care in each center, that is, to enable families, whether in a crisis or not, to send their child for one or several days to live in the center. As I indicated earlier, more than a few families did not want their child living permanently away from them, but they wanted to feel that there was a place to which they could safely send their child for one or several days, to give the family a "breather" or because of special circumstances. My plea went nowhere because in short order all beds were occupied. The possibility that a couple of beds might not always be used did not sit well with officialdom. If there is a bed, it must *always* be used. It never entered the minds of officialdom that respite care would reduce the pressure for long-term placement.

It is instructive here to recall that the 1965 Medicare legislation gave rise to the construction of thousands of nursing homes. Undergirding this legislation was the assumption that families caring for their aged, dependent, frail, or ailing parents were carrying a too heavy personal and financial burden and wished that there were nursing homes to which these parents could be sent. There was truth to that assumption, but it was not the whole truth. It took years (and nursing home scandals) before it was recognized that a fair number of nursing home–eligible people could remain in the community if there were appropriate supportive services and that not all families were ready to "dump" their parents into a nursing home. But that possibility did not inform the debate leading to the 1965 legislation. The nursing home would be *there*—use it! There were no alternatives. Every financial incentive in that legislation was intended to facilitate placement in a nursing home.

Another instructive example. Are there families who would be willing to serve as a long-term foster home placement for *severely* impaired mentally handicapped children who would always need the closest kind of care and supervision (e.g., children with cerebral palsy, spina bifida), the kinds of children for whom institutionalization was always considered the *only* appropriate placement? That question never crossed my mind or that of anyone else whom I knew. Why on earth would a family willingly assume such a burden? That fact is, as I later learned, that beginning in the late fifties or early sixties, a private organization was created precisely to seek long-term foster home placements for these kinds of almost totally dependent children.

A student of mine, Elizabeth Scarf Stone, interviewed these families for her doctoral dissertation. Reading that dissertation is an antidote to feelings of pessimism and cynicism about caring and compassion in people, some people, in our communities. What were some of the characteristics of these families? Most of them had one or more "normal" children of their own; they were stable, middle-class families; many of them were religious; all of them had a sense of obligation to give of themselves to these kinds of children who would ordinarily be consigned to spend their lives in an institution. They knew the responsibility they were assuming, and they assumed it willingly. No less important, they discharged their mission with amazing aplomb and success. Indeed, some of the families were seeking to overcome legal barriers to adopting such children!

I confess that I was humbled by this study because however strongly and articulately I fought against the proinstitutional (large or small) mind-set of officialdom, and for a better comprehension and use of community people and resources, it never occurred to me that placements of these kinds of children in these kinds of families were possible or, if possible, could be implemented successfully. When I would present my position, I invariably would be asked, "Are you denying, in light of your experience at Southbury, that institutions are not necessary for the profoundly mentally retarded, physically, neurologically impaired children who require constant care?" Up until Dr. Stone's study, I could not deny that necessity. Her study taught me that at least some of these children did not need to be warehoused. It taught me one other thing: the fact that an institution exists short-circuits the capacity to come up with bold and creative alternatives to institutionalization.

If it taught me that, it also confirmed in spades my belief that when people, professionals especially, affirm their support for a "community orientation," they have the most superficial understanding of the varieties of individuals and groups the community possesses, of how those varieties, some of them at least, have "assets" that can be utilized to help other individuals in mutually rewarding ways. Today we are used to hearing that "the community should be represented in development of any public policy that will, directly or indirectly, have consequences for a community." I agree. But far too often those words assume that in regard to a particular policy or problem, individuals in the community are homogeneous in terms of the values, ideas, and the willingness to act and contribute to the resolution of the particular problem. To policy makers, that assumption has one (unverbalized) virtue: it reduces to nil the necessity for thinking about and locating the actual or potential assets possessed by individuals and groups, assets relevant to a particular problem, such as how can we care for profoundly disabled people other than by institutionalizing them.

I have long been fascinated by how difficult it is when faced with a problem deliberately to force oneself seriously to determine the universe of alternatives available to you (me), that is, to go beyond the conventional wisdom or practice. Let me again illustrate this point by describing an experience I had over thirty years ago. The following is what I wrote about the experience (Sarason, Zitnay, and Grossman, 1972).

It is appropriate to ask a deceptively simple question: how do we understand why, in this country, at least, the pattern of residential care has been so consistent, i.e., a relatively large number of children are housed in a place staffed by a wide variety of professional and nonprofessional personnel? This is even true in a state like Connecticut where they have decentralized the state into regions in each of which there is a regional center. In each regional center there are residential facilities, and although the number of residents is far fewer than in the usual monstrous institutions, it is still true that the residents are in that regional center. It seems, unfortunately, to be the case that a large part of the answer to the question involves the failure explicitly and systematically to list and evaluate the universe of alternatives in regard to residential care.

There is more involved here than the weight of tradition, although that is an important factor. What I have been impressed by is that even in instances where the conditions for innovation were ripe, those who were responsible for creating the settings did not examine the alternative ways one could view and implement residential care. It is ironic that in planning buildings these same people can spend vast amounts of time creatively examining the alternatives for design and allocation of space, but fail to act and think similarly in regards to the alternatives to housing the children in one locale. Let me illustrate my point by relating the following experiences: On four occasions I had the opportunity to ask the following question of a group of individuals who either had or would have responsibility for creating an institution for mentally retarded children: *"What if you were given the responsibility to develop residential facilities with the restrictions that they could not be on 'institutional land,' no one of them could house more than 12 individuals, and no new buildings could be erected?"* The following, in chronological order, were the major reactions of the different groups.

1. Initially the groups responded with consternation, puzzlement, and curiosity. For some members of each of the groups, the question seemed to produce a blank mind, but for

others it seemed as if the question quickly brought to the surface all their dissatisfactions with the usual mode of residential care and stimulated consideration of alternatives.

2. In the early stages of discussion, the chief stumbling block was the restriction that "no new buildings could be erected." I should say that throughout the discussions I adopted a relatively nondirective approach and tried only to answer directly questions which would clarify the meaning of the initial question. For example, when asked if one could remodel existing structures, I indicated that this was, of course, permissible. When I was asked if there was any restriction as to where these houses or small buildings could be bought and rented, I said there were no such restrictions. The point deserving emphasis is that many individuals struggled for some time until they realized that there was no one way to act and think but rather that there was a potentially large universe of alternatives for action from which they could choose. In addition, as some individuals came to see, it was not necessary to choose only one alternative, i.e., one could and should proceed in different ways at the same time.

3. Midway in the meeting the behavior of the members began to change in rather dramatic ways. Whereas before most were hesitant, deliberate, and cautious in their remarks, they now seemed to respond as if they were engaged in an exciting, intellectual game in which one possibility led to thinking about other possibilities, and what at first seemed to be unrelated were then seen as crucially related. Faced with the task of creating settings they truly began to think and talk creatively.

4. *In two of the groups—and for reasons I cannot wholly account for—a plan for residential care evolved which brought together the renovation of substandard housing, training programs for nonprofessional personnel, volunteer services, and neighborhood involvement and responsibility. In short, these two groups were no longer dealing with mental retardation in its narrow*

aspects but in the context of some of the most crucial aspects of what has been termed the urban crisis.

One of the more experienced superintendents pointed out to his group that in the plan they had discussed "we are meeting more social problems, and providing more meaningful service to children and their families, at far less money than we are now spending." It was indeed remarkable how intellectually fertile the discussions in these two groups were. For example, one of the group members made the point that if these small housing units were strategically placed around our high schools they could be used by the schools in at least three ways: for educating these youngsters about mental retardation, for purposes of training child-care workers, and for enlisting volunteers for recreational and other purposes. Another group member, in the context of a discussion about food preparation in these small units, maintained that if neighborhood participation and responsibility were taken seriously, food preparation and feeding could be handled on a volunteer basis, besides which the food would probably taste better. In my opinion, the creative thinking and planning that went on in these two groups were, in part, a consequence of a process which permitted the members to think not only in terms of the retarded child but in the context of pressing urban problems which ordinarily are not viewed in relation to the field of mental retardation.

It is, of course, significant that the members could come up with approaches to residential care which they had not considered before and which deserve the most serious consideration. But what I consider of greater general significance is the fact that in the usual ways in which such settings are created the universe of alternatives is never described or thought through. It is my opinion that research on how settings are created will ultimately have a more beneficial impact on the quality and varieties of residential care than any other single

thing we might do. Up to now we have focussed research on
the recipients of residential care. I am suggesting that we will
learn a great deal about the recipients by turning our attention to the values, assumptions, and thought processes of
those who plan for the recipients. [p. 30]

When in the field of mental retardation deinstitutionalization
picked up steam, the thinking of the policy makers was parochial
in the extreme. Frequently, much too frequently, they were under
court pressure to reduce the number of residents in the large state
institutions. And if legal pressure was absent, economic pressures
to reduce spending played a significant role so that, for example, in
Connecticut and elsewhere, more than a few residents in these
institutions were for all practical purposes dumped into nursing
homes, which thereby transferred costs to the federal government
via existing social security legislation. I am reluctant to call this
moral chicanery because that implies that officialdom knew there
were better alternatives but for purely fiscal reasons chose to ignore
them. As best as I could determine, officialdom simply did not know
how to think other than in terms of the institutional setting. And
that is the point of this essay: *those responsible for deinstitutionalizing
the state's institutions had not the foggiest idea of what a community orientation meant or could mean, and if they had been capable of grasping
the idea, as one or two did, all were totally unsophisticated about how to
approach communities, the preparatory actions one needed to take, how
to develop constituencies, and what constitutes a realistic time perspective, which should never be confused with the single-year, fiscal perspective of the state legislature.* Deinstitutionalization was a doomed affair,
if only because those overseeing it (planning for it in offices in the
state capital is not oversight, unless flying blind is oversight) were
worse than amateurs in their understanding of what a community
is, the *predictable* problems they would encounter, and the steps they
should take to overcome or prevent or dilute the strength of these
obstacles. Their expertise was about institutions, which rendered
them incapable of comprehending action in complex communities.

They did not view the community as having assets they should locate and exploit; communities were their enemy, communities had caused the problem by dumping children into the state institutions, and it was unrealistic in the extreme to expect other than trouble and defeat from attempts to gain community acceptance and support. With attitudes like that, you never have to worry about whether you will fail. Failure is guaranteed. After many years of failure, it appears today that some lessons were learned, but at the expense of those who were supposed to be helped. Some people do overcome or learn to challenge conventional wisdom and practice. I urge the reader to read *Crossing the River* (Schwartz, 1992).

Is the story different in the case of our state mental hospitals? Psychotic and mentally retarded people are very different populations; they are viewed by society in different ways; and they require different modes of caring and treatment, modes that, in the case of psychotics, have varied considerably over the decades (e.g., electric shock treatment, injection of metrazol and other drugs, frontal lobotomy, different types of psychological therapies). However these populations differed, the institutions to which they were sent were very similar. Let me list some of these similarities.

1. In general, both types of institutions were warehouses. In fact, mental hospitals tended to have much larger populations. It was by no means rare for the mental hospital to house four or five or more thousand people, with the result, of course, that individual case and treatment were for all practical purposes nonexistent.

2. Professionals who took positions in either type of institution were rendered suspect by their professional communities. Why would any self-respecting professional seek to work in settings in which the utilization of their skills and their obligation to help and treat individuals obviously were next to impossible to realize? If you took a position there, you were regarded as mediocre (or worse), or it was assumed you wanted to be an administrator, or you had not been able to make it on the "outside," or you wanted to spend your remaining years in the comfortable residences provided the profes-

sional staff. In those predeinstitutionalization days, it was hard to fill professional positions.

3. However you define "care," the brute fact was that for most of each day patients were in the care of attendants, a transient and the most poorly paid population who literally had no preparation whatever for what they were doing. Nothing was ever done to enlarge their understanding of patients. In practice they were like prison guards, each of whom carried a chain of heavy keys to lock and unlock the doors of the closed wards. Their job was not to "care" but to keep the peace.

4. Each institution was bureaucratically organized, and the larger the institution, the more administratively layered it was. On paper the chains of responsibility were clear. In practice these settings were riddled by conflicts and ambiguities about who was responsible for whom and what. What may be termed "organizational craziness" was standard fare in conversations. In addition, the institution was overseen and controlled by a state department that was neither simply organized or small. Again, in practice the institution dealt with more than one department. Communication problems were frequent, especially in larger states. Institutional personnel tended to regard the department in the state capitol as insensitive, niggardly, arbitrary, and uncomprehending.

In the case of state hospitals, three factors contributed to the decision to proceed with deinstitutionalization. We are used to hearing that the development of new, more effective drugs was the crucial factor. That it was important goes without saying, although the effectiveness of the new drugs was overplayed just as their long-term effects were downplayed. No less important was the recognition that the hospitals were scandalously overcrowded and could not accommodate new patients. The third factor was economic: institutional costs were rising, and building new hospitals involved sums of money that neither legislators nor governors could or would expend. Building, staffing, and maintaining a hospital would run into many millions of dollars. The new psychoactive drugs were a ready answer to escalating budgets and the seemingly inexorable demand for more beds and buildings.

Deinstitutionalizing the state hospitals has been a moral, community catastrophe. Although in some states lessons have been learned, for at least three decades after deinstitutionalization began, countless people were dumped and harmed, and every negative stereotype of a state hospital patient was reinforced. This is by no means explained by economic factors and the appearance of new drugs. The failure of deinstitutionalization reflects other long-standing characteristics of the states' mental health system.

Before describing (again) these characteristics, let me substitute an imaginary script in place of the one played out in reality. Imagine that in those early years after World War II, state hospitals were not inhumanly overcrowded, economic pressures were weak or nonexistent, and the discoverers of the new drugs convince the policy makers that a significant number of patients could be sent back to the community. The policy makers agree, and they proceed with deinstitutionalization. Would the results have been other than what in reality happened? The answer is no because the discoverers of drugs, the policy makers, and institutional personnel had the most superficial understanding of what "return to the community" would and should require if patients stood a chance of being integrated in their communities.

Policy makers in the state capitol were rendered, by past experience, incapable of seriously thinking through the phenomenology of the returning patients, of their families, and of other community individuals and groups. They were incapable of seeing the obvious: unless a variety of options for community placement were developed, unless a variety of supportive services were available in the community, unless accepting and supportive constituencies were developed in the community, unless a realistic time perspective to accomplish these kinds of actions was adopted and appropriate budgets for these actions were made available—absent these actions, failure was likely, and, in the case of those patients who had spent several years or more in the hospital, failure was guaranteed.

Readers who have had no experience with state hospitals (or training schools) will have difficulty comprehending how self-absorbed these institutions were, how preoccupied both staff and patients were with what goes in the institutional setting. It was as if the institution was the world. It was a world of conflict, rivalries, police actions, blame assignment, rumors and gossip, informal and formal power struggles, and pitifully few occasions for personal or professional satisfaction, let alone growth. Everyone had a picture of what the institution should be, and everyone ended up disillusioned. They were as prepared to deal with communities as I am to go to the moon. I am being descriptive, not judgmental. They had become totally socialized in a total institution. Their overarching task was to adjust patients to life in the institution. When my wife and I left Southbury, we looked at each other and exclaimed, "We are free." Free from an encapsulated social and professional life that, to say the least, was inexorably confining and stultifying.

I said earlier that today it appears that there are some in officialdom who have learned something from the deinstitutionalization debacle. I know that this is the case in Connecticut where several years ago Dr. Albert Solnit, an internationally respected child psychiatrist and analyst with no institutional experience, became commissioner of mental health. I know of no other commissioner who came to his or her position with as much experience in dealing with communities. When I observe the programs he has initiated, I have two reactions: one is respect for and pride in what he is attempting to do, and the other is regret that those in earlier days who were gung ho for deinstitutionalization were completely incapable of his way of thinking even though there were some external critics, voices in the wilderness, who pointed out to them the complexities that "return to the community" implied and required.

It is apparently a kind of law that a society will move in the right direction only after a catastrophe has illuminated the consequences of inaction or the absence of preventive thinking. It took the Great Depression to bring about social security legislation as well as changes in the banking system and the securities arena. It took Pearl Harbor to wake people up to the futility of dealing with dynamic dictatorships. It took an escalating juvenile delinquency and deteriorating urban cities for the government to give up its hands-off stance. Following the Supreme Court's 1954 desegregation decision, it took the murders of civil rights activists, semi-insurrections, and riots to stimulate civil rights legislation. It took years for the society to recognize the plight and increasing numbers of older citizens and pass the Medicare legislation. And it took even longer to recognize that our health nonsystem was mammothly counterproductive on health *and* moral equity grounds. And it took decades for people to recognize that our "humane" public institutions (training schools, state hospitals, nursing homes) contributed to many instances of people's inhumanity to people.

11

The Blind Spot in the Health Care Nonsystem

It was not until 1993 that there was unanimous agreement about the necessity and justice of universal health insurance. Thus began the debate about means and ends: What would be the most effective and efficient means to achieve that end? That question explicitly assumed that in addition to universality of coverage, the means employed would in no way be at the expense of quality care. Indeed, the most frequent words in the ongoing debate have been *quality care*, words uttered in self-congratulatory terms as if it was self-evident that everyone knew two things: what quality care meant and that those who had the good fortune to have health insurance had enjoyed quality care. I have seriously followed the debate, and I have yet to read or hear anybody discuss or define quality care. The reason for the absence of discussion is that it is considered self-evident, therefore not in need of elaboration, that quality care refers to the *outcomes* of medical actions. If your appendix has been successfully removed, it is evident that you received quality care. If the treatment of a cancerous condition has caused a significant reduction or elimination of symptoms, it says something significant about quality care. If a broken limb has been reset and within a period of weeks or months you can use it in normal fashion, you say that you enjoyed a successful outcome. If after open-heart surgery you are able to resume activity, even jog and play golf or tennis, it is obvious you received quality care.

But what if the patient shows little or no improvement in his or her condition? Or what if the patient died? We are then provided with several answers. One is that current medical knowledge is too incomplete for successfully treating certain illnesses but that all that could and should have been done was tried. If the outcome was not successful, the treatment was the best available. No doubt in the future research will come up with knowledge making for successful outcomes. The second answer is that physicians differ widely in their knowledge and skill, a regrettable fact of life that the medical community is obliged to try to remedy. A variant of this answer is that the rate of successful outcomes for some of our major illnesses differs rather widely among hospitals, a statistic suggesting that unsuccessful outcomes may not be due only to the inadequate skill of a physician; that is, auxiliary personnel may play an adverse role.

The third answer is malpractice: the physician, or auxiliary personnel, or the hospital administration were simply negligent in their failure to use available and empirically verified knowledge. It is no secret that malpractice suits have two sources: one is based on what may be termed technical grounds, and the other derives from anger, resentment, fury in patients in regard to how they were treated as people, and what they should have been told and were not. Frequently, the two sources are related in the minds of those who sue, although that may not be discernible in legal briefs. The dramatic rise in malpractice suits in recent decades has been blamed, by the medical community at least, on greedy lawyers and ignorant, no less greedy patients. There probably is a kernel of truth to such blame assignment, but that by no means explains the frequency and strength of anger so many people have toward physicians, hospitals, and auxiliary personnel. If there is any complaint voiced by the medical community among themselves, it concerns a perceived hostile, uncooperative patient population that no longer holds that community in as high esteem as in earlier decades. I shall return to this complaint later in this chapter. What I wish to do now is to illustrate the limitations of the criterion of successful outcomes.

The term *robber baron* refers to those industrialists and financiers of the nineteenth century who accumulated fortunes at the expense of workers and others. The robber barons' practices were not always illegal; they were "doing their thing" regardless of its adverse consequences for others. From their standpoint, they were successful, and not infrequently their successes were greeted both with envy and admiration. In the main, however, the means by which those successes were achieved were considered unfair, and immoral and remedial legislation was enacted. Accumulating fortunes as an end could not be justified by means that were life-destroying for others. As an end the accumulation of fortunes was a justifiable effort quite compatible with American entrepreneurial individualism. But if the means for such accumulation meant the immoral exploitation of others, if they disregarded the health of others, if it means plunging and keeping others in a grinding, degrading poverty, then the successful outcome should not be tolerated. The successful outcome had to be judged by the means employed.

For a long time in our history, child labor was by no means frowned upon; many people depended on child labor for their "success." In Lowell, Massachusetts, the National Park Service took over some of the old textile producing mills—ghoulish-looking stone buildings—that in the nineteenth century were owned by people who made large fortunes, people of Yankee stock, moral pillars of their community, and recognized as those deserving praise and emulation. Lowell, Lawrence, Haverhill, and New Bedford were only some of the sites of this industry. Aside from being able to see what these mills were like, today's visitor to the Lowell site can watch a slide show that details how very young girls in England and Ireland were enticed to emigrate and work in the mills, the places in which they lived, and the restrictions placed on what they could do, when, and where. They were, for all practical purposes, indentured servants, a notch or two above slaves. You come away from the slide presentation troubled, if not aghast, by the acceptance of unjustified means for obtaining "successful" ends.

Examples from the long past are legion. Let us take a more recent example. It concerns "informed consent." What do you owe human beings who serve as subjects in your research or who will undergo a medical-surgical procedure you will perform? Until a couple of decades ago, the answer was that you owed them your good will, your knowledge and skill, your adherence to science and its methodologies. You did *not* owe them, you did not have to communicate to them, the probability of a successful outcome, the kinds of sequelae you should expect, whether you were an experimental or control subject, or that any aspect of decision making was a right you could exercise. As patient or research subject, your job was to trust someone else to do nothing potentially inimical to your psychological or bodily health. The most egregious example of deception and moral irresponsibility was the study of the efficacy of a new medication for the treatment of syphilis during the 1930s. There was an experimental group who received the medication and a control that did not. The control group was comprised of blacks; the experimental group was white. Enough said.

A personal experience is relevant here. It concerns Stanley Milgram's very well known study of obedience to authority. In that study, a subject was required to increase by steps the amount of electric current delivered to another person visible through a one-way window. In reality there was no electric current, although the gyrations and actions of the person visible through the window were quite realistic. A large percentage of the subjects obeyed the injunction to step up the current. Well, one night around 9:30 P.M. I received a call from a city alderman who had just served as a subject. He was, to indulge understatement, so troubled by his experience of causing pain to another person that he called a friend of his who was a psychologist to vent his anger. That friend was a friend of mine, and she suggested that in light of the fact that Milgram and I were in the same department, he should call me. Frankly, I do not recall (it was thirty or so years ago) what I said to the alderman, except that I would look into the matter. The next day I went to the chairman of our department (Claude Buxton) and told him the story. Apparently he had been concerned about Milgram's procedure and had insisted that he debrief each subject immediately after his participation, which in the case of the alderman he had not done. I relate this story to make the point that this alderman had been very upset by the experience. He thought he was participating in a study that would contribute to knowledge, a desirable end, but not in a study the means of which required injuring another person. If you read the research literature of that time, you come to two conclusions: Milgram's means were by no means atypical, and the willingness to deceive came easy to researchers for whom the end justified the means.

Another personal experience was in 1941–42 when, as a psychology intern at Worcester State Hospital, I observed patients undergoing electric shock therapy. Let me say right off that the psychiatrists were well-intentioned people seeking a means to alter positively the psychotic mind. Having said that, I must go on to say that they had no qualms about the means they were employing. In the name of scientific research, they felt justified in employing such means even though they had no basis for believing that such means would have other than short-term consequences. Having watched the assembly-line-like lineup of patients, each of whom was securely strapped to contain convulsions, each of whom was in a daze for days, and some of whom ended up with fractured bones and more, I had two reactions: I got sick to my stomach, and I was amazed, even envious, of the aplomb of the psychiatrists. I regarded myself as chickenhearted and the psychiatrists as courageous pioneers, even though in an inchoate way I knew something was morally wrong somewhere. Their ends were unassailable, but I could not say that for the means employed. Informed consent? From neither the patients nor their families was anything resembling informed consent obtained. Doctor knew best—do not ask any questions!

It took me a couple of years to realize that what I have described here pales before the fact that to the medical staff, these patients were not people but objects. Before, during, and after shock treatment, the relationship between physician and patient was impersonal. My observations of shock treatment were but extreme examples of what were characteristics of the transient, barely personal patient-doctor interactions generally in the hospital. I say transient because psychiatrists did not work in the wards—they *visited* them. Nurses and attendants "took care of" patients. This and more is well depicted in the film *One Flew over the Cuckoo's Nest*. If shock treatment was destabilizing, so was the ecology and staffing of wards.

I have no doubt that some patients were helped by shock treatment. But such successful outcomes are not compelling justification for the means employed. If nothing succeeds like success, it is also the case that nothing is more dangerous than success that ignores or grossly oversimplifies the means-ends dilemmas. To ignore them is to take a giant step down the slippery slope to an unintended, generalized immorality, at worst, and a gross insensitivity, at best.

Let us return to the current debate on health care reform in which the words *quality care* refer to the outcomes of health services (i.e., to the ends those services seek). What can be said about the means? What can be said about what patients experience before there is an outcome? And by *means* I refer to the quality of psychological care patients experience in their interactions with medical personnel, whether before or after a particular course of treatment. To illustrate the issues involved I shall use personal experience (as well as those of others). Lest I be accused of unfairly indulging subjectivity, I should emphasize that my conclusions are in every respect confirmed in the form of reports by medical school educators, today and in the past. More about those reports later, the conclusions of which are stated in general terms and need here to be preceded by concrete examples.

I came to visit my mother in her hospital room a week after she had been operated on for lymphatic cancer, a major site of which was behind the thyroid gland. Speech was impossible for her, because of both the surgery and an emergency tracheotomy two days later. We had been told that there might be temporary interference with speech. When I entered her room, she was crying and visibly agitated. I called the nurse, who could offer no explanation. Finally, my mother indicated that she wanted pencil and paper. The message she wrote said that, just before I had arrived, the surgeon had appeared, accompanied by several interns and residents. He explained to his younger colleagues my mother's condition, the type of surgery that had been performed, and that it had been necessary to sever several major vocal chords, following which he and the others left the room. That was how my mother found out that she would never talk above a whisper.

A second anecdote involved me as a patient. I had to go through an hour-and-a-half procedure that continuously "filmed" the activity of my heart. It was a painless, indeed fascinating, experience. Fascination aside, I was anxious about what the procedure would indicate. That was a Wednesday morning. I was told that it would take one or two days for the computer analysis of the filmed record and results to be placed in the hands of the cardiologist. Having heard nothing by the next Tuesday morning, I phoned the cardiologist's office and was told by the nurse, "Didn't they phone to tell you that there had been a malfunction in the computer and that another procedure would be necessary?" Angry, I called the radiologist's office and was told that they had called my home but no one had answered. Why, I asked, did they not call my office, the number for which I had given them? And why did they not try to get me over the weekend? I should also add that in the several different radiological procedures that were done, I never saw the radiologist, but I assume that he or she or they existed.

Two more anecdotes. Minutes after a woman delivered her child, still groggy and dazed from the experience, the mother was told that her child had mongolism (Down's syndrome). The second instance is that of a mother who had come for the first time to a pediatric clinic a few weeks after delivery. In the hall she met her doctor, who, in the process of saying hello and continuing down the hall, told her that her child was mentally retarded. Both instances took place in a prestigious medical center in 1976. Having been intimately involved in the field of mental retardation for over forty years, I can assure the reader that these instances are only somewhat extreme.

Another instance concerns the film version of *One Flew over the Cuckoo's Nest*. As I was viewing the film, I found myself caught between two strongly conflicting reactions. On the one hand, I was gripped by the artistry with which the struggle between McMurphy and the hospital in general, and Miss Ratched in particular, was developed. I indulged my disdain, indeed hatred, of nurse Ratched and my somewhat grudging admiration and respect for antihero McMurphy. I reacted internally with violence to the violence to which this patient was subjected. I have had enough experience with mental institutions to know that what Dorothea Dix described to the Massachusetts legislature in 1848, what Dr. Burton Blatt described to the same legislature in 1968, and what Dr. George Albee wrote in reaction to Frederic Wiseman's state hospital film, *Titicut Follies*, is well encapsulated in *One Flew over the Cuckoo's Nest*. (The reader should consult Blatt's [1970] book *Exodus from Pandemonium*, written after a stint as deputy commissioner in Massachusetts's Department of Mental Health.)

What I shall now report is based on *Parents Speak Out*, by Turnbull and Turnbull (1979), who are themselves parents of a retarded individual. One of the chapters is by Dr. Phillip Roos, a psychologist who, before becoming a parent of a retarded child, had written and lectured on parental reactions to such a situation. The first problem he discusses centers around the fact that the pediatrician, in contrast to Dr. Roos and his wife, did not feel that there was anything wrong with their child.

Clinging stubbornly to the conclusion that our daughter was "probably just fine," our pediatrician next referred us to a neurologist. Since this worthy was a consultant to the large state institution of which I was the superintendent, I felt confident that he would immediately recognize the obvious signs of severe retardation in our child. Imagine my consternation when, after failing to accomplish even a funduscopic (vision) examination on Val due to her extreme hyperactivity, the learned consultant cast a baleful eye on my wife and me and informed us that the child was quite normal. On the other hand, he continued, her parents were obviously neurotically anxious, and he would prescribe tranquilizers for us. I had suddenly been demoted from the role of a professional to that of "the parent as patient": the assumption by some professionals that parents of a retarded child are emotionally maladjusted and are prime candidates for counseling, psychotherapy, or tranquilizers. My attempts to point out the many indications of development delays and neurological disturbances were categorically dismissed as manifestations of my "emotional problems." I was witnessing another captivating professional reaction—the "deaf ear syndrome": the attitude on the part of some professionals that parents are complete ignoramuses so that any conclusion they reach regarding their own child is categorically ignored. Later I found that suggestions I would make regarding my own child would be totally dismissed by some professionals, while these same suggestions made as a professional about other children would be cherished by my colleagues as professional pearls of wisdom. Parenthetically, when I wrote to the neurologist years later to inform him that Val's condition had been clearly diagnosed as severe mental retardation and that she had been institutionalized, he did not reply. [pp. 14–15]

I do not present this excerpt to make the point that physicians make errors in diagnosis. They do, of course, and this happens all too frequently in regard to mental retardation. The purpose of this excerpt is to illustrate an even more frequent phenomenon: the physician's uncaring, uncompassionate attitude toward parents. For the sake of argument, let us assume that Dr. Roos and his wife were flagrantly "emotionally maladjusted" and in need of tranquilizers and psychotherapy. Does that in any way justify the neurologist's blunderbuss attack on the parents? Does it justify literally adding insult to injury? Does it justify confusing telling the truth with being helpful? What is at issue here is not a technical problem—how to communicate the diagnosis. What is at issue here is one's comprehension of the meanings that parents will attach to information that is inevitably upsetting and disorganizing. And by *comprehension* I mean that almost unreflective sense that one accepts, appreciates, and is prepared for the consequences of the fact that what parents need at the moment is caring and compassionate behavior. That does not mean that you avoid telling the truth as you see it; it does mean that you strive to express in words and action that what the parents are thinking and feeling is understandable to you, that, if you were in their place, you would feel as they do. To accept and appreciate what parents think and feel is not only to give them what they most need at that time; it is the beginning of a process whose goal is to intertwine two worlds: that of the parents and that of the clinician. To put it negatively, the goal is to avoid the feeling in clinician and parents that they are strangers to each other.

The following excerpt is from Burke's chapter in the Turnbulls' (1979) book:

When Becky was one year old, we moved to Gainesville, Florida. Our pediatrician in Billings had sent a letter of referral to Shands Hospital at the University of Florida. Our first visit to this large teaching hospital for Becky to be examined by the pediatric cardiologist and another, later visit to the same place for an examination by the pediatric neurologist are among my worst memories.

We arrived at the hospital at 8:00 A.M. and spent the whole day there. I filled out pages and pages of forms and questionnaires as I juggled my wiggly daughter. We were sent from this lab to that with instructions to "go to the third floor, turn left at the desk, go down three doors, turn right, and hand these cards and this form to the girl at the desk there," etc.

About 10:30 A.M. we were furnished with all the lab tests and were told to return to the pediatric cardiology clinic. There we were placed in a small examining room and I was told to undress Becky again and wait for the doctor. At 12:30 I went out to the desk and asked the nurse if we could go and get some lunch. They assured me that the doctor would come soon. A little later, after Becky had drunk several bottles of water (I had brought only one bottle of juice for her) and wet all the diapers I had brought for her, I asked the nurse to hold Becky for me for a minute. I couldn't lay her on the table or the chair because she'd fall and the floor was too cold to put her there. The problem was that I had to go to the bathroom and I didn't think I could manage it with Becky in my arms. The nurse grudgingly agreed but insisted I must be back in one minute. This episode increased my already rising feelings of anxiety and helplessness in the cold, impersonal place.

About 1:30 the resident physician came in and listened to Becky's chest and asked me some questions. He mentioned that she had a heart murmur. My fear and nervousness increased. At 3:00 the cardiologist came in and examined my sleeping daughter. She called the resident and asked him to listen to Becky's heart again and said "Where's the murmur now?" I hoped she was the one who was right.

After the cardiologist finished examining Becky, she told me that she had a normal EKG and her heart was a little enlarged which she assumed was the result of her earlier problems. She said that whatever problems Becky had had at birth had apparently corrected themselves. She advised us to return in one year for another checkup.

Then I asked her about Becky's motor development. She was over a year old and still couldn't sit up or crawl. I pointed out how stiff her legs were and how she stood on tiptoe when I stood her up. I explained that I had asked our family doctor about this and that he had told me that many children walk on their tiptoes when they are first learning to walk. She said, "I don't deal with legs, only with hearts, but if you are concerned about this, why don't you make an appointment with pediatric neurology? They are the ones who would deal with this sort of thing." She assumed that we could return the following week for such an appointment. She went out to the desk and said to the receptionist, "Please make an appointment for Mrs. Burke with pediatric neurology for next week." The receptionist laughed and said that the earliest appointment available would be in about eight weeks, so we took the earliest possible appointment.

From the vantage point of several years later, I am utterly unable to believe that the cardiologist did not know, or at least suspect what the problem was. I guess she didn't see any point in telling me that it was indeed an indication of a serious problem. By saying what she did, she avoided all discussion. It was frustrating for me to have to wait for an answer to that fearsome question, what is wrong? I think now that it is so painful to be the bearer of such dreadful news (that a child may have a permanent handicap condition) that physicians avoid any discussion of this sort whenever possible.
[pp. 86–87]

Fairness requires that I state that the book *Parents Speak Out* is not a catalogue of horrors in which parents do nothing but vent their spleen at clinicians seemingly devoid of the ability to be caring and compassionate. Needless to say, although clinicians do not come up smelling like roses, these highly educated and articulate parents distinguish for the reader the difference between caring and uncaring clinicians and settings. However much the accounts of these parents-contributors differ in details and emphasis, each of them criticizes the frequency with which caring and compassion is

absent from clinician behavior, and each emphasizes the inadequacies of the training of clinicians.

There is a problem in drawing conclusions from the book, and,
rather than state the problem, I will illustrate it by analogy to
another frequent medical situation: the individual with cancer. One
of my graduate students was married to a locally well known and
highly respected cancer specialist. What was remarkable about this
physician was the gulf he experienced between the interpersonal
support he gave to patients and what he wanted to give but felt he
did not know how to give. He did not blame external factors. It was
his problem, and the solution somehow had to come from within
him. He was also a specialist in the inadequacies of his medical
training for dealing with the social-familial-psychological consequences of learning that one had a cancerous condition. The reader
does not have to perform a great leap of faith to assume that Dr.
Leonard Farber was a caring and compassionate person who was not
satisfied with how well his actions reflected these motives. The
three of us discussed the issues and decided that it would be fruitful
if we could make direct observations of his transactions with his
patients. We worked out a simple observational schedule, permission for his wife (my student) to be present at examinations was
obtained from patients, and observations were made of all patients
who had appointments during a particular week. The most striking
finding had to do with the amount of time devoted to a patient.
Those patients who, like parents-contributors in the Turnbull book,
were highly educated people received twice as much time with Dr.
Farber as did those with a high school education or less; furthermore, the former far more than the latter asked questions and
received answers.

The reason I refer to this unpublished study is to suggest that
the level and quality of caring and compassionate behavior among
the clinicians with whom parents of retarded individuals interact
may be *overstated* in the Turnbulls' (1979) book. The parents in the
book, as is clear from reading it, were or became very assertive peo-

ple in response to the insensitivities they encountered. Most parents of retarded individuals, especially as one goes down the social class scale, retreat from these encounters further into their private worlds of discouragement and despair.

Parents Speak Out (Turnbull and Turnbull, 1979) is an instance of a genre of publications in which a family member expresses frustration and outrage deriving from experiences with diverse kinds of clinicians, mostly physicians, and the settings of which they are a part. There has been a veritable explosion of these publications in the post–World War II era. Mental retardation, autism, alcoholism, psychosis, learning disabilities, cardiac conditions, terminal illnesses, geriatric conditions—in regard to these and other conditions, some family members have been impelled to resort to print to describe, among other things, the percolating consequences of clinical behavior seemingly devoid of caring and compassion. When, today and in the past, medical educators cyclically bemoan the dilution of caring and compassionate feeling and action in physicians, they are not making a mountain out of a molehill. But their critiques apply to more than the medical clinician. And, I hasten to add, and as the report of the medical educators so clearly states, the problem inheres in the socialization process in which the student is shaped for the clinical role. To blame the individual clinician is akin to blaming the victim.

Finally, I return to a recent personal experience. As a result of an auto accident, in which my beloved wife of fifty years was instantly killed and I suffered a broken hip, a fractured arm, punctured lungs, and more, I spent two and a half months in three hospitals. I "enjoyed" a successful outcome: I can walk normally, and I can use the polio arm that was fractured to the same limited extent as before, although I have more aches and pains I could well do without. But I thank God for big favors! Sometimes. I am not about to present a litany of psychological horrors, nor am I in any way intent on indicting hospital personnel who, as I shall discuss later, I regard as I regarded myself: victims.

1. Never did anyone take the initiative to ask anything about what I was experiencing about the loss of my wife. It was as if that was verboten material that would upset me or, more likely, that they would not know how to handle except by the cliché "That is rough stuff." Over the two and a half months, no more than two people responded to my initiatives as if they truly wanted to be helpful. In each of these instances I was advised, "It would be a good idea to talk to a psychiatrist and get your feelings out," reflective of *their* fear that if they pursued the matter with me they would be confronted with a sobbing, crying, depressed man they would not know how to handle. The point here is that (with exceptions to be noted later) to the scores of personnel responsible for my care I was not a person but a body with injuries. Their job was to take care of my body, not *me*. The unverbalized message they communicated to me was "Let's stay away from feelings." These words are not being written by a person who expected that these people would sit down, listen to me, and express caring and compassion to soothe me, even for the moment. I wanted that, but I did not expect it. What I expected was at most a fleeting recognition that I was psychologically bleeding, a condition that they and I knew was beyond our powers to stop. I wanted some sense of *contact* between us, some sense that they *understood*. Unwillingly I retreated to and stayed within my private world. What I have said here has to be seen in light of the next point.

2. The process of hospitalization alerts you to two factors. The first is that you have become *dependent* on others for almost all of your needs, and in my case I was for a long time totally dependent, encased as I was in a body brace with one hand raised and extended as if performing a blessing. I had always to be on my back and needed help for my bodily needs and processes. Unwanted dependency brings in its wake fear, anxiety, anger, resentment, and more, all of which are enormously exacerbated by the second factor: the message that hospital personnel are busy people who do not have *time* to do all that they are expected to do or you expect them to do. So, when you press the call button and five minutes go by, ten

minutes, fifteen minutes, twenty minutes and no one comes, you should not feel guilty if you have murderous fantasies. Such times were not infrequent. On five occasions no one came until I yelled. On those occasions when someone came after an unconscionable wait, no one ever expressed regret. They rarely failed to tell me they were very busy, and on a few occasions I was told in so many words that waiting is the name of the game. If I had to sum up the modal stance of *almost all* personnel, it would go this way: "What do you want? I have to do it quickly because there are other patients I have to take care of." I was not, I was assured, a demanding patient. I could not bring myself to say, How can you be demanding of people on whom you were dependent in the most fundamental ways? Murderous fantasies are one thing; fear of retaliation and neglect for the expression of anger is an effective control over such expression.

3. At the end of my hospitalization, I made a list of all personnel (nurses, attendants, physicians, physical therapists) who when they entered my room I breathed a sigh of relief because by my criteria they were gracious, warm, friendly people. I felt I could ask them questions, tell them the latest joke I had heard, spar with them, and I did not feel that I had to talk quickly because they were on the run. The one word that characterizes them is a Yiddish one: *menschen.* They were there for me, not only for my body. Over two and a half months (in three different hospitals) I probably had sustained interactions with one hundred to one hundred fifty personnel. After writing the eighth name, my list was completed. Two were nurses, one was my orthopedist, another was an anesthesiologist, two were nurse's aides averaging twenty years of age, one was a cardiologist, and one was the director of the trauma clinic. It is not happenstance that six of the eight people were in Boston's Beth Israel Hospital, which is noted for its emphasis on caring and compassion for patients. (It was also the only one of the three hospitals whose meals were far more than edible.) On an absolute basis, the criticisms I voiced earlier are appropriate to Beth Israel. On a comparative basis, it is infinitely better than any hospital I have ever

been in as a patient. But what about the scores of those absent from the list? For the sake of brevity I shall only say that they were incapable of smiling, their manner businesslike in a cold, pejorative sense, and utterly uninterested in me. More than a few were hostile creatures. That may be too harsh, so let me just say they were unfriendly.[1]

In the post–World War II period, numerous books have been written by physicians (or members of their families) about their hospital experience as patients. At great length they describe events, feelings, and reactions similar to mine. The interested reader should also consult the reports of the Association of Medical Colleges, which decry a perceived dilution of caring and compassion in physicians.

Still another example of the cyclical concern for the lack of caring in the clinical endeavor is an article in the *New York Times* (Nelson, 1983). The headline of the article is "Can Doctors Learn Warmth?" The subheadline reads, "Concern over lack of compassion leads to nationwide action." Here are the first three paragraphs of the article:

Leading American medical professors and physicians are moving to correct what they regard as a serious problem in their profession: a lack of compassion in the treatment of patients.

"There is a groundswell in American medicine, this desire to encourage more ethical and humanistic concerns in physicians," Dr. John A. Benson, Jr., president of the American Board of Internal Medicine, said in a recent interview. "After

---

[1]The president of Beth Israel is Dr. Mitchell Rabkin, whom I had previously known and who chose the physicians who would care for me when I was flown up and transferred to Beth Israel. As my daughter Julie said to me, "What do people without contacts do?" I could say that if they are religious, they pray, if they are not religious, Lady Luck better be on their side. Dr. Rabkin is the epitome of a caring person. Within the limits of his many duties, he makes it his business personally to monitor the quality of patient care. A recent study listed the twenty corporations whose employees are most satisfied with their roles. All are private-sector organizations except for Beth Israel, which was in the top ten. That fact is testimony to Dr. Rabkin's efforts.

the technological progress that medicine made in the 60's and 70's, this is a swing of the pendulum back to the fact that we are doctors, and that we can do a lot better than we are doing now."

The movement is centered in medical schools, where some experts believe students can be dehumanized, and even brutalized, by the experience. Medical students are often physically and mentally overwhelmed by the demands placed upon them. They sometimes observe inhumane treatment of patients, and they themselves are not infrequently treated as ciphers by those above them in the medical hierarchy. As a result, these young would-be doctors begin, in turn, to view troublesome patients as ciphers.

The article then lists and discusses steps taken by the Association of Medical Colleges "to reassert the importance of compassion in the practice of medicine." (The verb *reassert* is well taken, because these "view with alarm" articles appear every ten years or so, their contents having predictable similarities.) First, a series of hearings was held around the country to pinpoint "lapses in the humanity of medical education." Second, educational programs emphasizing values, ethics, and compassion have been adopted in many medical schools. Third, medical certification boards are to give increased weight "to humanistic qualities in devising examinations and in monitoring the education of specialists." Fourth, there is an ongoing three-year study on the entire content of medical education. The article correctly notes that, although "doubts about whether physicians spend enough time caring for patients have been voiced for centuries," recent developments have exacerbated these doubts— for example, growth of specialization, third-party payments, exponential increase of and dependence on new and complex technology, and the ambience and process of medical education: socialization into the profession.

If I view the developments described in the article without enthusiasm or optimism, it is not because of any nihilistic or cynical proclivity on my part. There is a difference between pessimism rooted in temperament and that rooted in the actuarial basis provided by social history. Of course, one should take satisfaction, indeed pride, in the knowledge that there are people in the clinical professions who have the courage to be "whistle-blowers," to say out loud that the emperor may not only be naked but may also have a serious disease. But when whistle-blowing has the consequence of eliciting actions based on the wrong diagnosis, or on a conception of etiology discernibly invalid or demonstrably superficial, one may be pardoned if, with sinking heart, one finds oneself concluding, "Here we go again."

The concerns articulated in the article avoid confronting several questions. First, why have past efforts to make physicians more compassionate been ineffective? Indeed, why has the situation become worse? Second, to what extent do the criteria for selecting people for medical careers take account of "compassion"? Third, is it possible that selection criteria work at cross-purposes to the goal of selecting people high on the characteristic of compassion? Fourth, are the contexts of socialization (medical school, internship-residency) ones in which the characteristic of compassion gets diluted or even extinguished? In short, are we dealing with a situation and proposed remedies in no way genotypically different from what I discussed earlier in regard to the film *One Flew over the Cuckoo's Nest?*

The issues are not peculiar to a state hospital or to medical education; they are issues that arise whenever and wherever major societal institutions appear to be intractable to change in ways that society deems desirable. Today, for example, we are bombarded with reports critical of public education and containing remedies that are intended to improve the atmosphere and outcomes of schooling. As in the case of the current concerns of medical educators, the authors of these reports judge schools to be so seriously flawed as to imperil the public welfare; that is, if allowed to continue, these situations will inexorably have an adverse impact on the social fabric. There is another similarity in both instances: there is almost total amnesia for the historical fact that the reports of today are amazingly like those of previous decades.

There is one interesting and instructive dissimilarity. Whereas colleges of education have rarely, if ever, been in a situation of truly selecting people for the profession, medical schools have long had such a large pool of candidates from which to choose that they have steadily raised what they consider to be appropriate criteria for selection. And yet, despite such a large pool, these criteria have to no one's satisfaction led to more compassionate physicians. The skeptic could suggest that, if colleges of education were in a position to employ intellectual and educational criteria similar in principle and even substance to those used by medical schools (i.e., very high grade average from highly respected schools, high test scores on the Graduate Record Examination, etc.), we might well end up with future reports that are carbon copies of those of today and the past. On what basis do we call someone a skeptic because he or she sees no compelling evidence that the criteria are relevant for the selection of the kinds of people the profession and the larger society say they want? If the critics of education are clear about anything—and they are clear about few things—it is that entrants to the profession have to be more carefully selected, and I would guess that they would be ecstatic at the prospect of colleges of education employing the standards of educational and intellectual performance used by medical schools. Critics of medical education have always been gun-shy about facing the possibility that their criteria for selection play an important role in producing the problem of "lack of compassion." In fact, there has been less change in the process and criteria of selection of medical students than in any other aspect of medical training.

There is one more similarity between criticisms of public and medical education, a similarity that is far more serious than the critics realize in that it raises the "intractability" question: Can our purposes be realized within the context of the existing social structure and value system of our public and medical schools? Have these purposes in the past not been realized for the same reasons? If the answer to the first question is even a qualified no and to the second question even a qualified yes, then the situation is indeed serious, in that we are conceding that the problem is intractable in the existing contexts. The similarity can be put this way: Granted we may not be selecting by the most appropriate criteria and procedures, but even if we selected more appropriately, we still have to face the fact that, as soon as the person begins the socialization process into teaching and medicine, that person encounters an ambience, a set of pressures, a hierarchy of values on the basis of which one is judged worthy or unworthy, that literally changes the person's outlook and actions in undesirable ways. In the case of public education, the critic is referring to what the aspiring professional experiences in his or her training and in the culture of our schools, experiences that are frequently infantilizing, stultifying, and destructive of the spark of creativity and of the dynamisms of hope and motivation.

If that sounds extreme, it is because one has not listened to the critics from within and without the educational arena. The disdain with which the critics talk about the quality of the preparation of educational personnel in schools of education and about what life is like in our schools (and the amount of disdain expressed publicly pales compared to what is said privately) is enough to give the most dedicated students cause for rethinking career goals. And it is no different in the case of the critic of medical education who, on and between the lines, is drawing a picture of the medical school and hospital as akin to a jungle in which student-eating faculty and supervisors—driven by ambition, competitiveness, and the insatiable thirst for scientific knowledge, fame, and survival—turn the compassionate student into the noncompassionate clinician, a process always, of course, articulated and cloaked in the garments of efficiency, objectivity, necessity, and a presumed superior level of morality.

What the critics of these two societal institutions seem not to recognize is that they are describing contexts of socialization inimical to their goals of change, just as they were inimical to those in the past with similar goals. And when I say *inimical*, I mean that these contexts are intractable to the sought-for change, that, whatever the degree of change that will be accomplished, it will be very small, transient, and promptly forgotten even when a decade or so later the same viewing with alarm will take place. As I said earlier, one should be grateful that there are people who bring the issues to the social agenda. But the real significance of their role today inheres in their claim that the situation is not the same but worse. Whether or not the situation has deteriorated and will continue to do so—the existing "evidence" would not stand up in the courts of science—should not obscure the fact that many knowledgeable people believe that to be the case. And in the case of medical education and practice, I refer not only to many medical educators but to a significant portion of the general population to whom the adjective *compassion* does not readily come to mind when they reflect over their experiences with hospitals, physicians, and the allied professions.

There is irony in the fact that the concerns of medical educators about the lack of compassion are implicitly, and sometimes explicitly, based on a conception of the "social contagion of disease." Let me illustrate this point by an example from public education, another instance of parallelism between these two social arenas. The example concerns the Head Start program, which was initiated by President Lyndon Johnson in the sixties with much fanfare. Beginning as it did in the sizzling sixties, that program, which initially was a summer program, is not explainable outside of the sensitivities stimulated by racial conflict, the civil rights movement, and the war on poverty. There was one other major factor: the overwhelming evidence that socially and economically disadvantaged children, black and white, did poorly in school. The preschool Head Start program was intended as a way of preventing later school failure. That was the surface rationale. What did not get stated was the widely held view that the schools to which children from these strata went were inadequate on many grounds for normal passage by them through the grades; that is, their educational difficulties inhered less in any intellectual or social deficits and more in unstimulating, noncompassionate, unsupportive school environments, where the social atmosphere and substance of the curriculum extinguished rather than reinforced curiosity and interest. Put in another way: Head Start was to be a kind of inoculation against catching the disease of educational arrest that was so catchable or contagious in our schools. It did not take long before it became apparent that this preschool inoculation would need booster shots once the children entered school, and such shots took the form of the Follow Through program.

Nowhere today in discussion of their concerns do medical educators recognize the possibility that the culture of the medical school and hospital may be lethal to change by the efforts they have chosen. And yet they describe an atmosphere and ideology so powerful and encompassing, so successful in defeating all past similar efforts, that it should occasion no surprise if the medical student and neophyte catch the disease of "lack of compassion." What would require explanation would be if the outcome were otherwise.

I first became aware of this situation fifty years ago, when I was a member of a small child guidance unit in Yale's Department of Pediatrics. That unit was remarkable on two counts: it may have been the first of its kind in such a department, and it was headed by Dr. Edith Jackson, a well-known child psychoanalyst. In those days (the unit began before World War II), it was rare, and probably unique, that a psychoanalyst would have an important teaching position anywhere in a medical school. Soon after I joined the unit, I was made aware of how alien that unit was in the department. To put it succinctly, the goals of that unit were precisely those enunciated by the medical educators in the *New York Times* article (Nelson, 1983)—almost fifty years from the day I joined the unit.

Although the unit provided service primarily to children in the hospital or those referred from the outpatient clinic, its existence was justified as a teaching site for medical students, interns, and residents. To teach what? To teach understanding of and compassion for the psychological status of sick children and their families; put in another way, to enlarge the horizons of medical personnel about the dilution and prevention of misery attendant to the psychological trauma of hospitalization; to aid them to see that they had the responsibility to treat more than the physical condition; to get them to understand that to pigeonhole the psychological and physical into distinct categories was to have the most restricted views of "healing" and that to care for someone's well-being required sensitivity to and compassion for that being's social psychological state and context. There was no hard sell, if only because Edie Jackson was incapable of it. The hard-sell approach would have brought out into the open attitudes destructive of whatever surface courtesy and respect this unit enjoyed.

One such attitude was that whatever this unit did—and to members and students in the department, the goals of the unit had the characteristics of an inkblot—was in no way central to the field of *medicine*. And by *central* I mean that, if the unit were suddenly to disappear, there would be few if any mourners at the memorial service. Another attitude was that the techniques and practices employed in the unit did not meet the criteria of scientific validity and that there was no evidence that outcomes had scientific credibility. Finally, there was an attitude as influential as it was both subtle and disquieting to those who held it: Yes, what this unit wants us to understand and act on is very important, should be taken very seriously, and we need more of it if we are to become comfortable with it, but we have no *time* for it in either our training or our practice. To those (few) medical students and interns who had this attitude, what the unit stood for was a necessity that had the attributes of an unpurchasable luxury. To those (even fewer) residents and faculty members who shared this attitude, what the unit stood for was important only for those who wanted to specialize in matters psychological; it was necessary for them, but not for those seeking a career in "scientific medicine" and overwhelmed by the pressures such a career entailed. There was no disposition to recognize that the argument based on time constraints reflected a hierarchy of values and unreflectively justified specialization of role and function.

It was extraordinarily difficult for those of us in the unit to adjust to the fact that we were second- or third-class citizens in an institution devoted to the repair and prevention of the human misery that so often attends and surrounds illness. But, if it was difficult, it was not because of our need for status but because our conception of caring took far more into account than does the traditional conception of repair. I remember once saying to a faculty member in pediatrics that the unit of treatment should be not the child but the family. He looked at me as if I had just plumbed the depths of nonsense and then, in all seriousness, with only a trace of asperity, said, "Those who are not real physicians will never understand why medicine has made as much progress as it has."

I have heard that argument over the years, an argument that contains a kernel of truth coated with a glaze of rationalization. The most extreme example of this attitude was expressed by a former undergraduate student who had gone into pediatrics, married, and together with his wife was visiting me in my office. At one point, he said that one of the real pluses in their marriage was that they were both physicians, "and only physicians can live with and talk to physicians." He said this with complete and smug seriousness, unaware that he had indicted his own inability to understand and live with "foreigners," which included, I shall assume, many, if not all, of his patients. It is one thing to claim distinctiveness; it is quite another thing to confuse it with uniqueness. What is unusual in this example is not what this young man said to me. Physicians say that to each other all the time, as any half-candid physician and a voluminous literature (literary and scientific) will attest. What was unusual was that he said it to me, just as it would have been unusual if I had said to him how badly I felt that as a physician he would never understand—*could* never understand—what it was like to be a psychologist! To which he could have retorted with a smile, "But everybody is a psychologist of sorts." Is there anyone who is not a physician of sorts?

We have poured billions into medical research and education (physicians, nurses, and a variety of auxiliary-therapeutic personnel). Next to nothing has been given to support research on the quality of interactions between patients and medical personnel. That is not (at least was not in the past) because of a lack of money. It is almost wholly explainable by the fact that these personnel simply do not see that a problem exists, that uncaring and uncompassionate interactions are *unhealthy*, that many of them may have adverse consequences, that there are issues that cannot be prejudged or clarified by piously proclaiming good intentions, or suggesting that a course here and a workshop there will take care of the problem, or saying that there are always a few rotten apples at the bottom of the basket. *The problem is not one about individuals.* It is a problem that encompasses the criteria employed for selection of health personnel (not only physicians), the ambiance surrounding their training, the values espoused in theory and their unrelatedness with the values absorbed in practice, and the place in all of this of the most important question of all: what do you "owe" another person for whose care you are responsible? What of yourself are you *obliged* to give to that person? Do unto others as you would have others do unto you. Is that empty rhetoric or a moral imperative?

A colleague of mine, John Doris, asked this question: Imagine that you have to choose between passing on your genes to your children or passing on your code of morals. How would you choose and why? As I react to history, past and present, and respectful as I am of posterity's criteria for judgment, the choice is an easy one.

We are used to hearing about our health "system." Without denying that the provision of health services has some of the characteristics we associate with that label, its use has at least one very misleading connotation: it is a system geared to achieve agreed-upon ends, namely, the provision of quality care. Health professionals have done a most effective job of convincing the general public and the political community that those ends are being met, albeit there is room for improvement. And, yet, in that very same general public, there is a cauldron of resentment toward health professionals—whether in a private office, clinic, or hospital—for their interpersonal insensitivity that so often has scarring, lingering, and alienating effects.

Charles de Gaulle once plaintively asked, "How can you govern a nation that makes five hundred different cheeses?" In the spirit of that question, I would ask, "How can you say we have a health system providing quality care when it has a blind spot about means-ends issues that call into question the appropriateness of calling it a system—a label that suggests that the rhetoric about its ends are appropriately reflected in the means it displays?"

Science, we are told, is basically a moral enterprise in that its methodologies are intended to ensure that in the pursuit of knowledge the imperfections of people—their capacity to distort, misinterpret, overlook, and even fudge—are controlled. It is fair to say that science tries seriously to confront the frailties of the human observer. No one will deny that the provision of health care is a moral enterprise in that nothing should be done to injure patients. Do no harm! The blind spot I have discussed in this essay concerns kinds of harm that, however unintended, should not be tolerated. What truly bothers me is the tendency of health professionals to react to arguments like mine by saying that "really" the problems I describe are minuscule in importance. That response is not in the spirit of the morality of science but in that of the "true believer" who cannot distinguish between opinion and fact, between prejudging the validity of an argument and dispassionately studying and researching the claims of the argument.

Despite the billions of dollars given to health research, the blind spot I have discussed has gone unstudied. To me that speaks volumes about the role in the health care community of the frailties of self-protection, self-deception, and the self-congratulatory tendency. The reasons are many, but the most important reason is that no one wants data that may cause them or the so-called system to change.

References

Blatt, B. *Exodus from Pandemonium: Human Abuse and a Reformation of Public Policy.* Boston: Allyn & Bacon, 1970.

Boring, E. G. *A History of Experimental Psychology.* Englewood Cliffs, N.J.: Prentice Hall, 1957.

Crews, F. "The Unknown Freud." *New York Review of Books*, Nov. 18, 1993, pp. 55–66.

Douglas, C. *Translate This Darkness: The Life of Christiana Morgan.* New York: Simon & Schuster, 1993.

Feldman, D. H. *Nature's Gambit: Child Prodigies and the Development of Human Potential.* New York: Basic Books, 1986.

Fels, A. *New York Times Book Review*, Jan. 28, 1993, pp. 18–19.

Gambino, R. *Blood of My Blood: The Dilemma of the Italian-Americans.* Garden City, N.Y.: Anchor Press, 1974.

Garner, W. "Psychology Has a Rosy Past, Present, and Future." In F. Kessel (ed.), *Psychological Science and Human Affairs: Essays in Honor of William Bevan.* Boulder, Colo.: Westview Press, 1994.

Garner, W. "The Acquisition and Application of Knowledge: A Symbiotic Relation." *American Psychologist*, 1972, *27*, 941–946.

Ginzberg, E., and Bray, D. W. *The Uneducated.* New York: Columbia University Press, 1953.

Hilgard, E. "Prefatory Remarks to William James' Presidential Address to the American Psychological Association." In E. Hilgard (ed.), *American Psychology in Historical Perspective: Addresses of the Presidents of the American Psychological Association.* Washington, D.C.: American Psychological Association, 1978.

James, W. "Knowing Things Together." In E. Hilgard (ed.), *American Psychology in Historical Perspective: Addresses of the Presidents of the American Psychological Association.* Washington, D.C.: American Psychological Association, 1978. (Originally published in *Psychological Review*, 1895, *2*, 105–124.)

Johnson, A. B. *A Treatise on Language: Or the Relation Which Words Bear to Things.* Berkeley: University of California Press, 1947. (Originally published 1836.)

Kazin, A. "Love at Harvard." *New York Review of Books*, Jan. 28, 1993, pp. 3–5.

Kinsey, A. C., and others. *Sexual Behavior in the Human Male*. Philadelphia: W. B. Saunders, 1948.

Klee, E., Dressen, W., and Reiss, V. *"The Good Old Days": The Holocaust as Seen by Its Perpetrators and Bystanders*. New York: Free Press, 1991.

Lewinnek, E. "GI Blues." *The New Journal*, Apr. 1993, pp. 7–10.

Machiavelli, N. *The Prince*. New York: Mentor Books, 1952. (Originally published 1532.)

McCullough, D. *Truman*. New York: Simon & Schuster, 1992.

Miller, N. *Theodore Roosevelt: A Life*. New York: Morrow, 1992.

Murray, H. A. *Explorations in Personality: A Clinical and Experimental Study of Fifty Men of College Age*. New York: Oxford University Press, 1938.

Nelson, G. "Can Doctors Learn Warmth?" *New York Times*, Sept. 13, 1983, p. A4.

Nisbet, R. A. *The Degradation of the Academic Dogma: The University in America, 1945–1970*. New York: Basic Books, 1971.

Plato. "Phaedo: The Death Scene." *Euthyphro, Apology, and Crito*. New York: Bobbs-Merrill, 1948. (Originally published in 386 B.C.)

Robinson, F. G. *Love's Story Told: A Life of Henry A. Murray*. Cambridge, Mass.: Harvard University Press, 1993.

Santayana, G. "A Glimpse of Yale." *Harvard Monthly*, 1892.

Sarason, S. B. *The Making of an American Psychologist: An Autobiography*. San Francisco: Jossey-Bass, 1988.

Sarason, S. B. "Some Reflections on the APA Centennial," *Journal of Mind and Behavior*, 1993, 14(2), pp. 95–106.

Sarason, S. B. *The Case for Change: Rethinking the Preparation of Educators*. San Francisco: Jossey-Bass, 1993.

Sarason, S. B. *Letters to a Serious Education President*. Newbury Park, Calif.: Corwin Press, 1993.

Sarason, S. B., Zitnay, G., and Grossman, F. *The Creation of a Community Setting*. Syracuse, N.Y.: Syracuse University Press, 1972.

Schwartz, D. *Crossing the River*. Cambridge, Mass.: Brookline Books, 1992.

Silone, I. *The Story of a Humble Christian*. New York: HarperCollins, 1970.

Skinner, B. F. *Walden Two*. New York: Macmillan, 1948.

Todd, C. L., and Sonkin, R. *Alexander Bryan Johnson: Philosophical Banker*. Syracuse, N.Y.: Syracuse University Press, 1977.

Turnbull, H. R., III, and Turnbull, A. P. (eds.). *Parents Speak Out: Then and Now*. Columbus, Ohio: Merrill, 1979.